Daily Mail

INCOME TAX
GUIDE

1998–99

Daily Mail

INCOME TAX GUIDE

1998–99

For the year 6 April 1998 to
5 April 1999 in accordance with
the Budget proposals of March 1998 and the general law

EDITED BY

KENNETH R. TINGLEY

ORION BUSINESS
BOOKS

The right of Kenneth R. Tingley to be identified as the
author of this work has been asserted by him in accordance
with the Copyright, Designs and Patents Act, 1988

While every effort is made to ensure accuracy, the publishers,
the editor, Associated Newspapers Ltd, their assigns,
licensees and printers cannot accept any liability for any
errors or omissions contained herein nor liability for any
person acting or refraining from action as a result of the
information contained in this book. The editor regrets that
he cannot reply to personal tax problems.

First published in Great Britain in 1998 by
Orion Business
An imprint of the Orion Publishing Group Ltd
Orion House, 5 Upper St Martin's Lane,
London WC2H 9EA

A CIP catalogue record for this book is available
from the British Library

ISBN 0 75281 247 5

Photoset in Monotype Garamond by
Selwood Systems, Midsomer Norton

Printed in Great Britain by
Butler & Tanner Ltd, Frome and London

Contents

Rates and Allowances 1998–99

Income tax is charged on an individual's income at the following rates for 1998–99:

Lower rate	20 per cent on first £4,300
Basic rate	23 per cent on next £22,800
Higher rate	40 per cent on the remainder

Several allowances and reliefs may be deducted from income before calculating the sum chargeable to income tax. However, other allowances and reliefs support reductions on tax due at the reduced rate of 15 per cent or the lower rate of 20 per cent only and are not available for relief at rates exceeding these levels. Modifications are also required where income includes dividends and other income from savings.

Allowances 1998–99

Additional personal allowance for children
. . . . . £1,900

Blind person's allowance . . £1,330

Married couple's allowance:
age of elder spouse:
below 65 . . . . £1,900
65 to 74 . . . . £3,305
75 and over . . . £3,345

Personal allowance:
Taxpayer's age:
below 65 . . . . £4,195
65 to 74 . . . . £5,410
75 and over . . . £5,600

Widow's bereavement allowance £1,900

An introduction

THE 1997–98 EDITION of the Guide examined the many changes to the taxation structure of the United Kingdom which were introduced by the former Chancellor of the Exchequer in his Budget Statement of Tuesday, 26 November 1996. A new Labour Government was elected on 1 May 1997 and further amendments to the taxation structure were widely anticipated. These were not long in arriving. On Monday, 2 July 1997, the newly installed Chancellor, Mr Gordon Brown, delivered a Budget containing further significant changes, although many of these were not to apply until a later date.

Since 1993 it had been the practice to hold Budget Day at the end of November. This practice was abandoned, with Budget Day reverting to the Spring of 1998. In the event, Gordon Brown presented his full Budget Statement on Tuesday, 17 March 1998, outlining a mass of further proposals to amend the United Kingdom taxation structure.

The proposals, supplemented by a considerable volume of detail, are recorded in a Finance Bill. The contents of this Bill must be subjected to lengthy Parliamentary scrutiny, debate and amendment before becoming part of the law of the United Kingdom.

The proposed changes, together with the continuing legislation, are discussed on the following pages and numerous examples illustrate the calculation of liability to taxation. As the proposals announced on 17 March must be debated by Parliament it will not be overlooked that further amendments may be introduced at some later time before Royal Assent is eventually forthcoming.

Several significant changes in the treatment of investment income are being introduced on 6 April 1999. To avoid confusion with the treatment of income before this date a separate chapter, 'Investment Income after 5 April 1999', has been inserted towards the end of the Guide.

Self-assessment: the way ahead

The most fundamental reform in personal taxation for more than 50 years took place on 6 April 1996 with the introduction of self-assessment. This reform did not affect the amount of income tax and capital gains tax due to be paid, although some changes were made in an attempt to simplify the calculation of liability. The real effect was limited to arrangements for the payment of tax and to numerous compliance requirements which must be satisfied if payment and collection are to be achieved.

Who is affected by self-assessment?

Self-assessment directly affects all individuals receiving tax return forms, including the self-employed, members of a partnership, company directors, individuals having more than one source of income, and those with investment income liable to higher rate income tax. Tax returns will also be received by trustees administering settled funds and by personal representatives dealing with the estates of deceased persons. In addition, those having taxable income on which tax is due but who have not received a tax return must notify liability and will then be brought within self-assessment. In the first year of self-assessment some 9 million tax return forms were issued.

Many individuals receive their only income from a single source of employment and suffer income tax by deduction under the PAYE scheme. The deduction scheme also extends to others receiving a range of pensions. These individuals are not directly affected by self-assessment, but the situation may well change if an individual ceases employment and becomes self-employed, receives investment income, receives income from several different sources, or indeed is required to complete a tax return.

Payment of tax

The expression 'self-assessment' suggests that those within the new scheme must calculate their own tax liability and forward a remittance to the Inland Revenue. This may well be so, but taxpayers are provided with an option to forward a completed tax return at an early date. The Inland Revenue will then calculate the amount of tax due on the basis of information recorded in the return and notify the taxpayer who must arrange for the remittance of funds on or before the due date.

Some taxpayers will be required to make two payments on account with a subsequent balancing payment, or perhaps repayment where excessive tax has been suffered. Failure to make the required payments or to fully discharge liability on the due date will result in an obligation to pay interest, with a surcharge being imposed in cases of substantial delay.

Information

Before a tax return can be completed, detailed information must be provided and retained. This may involve the supply of information by others, notably employers. It follows that whilst those employers may not be directly affected by self-assessment, for example, where they are companies, they are indirectly involved by the need to supply information.

Companies

In its present form, self-assessment does not extend to companies residing in the United Kingdom. However, companies are to be brought within their own self-assessment regime for accounting periods ending after 30 June 1999.

Generally

This brief synopsis does no more than outline the broad thrust of self-assessment. A great deal of further comment is required if the numerous requirements are not to be overlooked and tax commitments properly discharged without incurring liability to interest, surcharges and penalties. These requirements are outlined in greater detail below and also on subsequent pages of the Guide. However, before proceeding it may be helpful to discuss briefly the system which applied before self-assessment was introduced on 6 April 1996.

THE OLD SYSTEM

The tax year 1995–96, ending on 5 April 1996, was the last year of the 'old system' before the introduction of self-assessment. It was a feature of this system that where no tax had been suffered (for example, on business profits), or liabilities arose at the higher rate on investment income, details had to be supplied to the Inland Revenue by completing a tax return form. This return also included details of any capital gains, together with claims for allowances and reliefs.

It then remained for the Inland Revenue to issue a notice of assessment identifying the amount of taxable income, profits or gains and showing the income tax and capital gains tax payable. There may well have been more than one notice of assessment where the individual received income from two or more different sources or realised capital gains. Should the taxpayer challenge the accuracy of an assessment, this would be made in the form of an appeal which was then settled by negotiation with the Inland Revenue, or determined on a hearing by Appeal Commissioners. Both income tax and capital gains tax became payable on a variety of different dates.

Tax returns

The last 'old style' tax return forms issued to individuals were those for the year ending on 5 April 1996. Most forms were issued during the month of April 1996 and required the insertion of income and capital gains, together with claims for allowances and reliefs. To avoid an obligation to discharge

interest, and perhaps penalties also, the completed forms had to be returned to the Inland Revenue not later than 31 October 1996.

Once the returns had been processed the Inland Revenue issued any assessments to income tax or capital gains tax for 1995–96 (year ending on 5 April 1996) which may have been required. Appeals then had to be made within strict time limits if the assessments were incorrect or were to be challenged. In the absence of a valid appeal the tax shown by an assessment became due and payable.

Payment of tax

Wages, salaries and other remuneration arising from an office or employment will usually be paid after deduction of income tax under the PAYE scheme. The deductions extend to tax at the lower rate, the basic rate and the higher rate where earnings are sufficiently substantial. Pensions paid by a former employer, or by persons administering a pension scheme will frequently be subject to PAYE deductions also. In addition, the deduction scheme is extended to include the taxation of statutory maternity and short-term sickness benefits paid by an employer.

Many payments of interest, together with various annual payments, will have been received net after deduction of income tax at the basic rate of 25 per cent which applied for 1995–96. No deduction of income tax will have been made from dividends paid by United Kingdom resident companies, but each dividend carried a tax credit of one-quarter and the recipient was not assessed to income tax at the lower or basic rates.

In those cases where the recipient of income was assessable directly to income tax for 1995–96 this tax generally fell due for payment on whichever was the later of:

a 1 January 1996, or
b 30 days after the date on which the assessment was made.

Income tax payable in this manner included tax at the lower rate, the basic rate and the higher rate where appropriate.

Tax payable on income arising from a trade, profession or vocation was discharged by two equal instalments in 1995–96, namely:

a 1 January 1996, and
b 1 July 1996.

Here also, tax extended to the lower rate, the basic rate and the higher rate.

Any higher rate income tax attributable to the

following income was separately charged:

a Dividends from United Kingdom companies.
b Investment income taxed at source at the basic rate of 25 per cent.

This tax became payable on 1 December 1996, or on the expiration of thirty days from the date of making the assessment, whichever was the later.

Capital gains tax attributable to gains arising in 1995–96 usually fell due for payment on 1 December 1996.

Where an assessment was under appeal an application could be made to defer payment of some or all of the tax pending determination of the disputed liability. This application usually had to be made within a period of 30 days from the issue of a notice of assessment and it was necessary to specify the grounds for believing that there had been an overcharge of tax.

SELF-ASSESSMENT

Tax returns

The 'old system' was replaced by self-assessment on 6 April 1996, the first day of the tax year 1996–97. The application of self-assessment relies heavily on the tax return. Most returns are issued in the month of April immediately following the end of the tax year to which they relate. For example, returns for 1997–98 (year ending on 5 April 1998) were mainly issued in the month of April 1998. Other returns may be issued later in the year for a variety of reasons, including the receipt of a request from a taxpayer.

The basic tax return form extends throughout a mere eight pages. The income section requires the insertion of details showing interest, dividends, pensions, social security benefits and a range of other items received. Space is made available to support claims for personal and other allowances, relief for pension contributions and any further outgoings which may qualify for tax relief. Those seeking repayment are provided with a space in which to make a formal claim. Other parts of the tax return form require the insertion of information which may be relevant for a raft of different matters.

In addition to the basic form, there are a number of supplementary pages dealing with the following:

a Employments
b Share schemes
c Self-employment
d Partnerships
e Land and property
f Foreign income
g Income from trusts and estates of deceased persons
h Capital gains
i Residence

A taxpayer who receives income, or who is affected by matters to be recorded on a supplementary page, will select the appropriate page, or pages, insert the required information and attach those pages to the basic return. The purpose of this approach is to avoid producing lengthy return forms relating to many matters which are of little or no interest to a large number of taxpayers.

When dispatching tax return forms, the Inland Revenue will enclose any supplementary pages which are thought to be relevant to a particular taxpayer. Indeed, some return forms will be extended by including the appropriate supplementary page, or pages, which are otherwise supplied on a loose-leaf basis. Should a taxpayer fail to receive a particular supplementary page requiring completion by him or her, an application for that page must be made to the Inland Revenue.

The importance of the tax return form cannot be overstated. Initially at least, the information recorded on a completed form will govern the calculation of income tax and capital gains tax payable. The submission of an incorrect form may well incur an obligation to discharge interest and penalties at a later date.

Reference should be made to page 135 for further information on the completion of tax returns.

Filing returns

Taxpayers are provided with a choice when delivering completed tax return forms to the Inland Revenue. One option is to include all information on the form and leave the Inland Revenue to calculate the amount of tax payable, or perhaps repayable. If this option is to be selected the form must be received by the Inland Revenue not later than 30 September following the end of the year of assessment to which it relates. If the return is issued after 31 July the delivery date falls two months after the date of issue, in substitution for 30 September. The Inland Revenue will then calculate the amount of tax due, based on the information recorded, and advise the taxpayer of this amount. No assessments will be raised and it remains for the taxpayer to discharge the appropriate amount of income tax or capital gains tax in due course.

Returns should also be submitted by 30 September where the Inland Revenue are required to collect outstanding income tax through the PAYE scheme.

This method of collection is usually available where the amount of tax outstanding does not exceed £1,000 and, of course, the individual receives income which is subject to deduction under the scheme.

The second option is to delay delivery of the completed return until 31 January following the end of the year of assessment. If this option is used, in addition to fully completing the return the taxpayer must calculate the amount of income tax and capital gains tax due. Should the return be issued after 31 October the delivery date is extended to fall three months after the issue date.

Many taxpayers will be content to adopt the first option and submit their completed return forms by 30 September following the end of the year of assessment. The advantage of this approach is that the Inland Revenue will then calculate the amount of tax payable, leaving the taxpayer to carefully check the accuracy of the calculation. The second option requires that the taxpayer must make his or her own calculation without the benefit of checking figures prepared by others.

1
THE TAX RETURN
THE CHOICE

During the month of April 1998 Andrew received a tax return form requiring completion for the year ended 5 April 1998 (1997–98). Once all information has been inserted Andrew retains the following choice:

a He may forward the return not later than 30 September 1998, thus requiring the Inland Revenue to calculate the amount of income tax and capital gains tax, if any, due; or

b He may delay forwarding the return until a later date, not falling after 31 January 1999, and enclose calculations showing income tax and capital gains tax, if any, payable.

Corrections
On receiving a completed tax return form, the Inland Revenue may carry out 'corrections' at any time during the succeeding nine-month period. This implies no more than correcting arithmetical and other obvious errors. It does not indicate any thorough examination of the information recorded on the return.

Amending the return
The taxpayer can subsequently amend a previously submitted return, usually within a period of twelve months from the filing date. However, this facility is withdrawn once the Inland Revenue notify the taxpayer that enquiries into his or her affairs are being made.

Inland Revenue enquiries
The Inland Revenue retain powers to enquire into the contents of any return. Notification that an enquiry will be commenced may be given to the taxpayer not later than twelve months after the filing date of 31 January. Should the return be filed, or an amended return be submitted by the taxpayer after 31 January, notification may be given at any time in a rather longer period. There are two types of enquiry, namely, an 'aspect' enquiry and a 'full' enquiry. The former will usually be restricted to limited areas of the information disclosed, perhaps the calculation of a chargeable gain. In contrast, full enquiries will involve a consideration of the return as a whole.

Most enquiries will reflect the suspicion of some irregularity or perhaps omission. However, a proportion of returns will be selected at random for enquiry to test the accuracy of self-assessment.

When any Inland Revenue enquiry is completed the taxpayer must be notified with details of the amendments, if any, which the Inland Revenue consider should be made. If the taxpayer is unable to agree to the amended calculations there is a right of appeal against the Inland Revenue findings.

Further action
Once the twelve-month period has elapsed following the filing date, usually 31 January or perhaps later if the submission of the return has been delayed, or has been amended without notice of an Inland Revenue enquiry being given, the rights of the Inland Revenue to examine the taxpayer's affairs are severely limited. However, 'discovery' assessments can be raised where, for example, it is shown that profits have not been assessed, tax payable has become insufficient, or excess relief has been granted. In the absence of fraudulent or negligent conduct, these assessments can be raised within a period of five years from 31 January following the end of the year of assessment involved. This is increased to twenty years where there is fraud or negligent conduct.

Late returns
Failure to submit the completed tax return form by the filing date, usually 31 January, may give rise to a fixed penalty of £100. This penalty is doubled to £200 if the failure continues throughout a period of six months.

2
THE TAX RETURN
TIME LIMITS

John delivered his completed tax return for the year ended 5 April 1998 on 14 January 1999. This established a normal filing date of 31 January 1999. Time limits within which action may be taken are as follows:

a Within a period of nine months commencing on the delivery date of 14 January and ending on 13 October 1999 the Inland Revenue may carry out 'corrections' to the return.
b Within a period of twelve months commencing on the filing date of 31 January 1999 and ending on 30 January 2000 John can amend the contents of his return. This facility will terminate earlier should the Inland Revenue issue a notice of enquiry.
c Also within a period of twelve months from the filing date of 31 January 1999, the Inland Revenue may give notice of an enquiry being made into the contents of the return. If an amendment to the return is made by John after 31 January 1999 a further twelve-month period will commence to run from the date on which the amendment is made and terminate on a subsequent quarter day.

The fixed penalty cannot exceed the amount of tax becoming due. In addition, it is possible for the penalty to be set aside if the taxpayer can offer a 'reasonable excuse' for his or her failure. The alleged existence of a 'reasonable excuse' as providing grounds for the removal of any penalty should be approached with considerable caution. It may be possible to illustrate such an excuse on the grounds of death, ill-health, or perhaps absence from the country, but reliance on the inability to understand a tax return or some fault of the taxpayer's agent is most unlikely to prove successful.

Should the failure to submit a return continue for more than twelve months, substantially increased penalties may become payable. It is also possible for the Inland Revenue to apply for the award of a daily penalty whilst the return remains outstanding.

Failure to file a return
Where a return has been issued but no completed return has been delivered by the individual, the Inland Revenue can make a determination of the estimated amount of tax due. There is no appeal against this determination. It can only be set aside by the taxpayer delivering a completed tax return form at a later date.

Absence of a return
Taxpayers having a liability to discharge income tax or capital gains tax for 1997–98 but who do not receive a tax return form should notify the Inland Revenue of liability not later than 5 October following the end of the year of assessment. If they do not, a liability to penalties may arise.

PAYMENT OF TAX
Self-assessment requires that income tax attributable to profits, gains or income for a tax year may, although not necessarily will, become payable in three stages, namely:

a An interim payment on account on or before 31 January falling shortly before the end of the tax year;
b A second interim payment on account on or before the following 31 July; and
c A balancing payment or repayment on the following 31 January, namely some ten months after the end of the tax year.

The final balancing adjustment will incorporate the difference between the aggregate amount, if any, paid by two instalments and the outstanding liability for the year.

A great deal of income will be received after deduction of income tax or, in the case of dividends, may carry a tax credit. It is only the additional tax, if any, that will become payable in this manner.

Capital gains tax is not discharged by instalments. The entire liability for a tax year must be discharged on or before 31 January following the end of the year of assessment in which the gain or gains arose.

Payments on account
The first payment on account of liability for a tax year falls due to be made on or before 31 January falling some two months before the end of the year itself. For example, if the tax year is 1997–98, ending on 5 April 1998, the first payment date is not later than 31 January 1998. It is apparent that the liability for the full year may well be unknown by 31 January and it is necessary to use a special approach based on the tax liability for the previous year.

The first step when calculating payments on account for 1997–98 is to establish the total income tax liability for the previous year, 1996–97. This will be increased by the amount of any Class 4 national insurance contributions.

The second step is to subtract from the aggregate tax and Class 4 contributions for the earlier year, the amount of income tax suffered by deduction. This will include:

a Income tax deducted, or that which is deemed to have been deducted.

b PAYE deductions suffered.

c Tax credits on dividends.

d Foreign tax relief.

─────────── 3 ───────────

PAYMENTS ON ACCOUNT EXEMPTION

The total income of Kevin for 1997–98 comprised:

Earnings from part-time employment (PAYE suffered £4,900).
Profits from a business.
Dividends (including tax credits of £200).

This income gave rise to a total tax liability of £5,950.

		£
Total tax for 1997–98		5,950
Less suffered by 'deduction':		
	£	
PAYE	4,900	
Tax credits	200	
		5,100
Tax assessed		£850

It is necessary to calculate whether payments on account for 1998–99 need to be made. The tax to be assessed exceeds £500 and the first exemption cannot be used. However, of the total liability for 1997–98, namely £5,950, the sum of £5,100 was suffered by deduction. This latter figure exceeds 80 per cent of the total liability and no payments on account need be made for 1998–99.

The balance of tax due for 1998–99 must be discharged not later than 31 January 2000.

───────────────────────

The net sum produced by this calculation may be used to establish the two payments on account for 1997–98 but there are two relaxations.

Firstly, no payment on account will be due if either:

a Income tax and Class 4 contribution liability for 1996–97, calculated net of tax deducted at source and tax credits on dividends, is less than £500; or

b More than 80 per cent of income tax and Class 4 contribution liability for 1996–97 was met by deduction of tax at source or from tax credits on dividends.

Secondly, where neither limit applies it remains possible for a claim to be submitted to reduce the amount of payments on account. This claim may be justified where it is considered that the amount of income tax and Class 4 contributions, if any, recoverable by self-assessment for 1997–98 has fallen when compared with the previous year. Although the Inland Revenue retain few powers to object to such a claim, a liability to interest may arise should the claim be found excessive.

Finally, the net sum remaining, if any, will be used to establish the amount of each payment on account of income tax which must be made for 1997–98 as follows:

a 31 January 1998 – 50 per cent of the net sum

b 31 July 1998 – 50 per cent of the net sum

The balance of income tax payable will fall due on 31 January 1999.

Capital gains tax is not subject to any payment on account and falls due on 31 January following the end of the year in which the liability arises.

A similar approach was made to establish payments on account for 1996–97 (based on information for 1995–96). However, there were some differences in the calculations required and the 80 per cent relaxation did not apply.

The approach used to determine payments on account for 1998–99 and future years is identical to that outlined above, with consideration being given to the liability for each previous year.

Other considerations

It must not be overlooked that two amounts of income tax may fall due for payment on each 31 January. For example, on 31 January 1999:

a the final balancing payment for 1997–98 (year to 5 April 1998) will fall due, and

b the first payment on account for 1998–99 (year to 5 April 1999) must be satisfied.

This can have unfortunate results where a new source of income arises, as illustrated by the examples on the opposite page.

Statements of Account

It is the practice of the Inland Revenue to issue Statements of Account some weeks before 31 January showing the amount of tax payable on the latter date. The provision of these Statements has no statutory effect but they do serve as a reminder to taxpayers. It is possible that a taxpayer who has filed a return form not later than 30 September fails to receive a Statement of Account. Where this occurs tax will usually become payable thirty days after the

4
PAYMENT OF TAX
1997–98

The total income tax liability of Sharon for 1996–97 was £5,400. Of this sum, £2,100 had been suffered by deduction leaving a balance of £3,300. Her income tax liability for the following year, 1997–98, amounted to £7,500, of which £1,900 was collected by deduction. Sharon had a capital gains tax liability of £980 for 1996–97 and a liability of £1,850 for 1997–98.

The tax payable for 1997–98 will fall due as follows:

Income tax

	£
31 January 1998 – 50% × £3,300 (£5,400 less £2,100)	1,650
31 July 1998 – 50% × £3,300 . .	1,650
Suffered by deduction . . .	1,900
31 January 1999 – Balancing payment	£2,300
Total tax liability for 1997–98 . . .	£7,500

Capital gains tax

31 January 1999 – Single payment .	£1,850

It will not be overlooked that on the basis of these figures the following payments on account will fall due for 1998–99:

31 January 1999 – 50% × £5,600 (£7,500 less £1,900)	£2,800
31 July 1999 – 50% × £5,600 . . .	£2,800

Statement is received, should this identify a payment date later than 31 January. No interest will be payable on late payment of income tax if this is satisfied within the thirty-day period.

Interest
Interest will be charged on any outstanding tax from the date tax was due for payment, until that on which the obligation is discharged. Interest, referred to as a repayment supplement, will become payable on any tax which must be repaid. Further information appears on page 139.

Surcharges
In addition, failure to discharge the balancing payment of income tax, usually on 31 January, within a period of 28 days may attract the imposition of a surcharge. This applies at the rate of 5 per cent of the unpaid tax and unpaid Class 4 national insurance contributions. Should tax remain outstanding for a six-month period a further 5 per cent surcharge is imposed. The calculation of this surcharge is not

5
PAYMENTS ON ACCOUNT
NEW SOURCE

For several years the only income of Peter was from an employment, with all tax being suffered under the PAYE deduction scheme. Peter terminated his employment on 5 April 1997 and commenced business as a self-employed computer specialist on the following day. Income tax due for 1997–98 was eventually agreed in the sum of £7,500.

There can be no payment on account for 1997–98 as all tax in the previous year, 1996–97, was suffered by deduction. Therefore, the entire liability of £7,500 for 1997–98 falls to be discharged on 31 January 1999. In addition, a payment on account for the following year, 1998–99, must also be made on 31 January 1999. On the assumption that Peter had acquired no other source of income, this payment will comprise £3,750 (50% × £7,500).

confined to income tax, but can also extend to any interest payable on unpaid tax.

Liability to interest, and to the surcharge also, extends to capital gains tax which is paid late.

Claims
Claims relating to events taking place in a year of assessment should be made on the tax return for that year. As it is possible to amend a return within a period of twelve months from the filing date, this step can be used to adjust previously submitted information within a period of some twenty-two months after the end of the year of assessment concerned.

Where, for any reason, a claim is not included in a return or an amended return, it can be made independently and the appropriate relief received or repayment made.

Claims related back
It has long been possible for certain pension contributions paid in a year of assessment to be treated as paid in an earlier year. This requires the submission of a special claim which will usually be made in a tax return. It will be apparent that where contributions are related back to an earlier year in this manner the tax burden for that year should be reduced. However, this is not the procedure adopted for payments actually made after 5 April 1996 and related back. The first step is to calculate the amount of any reduction of income tax which otherwise arises in the earlier year as a result of the claim. The tax actually attributable to the earlier year remains undisturbed. Relief is then given by:

a Direct repayment from the Inland Revenue, where tax has previously been paid;

b Setting the amount of the repayment against the tax due for the year contributions were actually paid; or

c Treating the amount of the repayment as a payment on account for the actual year contributions are paid.

The effect of this approach is not to reduce the tax actually paid in the earlier year when arriving at payments on account for the following year. As a result, the tax payable for the earlier year remains undisturbed when calculating liability to make payments on account in the following year. An exception did arise where pension contributions had been related back to 1995–96. In this situation tax payable for 1995–96 could be treated as reduced when determining the payments on account due for 1996–97.

It is possible for business losses arising in a year of assessment to be relieved in a previous year if a claim is made. Here also, the effect of such a claim is not to disturb the tax payable for the previous year. The amount of any relief attributable to the loss claim is given in a manner similar to that which applies where pension contributions are related back.

PARTNERSHIPS

Business profits of a partnership carried on by individuals were previously assessed to income tax by treating the partnership as a single unit. Therefore, a partnership assessment was made on the partnership and not on individual partners. This did not apply to the taxation of capital gains because, from the inception of capital gains tax, this tax has been borne by individuals and not by the partnership as a unit.

In the case of partnerships established before 6 April 1994 and continuing beyond 5 April 1997 ('old partnerships') the assessment of partnership profits in the name of a partnership continued for all years up to and including 1996–97. As a result, tax becoming payable on the business profits of a partnership for 1996–97 will be satisfied by two equal instalments falling due on 1 January 1997 and 1 July in the same year. The rules governing payments on account and balancing payments had no application to partnerships for 1996–97.

No partnership assessment can be raised for 1997–98 and future years. A representative of the partnership is required to complete an income tax return form showing details of all partnership profits, gains and income. This form is subject to the same filing date, 'corrections' and enquiry procedures as those which affect individuals.

The partnership return will disclose the allocation of profits, gains and income among the several partners. It is then the responsibility of each partner to record his or her share on the personal tax return. Each partner is responsible for discharging his or her payments on account and balancing payments to the exclusion of the remaining partners.

Although a partnership assessment was raised for 1996–97, individual partners were required to record their shares of profits, gains or income on personal tax returns. The possibility of double liability was avoided by each partner obtaining a credit against his or her tax liability for the share of income tax discharged by the partnership.

In the case of 'new partnerships' created after 5 April 1994 the special provisions for 1996–97 did not apply. Each partner was required to discharge his or her own liability for that year, and indeed all succeeding years.

The penalty of £100 or £200 which may result where a return is delivered late is increased where the return relates to a partnership. The amount of the penalty is increased in relation to the number of partners. For example, if there are five partners, a normal penalty of £100 will be increased to £500.

MAINTAINING RECORDS

The scheme of self-assessment requires the maintenance and availability of many records. Individuals carrying on a trade, profession or vocation must retain records relating to the basis period for 1996–97 and future years. These records need to be maintained until the later of:

a the completion of any Inland Revenue enquiry; or

b the fifth anniversary of the filing date, usually 31 January, for the period involved.

This applies also to individuals carrying on a Schedule A business and receiving income from letting property.

Persons not carrying on business must also retain records relating to the basis period for 1996–97 onwards. The retention period ends on the later of:

a the completion of any formal Inland Revenue enquiry; or

b twelve months after the filing date (usually 31 January).

All records and documents relating to taxation matters must be retained, although it is possible to use copies. A penalty may be imposed for any failure.

Directors and employees may receive information relating to benefits and other matters from their employers. The supply of this information is reviewed on page 71.

GENERALLY

Although the completion of a tax return form and new dates for discharging taxation identify the main significance of self-assessment, numerous changes have been made to the tax system in an attempt to achieve some measure of simplification. These changes include the withdrawal of the previous 'preceding year' basis of assessment and its replacement by a 'current year' basis. This change has affected all sole proprietors and also individuals carrying on business in partnership. Other changes include the fundamental amendment for the cal-culation of profits arising from letting property and the treatment of income distributed by personal representatives administering the estate of a deceased person.

Whilst this chapter has outlined the thrust of self-assessment, no tax return can safely be completed without the provision of information regarding the nature and calculation of taxable profits, gains and income. Many individuals not concerned with self-assessment, usually by reason of their income arising solely from an employment or pensions, will need to appreciate the nature and application of the tax system generally. Comments appearing on the following pages of the Guide deal with these matters and are of application both to individuals affected by self-assessment and to others where self-assess-ment has little or no immediate significance.

TIMETABLE OF MAIN EVENTS
PERIOD 1 JANUARY 1998 TO 31 MARCH 1999

Date	Event
31 January 1998	Deadline for filing tax returns for 1996–97.
	Balancing Payment due for 1996–97.
	First Payment on Account due for 1997–98.
April 1998	Inland Revenue issue tax return forms.
31 May 1998	Deadline for employers to provide 1997–98 P60 forms to relevant employees.
6 July 1998	Deadline for employers to provide 1997–98 P11D/P9D information to the Inland Revenue and to relevant employees.
31 July 1998	Second self-assessment payment on account for 1997–98.
30 September 1998	Deadline for the submission of tax returns for:
	a Inland Revenue calculation, and
	b where the taxpayer requires a balancing payment (below £1,000) collected through PAYE.
5 October 1998	Deadline for notification of chargeability for 1997–98.
31 January 1999	Deadline for filing tax returns for 1997–98.
	Balancing payment due for 1997–98.
	First payment on account due for 1998–99.

2

Liability to income tax

THE PERSONAL TAX SYSTEM

The system of income tax which applies for 1998–99 is based on taxable income arising, or that which is deemed to arise, during the year of assessment commencing on 6 April 1998 and ending on 5 April 1999. Many allowances and other reliefs available to individuals must be set against income chargeable to income tax. Where the allowances and reliefs exceed chargeable income there is unlikely to be any liability. If surplus income remains, the first £4,300 will be charged at the lower rate of 20 per cent and the next £22,800 charged at the basic rate of 23 per cent. Should chargeable income exceed £27,100 (£4,300 plus £22,800) the excess is taxed at the higher rate of 40 per cent. These rates apply generally to both earned and investment income but some adjustments may be required where a taxpayer receives income from savings. This income includes dividends and most other distributions from a company in addition to many items of interest. Adjustments will also be necessary for a number of allowances and reliefs, notably the married couple's allowance, where relief is given by deduction at the reduced rate of 15 per cent or 20 per cent and cannot extend to any rate exceeding these levels.

PAYE deductions made from earnings extend to income charged at all three rates, namely 20 per cent, 23 per cent and 40 per cent where earnings are sufficiently substantial. Tax at these rates will be collected simultaneously where a taxpayer must discharge liability on business and professional profits, rents and some other receipts. Where income is received, or is treated as received, after deduction

of income tax the taxpayer will be required to discharge any higher rate liability that may arise.

Tax relief on many, but not all, payments of mortgage interest is given under the MIRAS scheme by deducting income tax at the rate of 10 per cent from each qualifying payment made in 1998–99. Similar relief may be available on other payments made under deduction of income tax, although some deductions are made at the basic rate of 23 per cent and others at the reduced rate of 20 per cent or 12.5 per cent. This deduction procedure is merely a method of providing relief and has little effect on the net liability eventually borne.

The unified personal tax system incorporating income tax payable at all three rates is administered by the Inland Revenue.

Independent taxation

All individuals, whether married or single, receive a basic income tax personal allowance which may be increased for those aged 65 or over and further increased for those who have celebrated their 75th birthday. The amount of the increased personal allowance may be reduced where the individual's income exceeds stated limits. With the exception of severely limited transitional reliefs, any unused personal allowance of one spouse cannot be transferred to the other.

A married man whose wife is 'living with' him qualifies for a married couple's allowance. This allowance may be retained by the husband, shared in equal proportions with his wife or made entirely available to the wife. If the spouse to whom a married couple's allowance, or share of that allowance, has been allocated cannot fully absorb the allowance against income the excess may be transferred for the benefit of the other spouse.

Apart from the personal allowance and the married couple's allowance, the only remaining allowances comprise:

a An additional personal allowance for children
b A widow's bereavement allowance
c A blind person's allowance.

Of these three allowances, only the blind person's allowance can be transferred from one spouse to the other where it cannot be fully absorbed by the qualifying spouse.

Independent taxation of husband and wife commenced to apply on 6 April 1990. To ensure that independent taxation did not result in the reduction of allowances a small number of special transitional allowances were introduced. With the passage of time the number of claimants entitled to these special allowances has inevitably declined.

Capital gains tax is also subject to independent taxation, with all individuals being separately assessed. It is unnecessary to restrict the annual exemption to the combined gains of a husband and wife as each may obtain his or her separate exemption limit. However, it remains possible for assets to be transferred between a husband and wife 'living together' without incurring any capital gains tax commitments.

Self-assessment

The introduction of self-assessment on 6 April 1996 increased the compliance requirements which taxpayers must satisfy and also affected the date on which tax becomes payable. However, self-assessment does not, of itself, increase the tax burden and will have little, if any, effect on most employees and pensioners who discharge their entire tax commitment through the PAYE system.

Scotland

One of the functions available to a future Scottish Parliament is the power to impose a Scottish Variable Rate (SVR) of income tax. This will enable Parliament to vary the basic rate of income tax payable by Scottish taxpayers by a maximum of 3 per cent. For example, if the United Kingdom basic rate was say, 23 per cent, a resolution of the Scottish Parliament could increase this to a maximum of 26 per cent.

Notwithstanding the possible exercise of rate varying powers, SVR remains a United Kingdom

tax. Clearly, numerous problems could arise if two rates, namely the basic rate and the SVR applied simultaneously in different parts of the United Kingdom. These problems will be resolved by legislation to be published at some later date.

It is only that proportion of a person's income which is liable to tax at the basic rate which will be subject to SVR. The Scottish rate will not apply to income from savings or income taxed at the lower rate. Nor will it apply to the additional higher rate or to the special rates of tax payable on dividend income after 5 April 1999. Capital gains tax payable is calculated using income tax rates but this tax is unlikely to be brought within SVR.

Subject to these limitations, detailed rules will be introduced governing relief for pension contributions and other matters which affect the application of the basic rate.

PERSONS LIABLE TO PAY INCOME TAX

All individuals whose incomes exceed £4,195 may be liable to income tax for 1998–99, but there are increased exemption limits for those aged 65 or over. Most forms of income are assessable to income tax, although there are a number of exceptions. The following lists illustrate income which is, and that which is not, liable to tax in 1998–99. The lists are not intended to be exhaustive but provide an indication of the approach applied to many items of income experienced by a large number of taxpayers.

Following the introduction of Individual Savings Accounts on 6 April 1999 different rules may apply from that date governing income which is, or is not, exempt from income tax.

INCOME ASSESSABLE TO INCOME TAX

Annuities excluding the 'capital' portion of certain purchased life annuities.

Bank interest arising on deposits.

Benefits in kind made available to most directors of companies, and to employees earning £8,500 per annum or more. Certain benefits enjoyed by employees earning less than this sum may also be assessable.

Building society interest on deposits.

Christmas boxes to employees.

Dividends from companies.

Foster care contributions, should these exceed the cost of providing care.

Furnished letting receipts.

Interest on Government securities.

Interest on National Savings Income Bonds, Capital Bonds and First Option Bonds.

Pensions, whether voluntary or received under the terms of employment and whether received in respect of the recipient's services or those of another person.

Premiums from letting premises for periods which do not exceed fifty years (part only may be assessable).

Profits from businesses and professions.

Rents and other income from land and property.

Rent-free accommodation occupied by certain employees (income assessed by reference to a notional value).

Salaries, wages, bonuses, commission, and all other earnings from offices and employments. Voluntary payments made at the end of an employment and payments of compensation for loss of office are usually taxable, but liability may be limited to the excess of the aggregate sum received over £30,000.

Social security benefits. A list of those benefits which are taxable appears on page 188.

Tips received in connection with a business or employment.

INCOME NOT ASSESSABLE

Annuities paid to holders of the Victoria Cross, George Cross, Albert Medal, Edward Medal and certain other gallantry awards.

Benefits arising under some insurance policies and paid as the result of sickness or unemployment.

Bounty payments to members of the armed forces who voluntarily extend their service.

Compensation for loss of office and redundancy payments for loss of office, but where the aggregate receipts exceed £30,000 the excess is taxable.

Compensation for mis-sold personal pensions.

Covenanted payments made under a voluntary non-charitable deed of covenant.

Dividends arising under Personal Equity Plans.

Dividends on shares in Venture Capital Trusts.

Interest on contractual savings under the Save As You Earn scheme.

Interest on National Savings Certificates and Children's Bonus Bonds.

Interest arising under TESSA deposit schemes.

Jobwatch payments and training vouchers.

Maintenance payments under most Court Orders or agreements, although liability remains for payments under older arrangements.

National Lottery winnings.

National Savings Bank Interest. The first £70 of interest received on ordinary deposits with the National Savings Bank is exempt, but the excess will be taxable. This exemption does not extend to interest on investment deposits.

Payments in kind (where not convertible into cash or money's worth), except where received by most directors or by an employee earning £8,500 per annum or more. Certain benefits, received by employees earning less than this sum may also be taxable.

Premium Bond prizes.

Rent received under the 'rent a room' scheme where gross receipts do not exceed £4,250 or perhaps some lower figure.

Scholarship income.

Social security benefits. A list of those benefits which are not taxable appears on page 188.

Travel vouchers, warrants and allowances for members of the armed forces when travelling on leave.

Work incentive grants payable under government pilot schemes.

3

Allowances

APPLICATION OF ALLOWANCES

Individuals may be entitled to a range of allowances and reliefs, depending on personal circumstances. Most reliefs, dealt with in later chapters, are based on the amount of qualifying expenditure which an individual has incurred. In contrast, allowances are made available as of right and will apply to reduce or eliminate the amount of income tax payable. The availability of these allowances is reviewed in the present chapter. However, the method of providing relief for allowances must be carefully distinguished.

Some allowances, notably the personal allowance, are subtracted from the taxpayer's income and these reduce the amount of that income on which income tax must be paid. It follows that relief will be effectively obtained at the top rate of income tax suffered by the individual, whether 20 per cent, 23 per cent or 40 per cent.

Other allowances, including the married couple's allowance, are given as a deduction in calculating tax payable, usually at the rate of 15 per cent of the allowance. Therefore all taxpayers only obtain relief at this restricted rate whatever their maximum income tax commitment. Clearly, where income is small and there is little or no liability the application of relief at 15 per cent will only reduce tax payable to nil. The benefit of any excess allowance will then be lost.

HUSBAND AND WIFE 'LIVING TOGETHER'

The nature and amount of the allowances which a married couple can claim may be affected by whether a husband and wife are 'living together'. This relationship of 'living together' will be treated as satisfied unless the couple are:

a Separated under an order of a court of competent jurisdiction;

b Separated by deed of separation; or

c In fact separated in such circumstances that the separation is likely to be permanent.

PERSONAL ALLOWANCE

For 1998–99 all individuals are entitled to a personal allowance. The amount of this allowance is governed by the individual's age and in some cases by the level of income received.

Individuals below the age of 65 years receive a basic personal allowance of £4,195. The allowance

---

6
BASIC PERSONAL ALLOWANCE

Sue is 42 years of age and divorced. Her only income for 1998–99 is a salary of £16,000.

	£
Total income	16,000
Less Personal allowance . . .	4,195
	£11,805

Tax payable:

On first £4,300 at 20 per cent . .	860.00
On balance of £7,505 at 23 per cent	1,726.15
	£2,586.15

7
INCREASED PERSONAL ALLOWANCE

George is a widower aged 78. He receives a social security retirement pension of £3,364 and taxable income from letting properties of £8,750 for 1998–99.

Total income:

	£
Retirement pension	3,364
Letting income	8,750
	12,114
Less Personal allowance . . .	5,600
	£6,514

Tax payable:

On first £4,300 at 20 per cent . .	860.00
On balance of £2,214 at 23 per cent	509.22
	£1,369.22

The maximum personal allowance can be allowed as the taxpayer is over the age of 74 years and his income does not exceed £16,200.

8
MARGINAL PERSONAL ALLOWANCE

Ethel is a widow aged 69. In 1998–99 she receives aggregate income of £17,100 from a social security retirement pension and a company occupational pension scheme administered by her late husband's employers.

Total income:

	£
Pensions	17,100

	£	
Less Personal allowance . .	5,410	
Deduct one-half of excess over £16,200		
(£17,100 less £16,200)	450	4,960
		£12,140

Tax payable:

On first £4,300 at 20 per cent . .	860.00
On balance of £7,840 at 23 per cent	1,803.20
	£2,663.20

Part, or all, of the tax payable will be suffered by **PAYE** deducted from payments made by the previous employer's pension scheme.

9
LOSS OF MARGINAL PERSONAL ALLOWANCE

Applying the facts in Example 8, let it be assumed that the company pension was increased by, say £3,000, thereby increasing total income to £20,100.

The marginal personal allowance would then be calculated as follows:

	£
Maximum allowance	5,410
Deduct one-half of excess over £16,200	
(£20,100 less £16,200)	1,950
	£3,460

However, as the figure of £3,460 is less than the basic personal allowance of £4,195, no marginal personal allowance can be granted and the basic allowance only will be obtained. The calculation continues:

Total income:

	£
Pensions	20,100
Less personal allowance . . .	4,195
	£15,905

Tax payable:

On first £4,300 at 20 per cent . .	860.00
On balance of £11,605 at 23 per cent	2,669.15
	£3,529.15

is not affected by the amount of the individual's income.

For those who were 65 years of age or more at any time in the year ended 5 April 1999, the allowance may be increased to £5,410. A further increase to £5,600 is available to those who are 75 or over in the same year. In both cases the increased allowance will be forthcoming for an individual who died before reaching his or her 65th or 75th birthday if that age would otherwise have been achieved before 6 April 1999.

The amount of the increased allowance available to older taxpayers will be reduced if the total income of the individual exceeds £16,200 for 1998–99. Where this level is exceeded the increased personal allowance is reduced by one-half of the excess. This process continues until the personal allowance is reduced to the level of the basic allowance of £4,195 when no further reduction will be made. Where the taxpayer is a married man entitled to the married couple's allowance, the personal allowance will firstly be reduced, before reducing the married couple's allowance. When establishing the total income of an individual the income of that individual's spouse, if any, is ignored.

All individuals receive a personal allowance. Therefore both a husband and his wife will independently receive a personal allowance of £4,195, or some increased amount based on age, for 1998–99. Subject to a limited exception designed to smooth the introduction of independent taxation (see page 20), any unused personal allowance of one spouse cannot be transferred to the other.

Unlike some other allowances, relief for the personal allowance is not restricted to the reduced rate of 15 per cent, but is deducted from income when calculating the individual's top rate of tax.

The personal allowance is not confined to adults but can also be obtained by children of any age. There are, however, complex rules which prevent tax advantages being obtained by parents who transfer income-producing assets to their young children.

MARRIED COUPLE'S ALLOWANCE

Where a married man is 'living with' his wife throughout, or during any part of, the year ending on 5 April 1999, a married couple's allowance will be available. The amount of this allowance is also governed by the age of the parties to a marriage and perhaps by the level of the husband's income.

The basic married couple's allowance for 1998–99 is £1,900. This may be increased to £3,305 if either the husband or the wife is 65 years or over at any time in the year ending on 5 April 1999. A further increase to £3,345 will be forthcoming if either spouse is 75 or over at any time in the year. In the case of a spouse who died during the year but would otherwise have reached the age of 65 or 75 respectively before 6 April 1999, the appropriate increase will be available.

It has previously been shown that the increased personal allowance due to an individual over the age of 64 may be reduced where that individual's total income exceeds £16,200 for 1998–99. A similar restriction may apply when calculating the increased married couple's allowance. To prevent the same restriction being applied twice over, the order to be adopted is as follows:

a Calculate one-half of the husband's total income (not including any income for the wife) in excess of £16,200

b Reduce the personal allowance of the husband by the product of **a** but not beyond the basic allowance of £4,195

c Reduce the married couple's allowance by the

10
BASIC MARRIED COUPLE'S ALLOWANCE

Peter and his wife Katherine are both below the age of 65 and 'living together'. Peter has earnings of £20,000 in 1998–99. Katherine receives a salary of £10,500 and taxable benefits of £300 in the same year. No election has been made to transfer any part of the married couple's allowance.

Peter	£
Total income – earnings	20,000
Less Personal allowance . . .	4,195
	£15,805

Tax payable:	
On first £4,300 at 20 per cent . .	860.00
On balance of £11,505 at 23 per cent	2,646.15
	£3,506.15
Less Married couple's allowance – £1,900 at 15 per cent . . .	285.00
	£3,221.15

Katherine	
Total income:	£
Salary	10,500
Benefits	300
	10,800
Less Personal allowance . . .	4,195
	£6,605

Tax payable:	
On the first £4,300 at 20 per cent . .	860.00
On the balance of £2,305 at 23 per cent	530.15
	£1,390.15

product of **a**, less the amount of the reduction in **b**, but not beyond the basic married couple's allowance of £1,900.

The limitation under **c** is necessary to ensure that two different allowances are not both reduced by reference to the same amount of excess income. Subject to this, the reduction process continues until the married couple's allowance has been reduced to the basic allowance of £1,900 when no further reduction will take place.

A man may qualify for only one married couple's allowance for the year 1998–99, notwithstanding that one marriage terminates and a second marriage takes place in the same year.

A limit is placed on the amount of the married couple's allowance for 1998–99 where the marriage

———11———
MARGINAL MARRIED COUPLE'S ALLOWANCE

Joe and his wife Eileen are both 72 years of age and 'living together'. Joe's total income for 1998–99 is £19,100. Eileen has a total income of £10,000. No election has been made to transfer any part of the married couple's allowance.

Joe has an income of £19,100 which exceeds £16,200 by £2,900. Allowances must therefore be reduced by:

One-half × £2,900 = ... £1,450

The personal allowance must be reduced as follows:

Full allowance	5,410
Less restriction	1,215
Revised allowance	£4,195

A restriction is necessary to ensure that the allowance is not reduced below the basic allowance of £4,195.

The married couple's allowance then becomes:

	£	£
Full allowance . . .		3,305
Less restriction . .	1,450	
Deduction applied to personal allowance .	1,215	235
Revised allowance . . .		£3,070

Joe

	£
Total income	19,100
Less Personal allowance . . .	4,195
	£14,905

Tax payable:

On first £4,300 at 20 per cent . .	860.00
On balance of £10,605 at 23 per cent	2,439.15
	3,299.15
Less Married couple's allowance – £3,070 at 15 per cent	460.50
	£2,838.65

Eileen

	£
Total income	10,000
Less Personal allowance . . .	5,410
Tax chargeable on	4,590

Tax payable:

On first £4,300 at 20 per cent .	860.00
On balance of £290 at 23 per cent	66.70
	926.70

———12———
MARRIED COUPLE'S ALLOWANCE – TRANSFER

Due to adverse trading conditions the assessable business profits of Roy for 1998–99 were only £4,705. He was 'living with' his wife Jane throughout the year and her income comprised a salary of £13,000. Neither spouse had any other income and both were under the age of 65. No election has yet been made to transfer any part of the married couple's allowance.

Roy is entitled to a personal allowance of £4,195 and a married couple's allowance of £1,900. These allowances are more than sufficient to eliminate any income tax liability as shown below.

	£
Total income	4,705
Less Personal allowance . . .	4,195
	£510

Tax payable:

On £510 at 20 per cent . . .	102.00
Less Married couple's allowance £680 at 15 per cent	102.00
Tax payable	NIL

The balance of the married couple's allowance, namely £1,220 (£1,900 less £680) is unused. Roy may transfer this unused part to his wife. If he agrees, the liability of Jane becomes:

	£
Total income	13,000
Less Personal allowance . . .	4,195
	£8,805

Tax payable:

On first £4,300 at 20 per cent . .	860.00
On balance of £4,505 at 23 per cent	1,036.15
	1,896.15
Less Married couple's allowance – £1,220 at 15 per cent	183.00
	£1,713.15

takes place after 5 May 1999. This limitation is discussed on page 128.

As a transitional measure, the married couple's allowance may occasionally be available to a husband who separated from his wife before 6 April 1990 (see page 22). Further transitional relief may be obtained by elderly persons who would otherwise

13

MARRIED COUPLE'S ALLOWANCE – ELECTION

Adapting the facts in Example 10, on page 15, let it be assumed that an election was made by Katherine to take one-half of the married couple's allowance.

Peter

	£
Total income – earnings	20,000
Less Personal allowance . . .	4,195
	£15,805

Tax payable:

On first £4,300 at 20 per cent . .	860.00
On balance of £11,505 at 23 per cent	2,646.15
	3,506.15
Less Married couple's allowance – £950 at 15 per cent	142.50
	£3,363.65

Katherine

Total income:	£
Salary	10,500
Benefits	300
	10,800
Less Personal allowance . . .	4,195
	£6,605

Tax payable:

On first £4,300 at 20 per cent . .	860.00
On balance of £2,305 at 23 per cent	530.15
	1,390.15
Less Married couple's allowance – £950 at 15 per cent	142.50
	£1,247.65

suffer a disadvantage from the introduction of independent taxation (see page 20).

Married couples are provided with the following alternatives where a married couple's allowance is available for 1998–99.

a To take no action with the allowance being allocated to the husband only

b For the wife to elect, as of right, to take one half of the basic allowance of £1,900, leaving the remaining one-half allocated to the husband

c For the couple to elect jointly that the entire basic married couple's allowance should be given to the wife, with no part of that allowance being absorbed by the husband.

The elections available under **b** and **c** must be restricted to the basic married couple's allowance of £1,900. It is not possible for individuals over the age of 64 years and receiving an increased allowance to include the amount of the increase in any election.

Subject to two exceptions, an election will only be effective for a year of assessment if it is made before the commencement of that year on 6 April. The first exception enables the election to be made not later than the following 5 May, if HM Inspector of Taxes was notified before the previous 6 April that an election would be forthcoming. The second exception deals with the year of marriage and enables an election to be made at any time in that year.

Once made, an election continues indefinitely for each succeeding year until it is withdrawn. The time limits for withdrawal are similar to those which govern the ability to make an election.

Where a joint election has been submitted under **c** for the wife to take the entire basic married couple's allowance, the husband can subsequently elect to retrieve one-half of that allowance. This election also must be made within the normal time limits.

It is possible that the husband or wife to whom all or part of the basic married couple's allowance has been allocated cannot utilise the entire allowance due to an absence of income. The spouse involved may then give written notice transferring the unabsorbed part to the other spouse. This option is also available to a husband who obtains that part of the married couple's allowance in excess of the basic allowance which he cannot use.

Rate of relief

Relief for the married couple's allowance is restricted to 15 per cent. This restriction is achieved by subtracting relief, calculated at the rate of 15 per cent, from the amount of tax otherwise payable for 1998–99. The relief is not given by deducting that allowance from the taxpayers' total income.

For the year 1999–2000, commencing on 6 April 1999, relief will be reduced from 15 per cent to 10 per cent.

ADDITIONAL PERSONAL ALLOWANCE

An additional personal allowance of £1,900 may be available for 1998–99 to:

a A woman who is not, throughout the year ended 5 April 1999, married and living with her husband

b A man who is neither married nor living with his wife for the whole or any part of the year. A man

14
ADDITIONAL PERSONAL ALLOWANCE

Peggy is a divorced mother aged 43, with an eleven-year-old daughter and a nine-year-old son living at home. She has not remarried and earns a salary of £14,000 for 1998–99.

	£
Total income	14,000
Less Personal allowance . . .	4,195
	£9,805

Tax payable:

On first £4,300 at 20 per cent . .	860.00
On balance of £5,505 at 23 per cent .	1,266.15
	2,126.15
Less Additional personal allowance –	
£1,900 at 15 per cent . . .	285.00
	£1,841.15

---

separated from his wife but who may claim the special transitional married couple's allowance discussed on page 22 must be excluded

c A man who, for the whole or any part of the year, is a married man living with his wife, if the wife is totally incapacitated by physical or mental infirmity throughout the entire year.

d A woman who, for the whole or any part of the year, is a married woman living with her husband, if the husband is totally incapacitated by physical or mental infirmity throughout the entire year.

The category in **d** was added for the first time from 6 April 1997.

To obtain the additional personal allowance the claimant must show that a qualifying child is resident with him or her for the whole or part of the year. Only one allowance of £1,900 is available, notwithstanding the number of qualifying children.

The expression 'qualifying child' means a child:

a Born during the year ending on 5 April 1999, or

b Under the age of 16 years on 6 April 1998, or

c Over the age of 16 on 6 April 1998, and either receiving full-time instruction at a university, college, school or other educational establishment or undergoing training for a trade, profession or vocation throughout a minimum two-year period.

It is also necessary to demonstrate that the qualifying child:

a Is a child of the claimant, or

b Not being a child of the claimant, was either born during the year ended 5 April 1999, or under the age of 18 years on 6 April 1998, and maintained for the whole or part of the succeeding twelve-month period by the claimant at his or her own expense.

'Child' includes a stepchild, an illegitimate child if the parents have subsequently married, and an adopted child under the age of 18 years at the time of the adoption.

A woman may be married and living with her husband during part of the year of assessment. She will only qualify for the additional personal allowance if the qualifying child is resident with her during that part of the year when she was not living with her husband, i.e. following separation or death.

A man who marries during the year may elect to forgo the married couple's allowance and obtain the additional personal allowance for that year should that allowance otherwise be available; a course of action which would usually be advantageous.

Where a man and woman are unmarried but living together as husband and wife it is not possible for both to obtain the full additional personal allowance for different children. In this situation the claim must be limited to the youngest of the qualifying children only. In those cases where two or more individuals can each claim the allowance for the same child, the allowance can be divided between them in whatever proportions may be agreed.

The additional personal allowance will often be claimed by a separated spouse or divorced former spouse, having custody of a child or children. It will also be available to other single persons, including widows, and a married man or woman with an incapacitated spouse, if of course there is at least one qualifying child.

An individual who qualifies for the additional personal allowance of £1,900 also receives the lower personal allowance of £4,195 (or perhaps more if the individual is over 64). These two allowances are identical in amount to the personal allowance and the married couple's allowance available to a married man. It will therefore be apparent that a single parent family is effectively taxed on a basis similar to that of a married man 'living with' his wife.

No part of the additional personal allowance can be transferred as the allowance is available only to the claimant.

Rate of relief

Relief for the additional personal allowance is given at the rate of 15 per cent. Like the married couple's allowance, relief is applied by subtracting the relief from tax otherwise payable for 1998–99.

The level of relief will be reduced from 15 per cent to 10 per cent for 1999–2000.

WIDOW'S BEREAVEMENT ALLOWANCE

Where a husband and wife are 'living together' and the husband dies, the widow is entitled to a widow's bereavement allowance. The allowance is available for the year in which death occurs. It will also be available for the following year only, unless the widow remarries in the year of her late husband's death. For 1998–99 the amount of the allowance is £1,900.

A widow entitled to the widow's bereavement allowance of £1,900 for 1998–99 also receives a personal allowance of £4,195 (or perhaps some greater amount if the widow is over 64). These allowances are identical to the personal allowance

---

— 15 —
WIDOW'S BEREAVEMENT ALLOWANCE

John and Margaret, both aged 50 years, were 'living together' until 15 October 1998, when John died. The two children of the marriage, aged fourteen and eleven, continued to reside with their mother. Margaret's total income for 1998–99, comprising a salary, a pension and taxable social security benefits, amounted to £13,200. No part of the married couple's allowance was transferred. The tax payable by Margaret will be calculated as follows:

	£
Total income	13,200
Less Personal allowance . . .	4,195
	£9,005

Tax payable:	
On first £4,300 at 20 per cent . .	860.00
On balance of £4,705 at 23 per cent .	1,082.15
	1,942.15

	£
Less Widow's bereavement allowance – £1,900 at 15 per cent	285.00
Additional personal allowance – £1,900 at 15 per cent	285.00
	570.00
	£1,372.15

and married couple's allowance available to a married man 'living with' his wife. In addition, a widow with a qualifying child or children may also obtain the additional personal allowance of £1,900.

It is a necessary requirement that immediately before the time of his death the husband and wife were 'living together'. The widow's bereavement allowance will not usually be available if the parties were separated at that time.

The widow's bereavement allowance is available only for the year of assessment in which the husband dies and for the immediately following year and cannot be obtained for future years. The allowance is confined to widows and there is no similar allowance for widowers.

Further information on the liability of parties to a marriage where one spouse dies will be found on page 129.

The widow's bereavement allowance is available to the widow only and cannot be transferred to any other person.

Rate of relief

The widow's bereavement allowance is given at the rate of 15 per cent for 1998–99 and must be subtracted from income tax otherwise payable.

For 1999–2000 the allowance will be reduced from 15 per cent to 10 per cent.

BLIND PERSON'S ALLOWANCE

An individual who, at any time in the year ending on 5 April 1999, is registered as blind on a register maintained by a local authority may obtain a blind person's allowance of £1,330. Although the allowance is only available for a year of assessment during which registration has been made, it may also be granted in the year before initial registration, if proof of blindness was available in that earlier year.

The blind person's allowance available to a husband may exceed the balance of total income remaining after making deductions for other allowances and reliefs. In this situation, if the husband is a married man living with his wife any unused excess may be transferred to the wife.

It is possible that the wife cannot use all or part of her own blind person's allowance. She may then transfer the unused allowance to her husband.

A transfer from either spouse to the other will only be effective for 1998–99 if it is evidenced by written notice given by the transferor within a period of nearly six years ending on 31 January 2005.

Unlike some other allowances, relief for the blind person's allowance is not restricted to 15 per cent

16
BLIND PERSON'S ALLOWANCE

Eric is a single man aged 35 and registered as blind. His only income for 1998–99 is a salary of £12,000.

	£	£
Total income . . .		12,000
Less Personal allowance . .	4,195	
Blind person's allowance	1,330	5,525
		£6,475

Tax payable:

On first £4,300 at 20 per cent . .	860.00
On balance of £2,175 at 23 per cent	500.25
	£1,360.25

but can be subtracted from total income.

TRANSITIONAL RELIEFS

When changing from the old pre-April 1990 system of taxing husbands and wives to the present system of independent taxation it was the intention that the change should not result in any increased income tax liability due to the reduction in, or loss of, allowances.

There were, however, three situations where a fall in allowances could occur and special transitional relief had to be introduced to offset this fall. These situations comprised:

a Husbands with older wives
b Husbands with insufficient income to absorb the personal allowance
c Separated couples.

The problem experienced by husbands with older wives arose where the older spouse was above the age of 64 years, or perhaps 74 years. The legislation in operation before 6 April 1990 provided the husband with a married man's personal allowance (often referred to as an age allowance) based on the age of the older spouse. Following the introduction of independent taxation on 6 April 1990 the personal allowance available to an individual is based on that individual's age and not on the age of the spouse. The loss of the increased personal allowance could therefore result in increased income tax liability. This possibility was removed by providing the husband with a special transitional personal allowance in place of the personal allowance which would otherwise be available. However, subsequent increases in the rate of the personal allowance removed the need for this particular transitional relief and it can have no application for 1998–99.

The two remaining transitional reliefs continue and their application is outlined below. When approaching this matter, it must be recognised that transitional reliefs can only affect couples who were married before 6 April 1990 and can have no application to those who marry subsequently. It must also be stressed that the very great majority of taxpayers will not be affected by these special transitional reliefs as with the passing of time the restricted number of claimants must inevitably reduce further.

TRANSITIONAL RELIEF – HUSBANDS WITH LOW INCOMES

Where the income of a husband is insufficient to absorb the personal allowance it is not normally possible to transfer any unused part of that allowance to his wife. However, it may be possible for the wife to obtain the benefit of the unused allowance where the parties were married before 6 April 1990. The first step is to establish the amount, if any, of the husband's unused personal allowance which was transferred to the wife in 1990–91, namely, the tax year ending on 5 April 1991. For the purpose of this calculation a distinction had to be made between marriages taking place before 6 April 1989 and those taking place on or after that date but before 6 April 1990.

Marriage before 6 April 1989

To obtain the transitional allowance for 1990–91 in the case of marriages taking place before 6 April 1989, it was a requirement that:

a A husband and wife were living together for the whole or part of both 1989–90 and 1990–91;
b No wife's earnings election was in operation for 1989–90; and
c The allowances available to the husband for 1989–90 (including married man's personal allowance, wife's earned income allowance and blind person's allowance) exceeded the aggregate of:

i the husband's total income for 1990–91, and
ii the allowances available to the wife for 1990–91 (including married couple's allowance and blind person's allowance).

Where these requirements were satisfied and there was such an excess, the wife could obtain a special transitional allowance for 1990–91 equal to that excess.

——— 17 ———
TRANSITIONAL ALLOWANCE – HUSBAND WITH LOW INCOME

Brian and Mary, both under the age of 65, had been married for many years. In 1990–91 Brian was unable to use any part of his married couple's allowance and the entire allowance of £1,720 was transferred to Mary. A claim was also made under the special transitional provisions for part of Brian's personal allowance to be transferred to his wife. As a result, £650 was transferred. Similar claims were made in each of the years 1991–92 to 1997–98, which resulted in a transfer of £300 in the later year. The entire married couple's allowance was transferred in each year.

The following information was obtained for 1998–99:

a Brian's total income was £3,800

b Mary's income was £19,500

c The married couple's allowance of £1,900 was transferred by Brian to Mary

The special transitional allowance representing part of Brian's personal allowance which can be transferred to Mary will be the lower figure produced by the following calculations:

	£	£
i Transitional allowance for 1997–98	.	300
Less Increase in allowances to Mary:		
1998–99 £4,195 + £1,900	6,095	
1997–98 £4,045 + £1,830	5,875	220
		£80

	£
ii Brian's personal allowance 1998–99	4,195
Less Income 1998–99 . . .	3,800
	£395

The smaller figure is £80 and this will comprise the special transitional allowance available to Mary for 1998–99.

Brian has no income tax liability for 1998–99 and the tax payable by Mary becomes:

	£	£
Total income		19,500
Less Personal allowance . .	4,195	
Special transitional allowance . .	80	4,275
		£15,225

Tax payable:

On first £4,300 at 20 per cent . .	860.00
On balance of £10,925 at 23 per cent	2,512.75
	3,372.75
Less Married couple's allowance – £1,900	
at 15 per cent	285.00
	£3,087.75

Transitional relief will continue for future years until it is overtaken by increases in allowances or Brian's ability to use his personal allowance in full.

Marriage after 5 April 1989

To obtain the transitional allowance for 1990–91 in the case of marriages taking place during the year 1989–90 it had to be shown that:

a A husband and wife were 'living together' for the whole or part of 1990–91; and

b The allowances available to the husband for 1989–90 (disregarding any wife's earned income relief) exceeded his total income for 1990–91.

Where these requirements were satisfied and such an excess arose, the wife could obtain a special transitional allowance equal to the amount of that excess. However, if the allowances available to the wife for 1990–91 (including married couple's allowance and blind person's allowance) exceeded the lower of:

a The wife's total income for 1989–90, and

b The allowances available to the wife for 1989–90 (excluding any additional personal allowance, widow's bereavement allowance or allowances transferred from the husband),

the transitional allowance had to be reduced by the excess, or perhaps eliminated.

The transitional allowance was not available for 1990–91 unless the husband provided written consent within a period of six years after 5 April 1991. It was also necessary for the husband to transfer the married couple's allowance and any blind person's allowance to his wife.

The allowance for 1998–99

If the special transitional allowance is to be obtained for 1998–99 it must be shown that:

a The transitional allowance was made to the wife for 1990–91;

b The transitional allowance was also made to the wife for each of the years 1991–92, to 1997–98 inclusive; and

c The same couple are 'living together' throughout or during some part of 1998–99.

Where these requirements are satisfied, the transitional allowance capable of being transferred to the wife for 1998–99 will comprise the smaller of:

a the transitional allowance given to the wife in 1997–98, less any increase in the personal allowance and married couple's allowance given to the wife for 1998–99 over that for the previous year;

b the husband's personal allowance for 1998–99 which he cannot use.

This calculation ensures that once there is a year

in which the transitional allowance is not available, or not claimed, no allowance will be forthcoming in any future year.

TRANSITIONAL RELIEF – SEPARATED COUPLES

For 1989–90 and earlier years an increased married man's personal allowance was available to a husband 'living with' his wife, unless a wife's earnings election was in force. Exceptionally, the married man's allowance could be obtained by a husband separated from his wife if she was wholly maintained by him and the husband obtained no tax relief for the cost of providing maintenance. As no married couple's allowance can be obtained in this situation for 1990–91 and future years, the separated husband could be at a disadvantage from the introduction of independent taxation. To remove this possibility a special transitional married couple's allowance may be available. This allowance can only be obtained if:

a The couple ceased to live together before 6 April 1990;

b The couple have remained husband and wife;

c The wife has been wholly maintained by her husband;

d The husband cannot obtain any tax relief for sums paid as maintenance to his wife; and

e The husband was entitled to the married man's personal allowance for 1989–90.

Where these several requirements are satisfied the husband can obtain a special transitional married couple's allowance, based on the age of the older party. The husband cannot transfer any part of an unused married couple's allowance to his separated wife, the wife cannot claim a special transitional personal allowance where the husband's income is small, and any blind person's allowance cannot be transferred between the parties.

The special transitional married couple's allowance continues for successive tax years until the conditions shown above cease to be satisfied. Once this stage has been reached no further transitional relief will be available.

Rate of relief

In line with restrictions which apply to the married couple's allowance, the special married couple's allowance produces relief at the reduced rate of 15 per cent for 1998–99. Relief will be reduced from 15 per cent to 10 per cent for 1999–2000.

INDEXATION

The tax legislation contains provisions for index-linking the several allowances discussed above. Index-linking is achieved by increasing the allowances in line with changes in the retail prices index. Similar index-linking may be applied to income tax rate bands. However, Parliament may disregard changes in the retail prices index and impose some increased or smaller adjustment, or no adjustment at all.

In the event, all allowances for 1998–99 were increased in line with changes in the retail prices index for the period ended on 30 September 1997. The upper limits in both the lower rate and basic rate tax bands were also increased on a similar basis.

HOW TO OBTAIN ALLOWANCES

The several allowances are given in arriving at the amount of income tax payable, or in fixing the code number used for PAYE purposes. Allowances cannot be granted unless the Inland Revenue are informed of the taxpayer's personal circumstances and for this purpose a proper claim must be made. This claim may well involve completing a tax return. Where the only income of the individual arises from an employment to which the PAYE deduction procedure applies, no further action will be necessary. However, where self-assessment is relevant the allowances and reliefs claimed will be taken into the calculation of tax payable.

The completion of the claim portion of a tax return is straightforward but the information relating to allowances must be inserted as follows:

Personal allowance

All individuals automatically receive a basic personal allowance. Those who were over the age of 64 at any time in the tax year and who wish to claim an increased allowance should tick the appropriate box and record their date of birth elsewhere on the return form. This will enable any increased personal allowance to be calculated. There is a further space for those wishing to claim the special transitional personal allowance.

Blind person's allowance

The date of registration and the name of the local authority with whom registration was made should be recorded.

Married couple's allowance

A man must insert the full Christian or other forenames of his wife. The date of marriage should also be inserted if this occurred during the tax year for which the claim is made. Special boxes require completion if all or one-half of the married couple's allowance is to be made available to a wife.

Additional personal allowance

It is necessary to indicate whether the qualifying child for whom an allowance is claimed resides with the claimant. Details of the child's age and other information should be given, together with the name and address of any other person claiming the allowance for the same child.

Widow's bereavement allowance

The date of the late husband's death must be inserted.

Generally

It is important that the claim portion of the tax return, and indeed all parts of the return, are completed properly. For those affected by self-assessment the recorded information will be used to calculate the amount of tax payable, or perhaps repayable. The provision of inaccurate information may well have serious repercussions, particularly where too little tax has been paid. Many taxpayers arrange to have their affairs handled by qualified accountants who are expert in tax matters and can ensure that allowances are properly claimed and that no more tax is paid than the law requires.

4

Pension contributions

PENSIONS FROM THE STATE

The provision of a pension or lump sum payment arising on retirement, disablement or some other event is of considerable importance. Most individuals will qualify for pensions or other social security benefits provided by the State. These may arise in several differing forms but there are two main headings. Firstly, there is a general entitlement to the basic social security retirement pension. Secondly, an additional pension may be due under the State Earnings-Related Pension Scheme (SERPS) which is available to those who have been in employment. The level of the basic retirement pension is determined annually, with increases becoming payable from the beginning of April. In contrast, the additional pension provided by SERPS is governed by the amount of Class 1 national insurance contributions paid within upper and lower limits. The volume of additional pension payments is growing as contributors reach retirement age and in an attempt to reduce the escalating cost the value of this pension (but not the retirement pension) will fall from a future date.

It has long been possible to 'contract out' from the SERPS scheme, where a satisfactory alternative pension arrangement was made under a scheme linked with an individual's employment. At earlier times contracting out implied a reduction in both primary and secondary Class 1 contributions to eliminate the SERPS element of those contributions. However, following the introduction of personal pension schemes, the ability to contract out was increased without directly reducing the level of contributions. Contracting out may also be achieved by employees contributing additional voluntary contributions. Changes in the amount of rebates and other advantages from contracting out have been introduced from time to time.

There are now no particular taxation reliefs or advantages which can be obtained when securing title to the basic retirement pension or the additional pension, or indeed other social security benefits. Previously relief was available for Class 4 contributions paid by the self-employed but this relief was withdrawn on 6 April 1996.

Many individuals will increase the future level of retirement and other benefits by involvement in an employer's occupational pension scheme, a retirement annuity scheme or a personal pension scheme during their working lives. Indeed, it seems likely that the range of available arrangements will be increased by the introduction of stakeholder pensions at some later date. In the meantime the treatment of existing arrangements for taxation purposes is discussed below.

OCCUPATIONAL PENSION SCHEMES

Many directors and employees pay contributions to an approved occupational pension scheme or superannuation fund. Individual arrangements differ but are designed to provide pensions or other benefits in the event of an individual's retirement or death. The rules of the scheme or fund must be approved by the Inland Revenue before tax relief can be obtained, both by the contributors and by trustees or other persons administering the arrangements.

Maximum annual contributions paid by a director or employee must generally be limited to 15 per cent of earnings. Contributions payable under most occupational pension schemes usually fall below, perhaps substantially below, this limit but it is possible for individuals to make additional voluntary contributions (AVC's) provided the aggregate limit of 15 per cent is not exceeded. AVC's may be paid to trustees or others administering an occupational pension scheme. Alternatively, it is possible to make 'free standing' AVC's to an insurance company or other qualifying institution of the employee's choice.

Any contributions paid to trustees or others administering an approved occupational pension scheme qualify for tax relief when calculating the liability of the payer. Relief is usually given by deducting the approved contributions from earnings arising from the office or employment. This ensures that the earnings chargeable to income tax are reduced by the amount of the approved contributions and PAYE deductions are limited to the net sum. However, where 'free standing' AVC's are paid these are usually discharged after deducting income tax at the basic rate of 23 per cent for 1998–99. This provides full relief at that rate but where the contributor is liable to the higher rate of 40 per cent further relief will be forthcoming. The 20 per cent lower rate income tax band does not affect the ability of a contributor to deduct, and to retain, tax at the basic rate from payments of 'free standing' AVC's.

Difficulties may sometimes arise in determining whether the amount of contributions to be paid on 'free standing' AVC's will exceed the permissible limit. This can only be verified if detailed information is forthcoming on the amount of contributions made to the employer's scheme. However, unless the AVC's exceed £2,400 in any year a check will only be applied when the contributor retires. Any excess contributions will then be returned, subject to a tax charge, which is imposed at the rate of 33 per cent for returns made in 1998–99.

The primary purpose of paying contributions is to provide a pension to the contributor on retirement, or to the spouse or dependants of the contributor following death. For older contributors the pension will usually be limited to two-thirds of final salary. Whilst the two-thirds approach is retained, an initial earnings cap of £60,000 was placed on the maximum amount of final salary to be recognised for new schemes introduced after 13 March 1989,

and for individuals joining existing schemes after 31 May in the same year.

However, the initial ceiling is capable of being index-linked to changes in the retail prices index. As a result, the earnings cap has been increased on several occasions since its introduction in 1989. The cap for 1998–99 and the previous six years is shown by the following table.

Year of assessment	Amount £
1992–93.	75,000
1993–94.	75,000
1994–95.	76,800
1995–96.	78,600
1996–97.	82,200
1997–98.	84,000
1998–99.	87,600

It is often possible to take a tax-free lump sum at retirement and a reduced pension subsequently. For those joining after the dates mentioned above the maximum lump sum is usually limited to one-and-a-half times the earnings cap at the time of retirement.

The maximum pension and other benefits which can be provided by an approved occupational pension scheme may be considered insufficient by the prospective pensioner. However, it is possible for an employer to set up an unapproved 'top-up' scheme providing additional pension rights. Contributions to this scheme will not secure tax reliefs and there are other taxation disadvantages, but the existence of an unapproved scheme will not, of itself, affect recognition of a different qualifying approved scheme.

Occupational pension schemes remain unaffected by the introduction of personal pension schemes, but it is not mandatory for an employee to become, or indeed remain, a member of an employer's scheme.

RETIREMENT ANNUITIES

Self-employed individuals, together with directors and employees not in pensionable employment, cannot obtain membership of an occupational pension scheme. For many years, however, it has been possible for these individuals to secure annuities or lump sums payable on retirement or death under retirement annuity arrangements. Premiums paid to obtain an annuity or lump sum may entitle the payer to tax relief if, but only if, a number of conditions are satisfied. Both the conditions governing relief and the application of that relief are briefly discussed below, but it is not possible to conclude *new* retirement annuity arrangements after 1 July 1988. Contributions paid after this date in respect of arrangements concluded previously will, however, continue to obtain relief. The inability to conclude new retirement annuity arrangements is explained by the introduction of personal pension schemes, discussed later, which retain most but not all of the features to be found in retirement annuity arrangements.

It is a necessary requirement that the retirement annuity contract or other document is drafted in a form approved by the Inland Revenue but in general the contract will:

a Provide the taxpayer with a life annuity in retirement;

b Provide an annuity for the spouse of the taxpayer or for one or more dependants of that individual; or

c Provide a lump sum on the death of the individual before he or she attains the age of 75.

Where these requirements are satisfied, any premiums paid qualify for relief in calculating liability to income tax. Premiums paid in a year of assessment are primarily allocated to that year. However, the taxpayer may elect to treat the payments as having been made in the previous year, or in a year falling two years before the year of payment if there were no net relevant earnings in the previous year. Individuals deriving relevant earnings from Lloyd's underwriting activities may relate premiums paid back to even earlier years. Following the introduction of self-assessment, where premiums paid after 5 April 1996 are related back to an earlier year the method used to provide relief is identical to that outlined on page 28 for personal pension contributions.

Relief for premiums paid, or treated as paid, in a year of assessment is not to exceed 17.5 per cent of the contributor's net relevant earnings for that year. This percentage may be increased to the levels shown by the following table for 1998–99 for those over the age of 50 on 6 April 1998:

Age on 6 April 1998	Percentage
51 to 55.	20
56 to 60.	22.5
61 and above .	27.5

'Net relevant earnings' represent the taxpayer's earned income, after subtracting capital allowances and losses. Personal outgoings, such as mortgage interest, may be ignored. The earnings cap of £87,600 which applies to restrict the amount of earnings on which personal pension scheme contributions can be based has no direct application to retirement annuity premiums.

Where the premiums relate to a contract falling under **b** or **c** above, the allowable premiums are limited to 5 per cent of the individual's net relevant earnings for the year of assessment. However, the figure of 17.5 per cent, suitably increased for older taxpayers, represents the maximum relief which can be obtained for all premiums falling under **a, b** and **c** paid by the claimant. This maximum figure cannot be further increased by the addition of premiums falling within the 5 per cent restriction.

It is possible that the full potential relief for a year of assessment has not been obtained, due to an absence of sufficient premiums paid. This unused relief may be carried forward for a maximum period of 6 years and applied to relieve premiums paid which exceed the 17.5 per cent (or higher) limitation in future years. The relief is given for the year of assessment in which premiums are paid, or treated as having been paid, and not for the year in which the unused relief arose. Once the six-year period has expired the unused relief can no longer be carried forward and will be lost.

Unused retirement annuity relief can be carried forward in this manner and set against future excess contributions paid under personal pension schemes.

PERSONAL PENSION SCHEMES

On 1 July 1988, personal pension schemes were introduced in substitution for retirement annuity contracts. Personal pension schemes do not replace occupational pension schemes, which continue largely undisturbed. Overlapping is avoided by ensuring that earnings from a pensionable employment carrying membership of an occupational pension scheme cannot be taken into account when calculating relief under personal pension scheme arrangements. Thus an individual whose sole source of income arises from an employment, and who is a member of the employer's occupational pension scheme, cannot contribute to a personal pension scheme unless he ceases membership of the employer's scheme. An individual who receives earnings supporting membership of an occupational pension scheme and who also receives non-pensionable earnings from a different source may incorporate the latter earnings in a personal pension scheme. Any shortfall in benefits arising under an occupational pension scheme can be overcome by contemplating the payment of AVC's, either to trustees administering the scheme or under 'free standing' contracts.

With the exception of retirement annuity arrangements commenced before 1 July 1988, and which continue subsequently, personal pension schemes entirely replace those arrangements. This is achieved by precluding the introduction of any new retirement annuity arrangements on and after 1 July 1988.

As the name implies, personal pension schemes are 'personal' to the individual concerned. A scheme is retained when an individual changes jobs or becomes self-employed, although arrangements may be made to transfer from a personal pension scheme to an occupational pension scheme where an individual becomes a member of such a scheme.

Scheme requirements

Contracts for personal pension schemes are made between the individual and an approved institution including assurance companies, banks, building societies and friendly societies, among others. Each contract must be approved by the Inland Revenue and provide one or more of the following benefits:

a An annuity payable to the contributor and commencing on reaching an age between 50 and 75 years. A reduced age may apply by reason of early retirement on the grounds of ill-health, or perhaps engagement in an occupation where it is customary to retire before reaching 50;

b A lump sum not exceeding 25 per cent of the value of the annuity when it first becomes payable, with a correspondingly reduced future annuity;

c An annuity payable to the surviving spouse or dependants on the death of the contributor;

d A lump sum payable on the death of the contributor before reaching the age of 75;

e The return of contributions with interest and bonuses on the death of the contributor.

Allocation of contributions

Contributions paid under a qualifying personal pension scheme entitle the contributor to tax relief. It is possible for an individual to contemplate involvement in two or more schemes simultaneously, but a limit is placed on the aggregate relief which will be forthcoming for contributions paid.

Any contributions paid in a year of assessment ending on 5 April will be primarily allocated to that year. However, after the end of the year of assessment in which payment is actually made the taxpayer may elect for contributions to be treated as paid in

18
ALLOCATION OF CONTRIBUTIONS

On 29 September 1998 Harry paid a qualifying personal pension contribution of £6,000 (gross). In the absence of an election the contribution will be treated as paid in the actual year of payment, namely 1998–99.

However, not later than 31 January 2000 Harry may elect to treat the contribution as having been paid in 1997–98 (or perhaps in 1996–97 if there were no net relevant earnings for 1997–98).

By re-allocating the contribution in this manner it may be possible to obtain relief for an earlier year which would otherwise be lost.

the previous year, or perhaps earlier if there were no relevant earnings in the previous year or earnings arose from Lloyd's underwriting activities. For contributions paid after 5 April 1996 the election must be made not later than 31 January falling some ten months after the end of the year of assessment in which payment was actually made.

Limitations on relief

The maximum contributions paid, or deemed to be paid, in a year of assessment and which qualify for relief in that year are not to exceed 17.5 per cent of net relevant earnings. This percentage may be increased to the following levels for 1998–99 for those over the age of 35 on 6 April 1998:

Age on 6 April 1998					Percentage
36 to 45.	.	.	.	.	20
46 to 50.	.	.	.	.	25
51 to 55.	.	.	.	.	30
56 to 60.	.	.	.	.	35
61 and above .	.	.	.	.	40

Where the personal pension scheme produces entitlement to a lump sum falling under **d** above, the maximum contributions qualifying for relief and attributable to that scheme are not to exceed 5 per cent of net relevant earnings. This limitation of 5 per cent is not to increase the total relief above the 17.5 per cent (or higher amount for older taxpayers) level.

When applying the appropriate percentage to net relevant earnings for 1989–90, any excess of those earnings above £60,000 had to be disregarded. This was in line with the earnings cap which applied to members of an occupational pension scheme. However, the limit may be increased annually as the retail prices index increases. Several increases have taken place and the figures for 1998–99, together with those for the previous six years are shown by the table below.

Year of assessment	Maximum £
1992–93.	75,000
1993–94.	75,000
1994–95.	76,800
1995–96.	78,600
1996–97.	82,200
1997–98.	84,000
1998–99.	87,600

Occasionally, both an employee and his or her employer may pay contributions to a personal pension scheme taken out by the employee. Any contributions discharged by the employer will be subtracted from the maximum amount on which the employee can otherwise obtain relief.

'Net relevant earnings' will comprise most items of income arising from an employment, office, trade or profession, after subtracting capital allowances and losses, among other items. There must be excluded earnings from an office or employment which entitles the employee to membership of an occupational pension scheme.

Method of providing relief
Personal pension contributions actually paid in a year of assessment may either be:

a Treated as paid in the year of payment; or
b Related back to an earlier year, if of course a suitable election is made.

Payments made before 6 April 1996 and dealt with under either heading reduced the amount of income tax payable for the year of assessment to

---

19
CALCULATION OF RELIEF NO RELATING BACK

Sandra, a single woman aged 34, had profits of £40,000 assessable for 1998–99. On 24 November 1998, she paid a contribution of £6,000 under an approved personal pension scheme. The contribution remained allocated to the year of payment.

	£
Total income	40,000
Less contribution	6,000
	34,000
Less Personal allowance . .	4,195
	£29,805

Tax payable:	£
Lower rate:	
On first £4,300 at 20 per cent . .	860.00
Basic rate:	
On next £22,800 at 23 per cent .	5,244.00
Higher rate:	
On balance of £2,705 at 40 per cent .	1,082.00
	£7,186.00

20
CALCULATION OF RELIEF RELATING BACK

John is a single man aged 40. He had profits of £40,000 assessable for 1997–98. Apart from the personal allowance there were no deductions or allowances. The income tax payable became:

	£
Total income	40,000
Less personal allowance . . .	4,045
	£35,955

Tax payable	
Lower rate:	£
On first £4,100 at 20 per cent . .	820.00
Basic rate:	
On next £22,000 at 23 per cent .	5,060.00
Higher rate:	
On balance of £9,855 at 40 per cent .	3,942.00
	£9,822.00

On 24 November 1998 John paid a contribution of £6,000 under an approved personal pension scheme. This contribution was actually paid in 1998–99 but John filed an election to treat it as paid in 1997–98.

If the contribution of £6,000 had actually been paid in 1997–98 tax would be payable on £29,955 (not £35,955). As a result tax at the higher rate of 40 per cent would be reduced by

£6,000 at 40 per cent =	£2,400

However, the tax liability for 1997–98 remains in the original sum of £9,822. The relief of £2,400 will be given, at John's option,

a By repayment,
b By set-off against liability for 1998–99, or
c By treating £2,400 as a payment on account for tax due for 1998–99.

——— 21 ———
CARRYING FORWARD UNUSED RELIEF

In the absence of sufficient premiums paid, Andrew had the following amounts of unused relief for earlier years:

		£
1992–93	. . . . . .	740
1993–94	. . . . . .	1,620
1994–95	. . . . . .	5,800
1995–96	. . . . . .	2,900
1996–97	. . . . . .	3,250
1997–98	. . . . . .	1,760

Andrew's net relevant earnings for 1998–99 were £42,000. During 1998–99 he paid contributions of £17,000 on a qualifying personal pension scheme policy which remained allocated to the year of payment. Assuming Andrew was 40 years of age on 6 April 1998, and therefore qualified for the increased relief calculated at the rate of 20 per cent, these contributions will be absorbed as follows:

		£
Maximum relief for 1998–99		
20 per cent of £42,000 .	. . .	8,400
Unused relief brought forward (earlier year first)		
1992–93	. . . . .	740
1993–94	. . . . .	1,620
1994–95	. . . . .	5,800
1995–96	. . . . .	440
Total relief available for 1998–99	. .	£17,000

Unused relief available for future years (subject to six-year time limit)

		£
1995–96	. . . . .	2,460
1996–97	. . . . .	3,250
1997–98	. . . . .	1,760
1998–99	. . . . .	NIL

If Andrew is a married man with no other income, and entitled to the full married couple's allowance, the tax payable for 1998–99 becomes:

		£
Total income:		
Business profits .	. . .	42,000
Deduct personal pension contributions	.	17,000
		25,000
Less Personal allowance	. . .	4,195
		£20,805
Tax payable:		
On first £4,300 at 20 per cent	. .	860.00
On balance of £16,505 at 23 per cent	.	3,796.15
		4,656.15
Less Married couple's allowance – £1,900		
at 15 per cent .	. . . .	285.00
		£4,371.15

which those payments were allocated. However, a rather different system applies for personal pension contributions paid after 5 April 1996.

Where these more recent contributions are allocated to the year of payment, the former approach remains undisturbed. The qualifying payments will be relieved against income chargeable to income tax with liability being discharged under the normal self-assessment procedure.

A different approach emerges where contributions paid in one year are related back to an earlier year. The first step is then to calculate the amount of the reduction in income tax due for the earlier year by reason of the related back contributions. However, the amount of income tax payable for the earlier year remains undisturbed and this may well govern the calculation of payments on account of liability which must be discharged under the self-assessment regime for the later year.

An amount representing the reduction in income tax liability for the previous year may be relieved:

a By repayment of tax previously paid;
b By set-off against outstanding income tax liabilities; or
c By treating the amount repayable as a payment made on account for the year in which contributions were actually paid.

This approach was considered advisable to avoid any re-calculation of tax payable for the earlier year to which contributions had been related back.

However, in recognition of the widespread confusion which arose from the introduction of the revised approach, a special relaxation was made for contributions paid in 1996–97 and related back to 1995–96. In this situation the assessment for 1995–96 was amended to produce a reduced liability governing the calculation of payments on account for the following year, 1996–97. It must be emphasised that this special relaxation has no application to any further contributions.

Those contemplating the payment of future contributions which are to be related back should be aware that they will not affect the calculation of payments of income tax on account for the later year. Frequently it will not be possible to avoid this problem but where circumstances permit it is advisable to satisfy contributions shortly before 5 April and to avoid the need to relate those contributions back to an earlier year.

Similar comments apply to retirement annuity contributions which are related back to an earlier year.

Reference is made on page 84 to business losses incurred in a year of assessment which can be related back to the previous year. Here also, loss relief attributable to that previous year will be dealt with in a manner identical to that which applies to related back personal pension contributions.

Unused relief

Contributions allocated to a year of assessment may fall below the maximum available relief calculated by applying the 17.5 per cent, or some other increased, level. The unused relief may then be carried forward for a maximum period of 6 years and applied to relieve contributions paid in a future year which exceed the 17.5 per cent (or other) limit for that year. Relief is given for the year in which contributions are paid, or treated as paid, and not in the year during which unused relief arose.

Once the six year period has expired any remaining unused relief must be abandoned.

Mixed contributions

It is possible for an individual to pay both retirement annuity contributions and personal pension scheme contributions in the same year of assessment. Where relief is available for both, retirement annuity contributions are afforded priority. Before contemplating payments under both headings in the same year expert advice may well be required. This will recognise that whilst the earnings cap does not apply to retirement annuity arrangements, those arrangements may attract a reduced percentage of earnings supporting relief.

Deduction of tax

Personal pension scheme contributions made in 1998–99 will be discharged net, after deducting income tax at the basic rate of 23 per cent where the relevant earnings are assessable under Schedule E. Deduction and retention of tax in this manner provides the contributor with relief at the basic rate.

This remains unaffected by the lower rate band of 20 per cent, although further relief may be due to those suffering tax at the higher rate. Other contributions, namely those discharged by self-employed individuals, are paid gross and relieved in the normal manner by self-assessment.

Contracting out

As an inducement to invest in a personal pension scheme employees are provided with a 'contracting out' option. This is limited to those paying Class 1 national insurance contributions and can have no application to the self-employed. The purpose of contracting out is to remove the SERPS contribution element from Class 1 contributions. Unlike contracting out for members of an occupational pension scheme, the full Class 1 contributions are paid both by the employer and by the employee. The Department of Social Security will then pay 'minimum contributions' to the employee's own personal pension scheme. These 'contributions' identify a rebate of Class 1 contributions, representing the SERPS element, together with an incentive payment.

Contracting out will only be permitted where the personal pension scheme provides a pension equal to that otherwise due under SERPS. Thus before electing to contract out individuals must recognise the loss of a future SERPS additional pension. Contracting out may also be possible for employees who contribute towards 'free standing' AVC's which provide a sufficiently substantial alternative pension.

Husband and wife

Independent taxation requires that the relevant earnings of a husband and his wife are calculated separately and relief given to each individual without regard to the affairs of the other.

Taking an annuity

When a benefit is first taken from a personal pension scheme and an annuity becomes payable, a suitable annuity must be purchased with proceeds from the scheme. If annuity rates are low this purchase will provide a lower annuity in contrast to that which could be obtained if annuity rates were high. In recognition of this possibility a scheme member may exercise his or her right to defer taking an annuity to a date not later than the 75th birthday. This will enable the purchase of an annuity to be deferred until, hopefully, annuity rates improve and an increased annuity will be forthcoming. Pending such a purchase the member must withdraw income from the scheme, subject to maximum and minimum limits. Sums withdrawn are taxed under the PAYE scheme of deduction.

An annuity need not necessarily be purchased from a financial institution in the United Kingdom. It is possible for the annuity to be obtained from a limited range of approved insurance companies operating in a Member State of the European Community. However, the overseas body must have a representative in the United Kingdom. The existence of United Kingdom representation is required to ensure that the PAYE scheme of tax deduction will apply to future payments of any annuity. This scheme now applies generally to all annuities paid under personal pension scheme arrangements.

Compensation for mis-sold pensions

The introduction of personal pension scheme arrangements persuaded many individuals to transfer from, opt out of or refrain from joining, an occupational pension scheme and to take out a personal pension, buy-out contract or retirement annuity contract. This has led to widespread allegations that a large number of individuals were wrongly advised and became the victims of mis-selling. To obtain redress for the financial loss suffered those allegedly responsible for mis-selling are to provide compensation. This may take the form of payments to an occupational pension scheme, personal pension scheme, buy-out contract or retirement annuity contract for the benefit of the victim. In some situations lump sums may be received by individuals as the result of court awards or out of court settlements. Arguably, some compensation of this nature could become chargeable to income tax or capital gains tax. However, where compensation is attributable to bad investment advice given between 29 April 1988 and 30 June 1994 inclusive no liability to income tax or capital gains tax will be incurred.

This exemption does not apply to any annuities arising from the compensation. The annuities will continue to be treated as income and subjected to income tax in the normal manner.

As part of the arrangements the victims of mis-selling may be reinstated in an occupational pension scheme. In recognition that changes have been made in the treatment of such schemes, reinstatement will be treated as applying from the date an individual left a scheme or from the date he or she would otherwise have joined but for the mis-selling.

Pension scheme funding

Most forms of income received by pension funds are exempt from liability to taxation. Where income tax has been deducted, with only the net sum remaining being received, the tax suffered may usually be repaid. This previously enabled pension funds to obtain repayment of tax credits attaching to dividends from United Kingdom companies.

However, the ability to recover the amount of tax credits ceased to apply for dividends and other distributions arising on and after 2 July 1997. From that date the income of pension funds will be limited to the actual amount of the dividend or distribution without an addition for the tax credit. Clearly, the effect is to substantially reduce the level of income which certain pension funds may receive. For example, a cash dividend of £80 received in 1996–97 or 1997–98 (before 2 July 1997) carries a tax credit of £20, representing one-fifth of the total sum received. The same dividend arising subsequently represents income of only £80, an effective reduction of one-fifth.

The removal of relief for tax credits affects all pension funds, including occupational pension schemes and funds used to invest contributions under retirement annuity scheme or personal pension scheme arrangements. Unless the effective reduction in income attributable to dividends can be made good from other investments, it does seem inevitable that either contributions to pension scheme arrangements will have to be increased or the future level of pension benefits will be reduced.

5

Interest paid

MANY INDIVIDUALS make payments of interest, particularly on mortgages or loans obtained to acquire their own homes. These individuals are entitled to income tax relief for interest paid if, but only if, a number of conditions are satisfied. When approaching this matter there are two quite separate problems to be resolved, namely the identity of the interest which qualifies for relief and also the manner in which that relief can be granted. Relief is now severely restricted to the reduced rate of 10 per cent for payments of mortgage interest but this restriction does not extend to other qualifying interest payments.

No relief will be forthcoming for payments of interest on a bank overdraft or similar facility, unless those payments can be included in the calculation of business profits. Relief for other payments which do not comprise a business outlay will only be available if interest is payable on a debt incurred to finance expenditure falling under one of the headings discussed below. If the requirements of these headings are not satisfied the interest cannot qualify for relief when calculating the payer's liability to income tax.

PRIVATE RESIDENCES – MORTGAGE INTEREST

Occupation by borrower

Interest paid on a loan applied to acquire land or buildings in the United Kingdom or the Republic of Ireland will qualify for relief, if at the time the interest is paid the property is used as the borrower's only or main residence. Relief also extends to interest paid on a loan to purchase caravans and houseboats used for a similar purpose.

For interest paid within a period of twelve months, or perhaps longer at the discretion of the Inland Revenue, from the date of borrowing, relief will also be available should the property be used for a qualifying purpose at any time within the twelve-month period. In such cases it is immaterial whether the property was actually used at the time interest was paid.

The fall in property values which occurred in the early nineteen nineties created many situations, known as 'negative equity', where the value of a property became less than the outstanding mortgage. This could often prevent the owner of that property finding a purchaser and acquiring a new home as the sale proceeds may well be insufficient to discharge the outstanding mortgage. However, it may occasionally be possible to overcome this difficulty and retain an entitlement to interest relief if:

a Interest is being paid on a qualifying loan used to acquire the old property; and

b The lender agrees to substitute the new home for the old as security for the existing loan.

Although this arrangement will not result in the old loan being applied to acquire the new home, relief for interest paid will be forthcoming if the new home is a qualifying residence. Before agreeing to this 'substitute' arrangement, lenders will be anxious to ensure that the value of any security is not eroded.

Partial residential use

It will sometimes be found that a single loan is obtained to acquire property which is partly occupied as the borrower's residence and partly used exclusively for business purposes. By concession, it is then possible to allocate the loan into two distinct parts, one reflecting the portion attributable to residential use and the other representing the part attributable to business use. Interest paid on that part of the loan allocated to qualifying residential use may be relieved in the manner discussed below. The remaining interest attributable to the business part may then be included in the calculation of business profits.

Occupation by dependent relatives and others

In limited situations relief may also be available for interest paid on a loan applied before 6 April 1988 to purchase land, buildings, caravans and houseboats used as the only or main residence of:

a A dependent relative of the borrower; or
b A former or separated spouse of the borrower.

Occupation by a dependent relative will only be recognised if the property is provided rent-free and without other consideration. The expression 'dependent relative' when applied to an individual identifies a relative of that individual, or his spouse, who is incapacitated by old age or infirmity from maintaining himself. It also includes the mother or mother-in-law of the individual if she is widowed, living apart from her husband or divorced.

This relief for property occupied by a dependent relative, a former spouse or a separated spouse is only available where the loan was applied before 6 April 1988. No relief will be forthcoming for interest on loans applied on or after that date. It also remains a condition for obtaining relief that the individual occupying property before 6 April 1988 continues to occupy the same property when future payments of interest are made on 'old' loans. Should the 'old' loan be replaced by a new loan, no relief can be allowed for interest on the replacement loan.

Improvement loans

Relief was previously available for interest paid on a loan applied to improve property occupied as a qualifying residence by the borrower, a dependent relative or a former or separated spouse. However, relief cannot apply to interest on any home improvement loan granted after 5 April 1988, unless the loan is used to finance the construction of a new building for occupation by the borrower and otherwise satisfies the remaining requirements governing relief. Interest on qualifying improvement loans obtained before 6 April 1988 continues to obtain relief but, should such a loan be replaced by a new loan on or after this date, no relief will be available for interest on the replacement loan.

Limitations of relief

A limitation is placed on the maximum amount of interest paid by an individual in the year ending on 5 April 1999 which can qualify for relief. This limitation is imposed by restricting relief to interest on loans of £30,000. It is the amount of the qualifying loan, or loans, which establishes relief and not the amount of interest paid. £30,000 is an overriding maximum, incorporating all qualifying loans attributable to residences and falling under this heading. In those situations where the aggregate loans exceed £30,000, relief is limited to interest on the first £30,000. Any loans applied after 5 April 1988 which fail to qualify for relief may be disregarded when calculating the limit.

Notwithstanding the system of independent taxation, a husband and wife 'living together' cannot each obtain the benefit of the £30,000 limit. This limit applies to the aggregate amount of qualifying loans made to a husband and his wife. As will be seen later (page 39) there is some flexibility in selecting the spouse who can be treated as having paid interest qualifying for relief. Unfortunately, this flexibility has lost a great deal of its former attraction with relief being restricted to a mere 10 per cent.

A problem may sometimes arise where a man and a woman were each obtaining relief for interest paid on qualifying loans. If the couple subsequently marry, the limit of £30,000 will apply to the aggregate loans of both. This could result in a substantial reduction in the amount of future interest qualifying for relief.

Joint owners

The ceiling of £30,000 was previously applied to loans made to an individual, with an aggregate limitation of £30,000 for husband and wife 'living together'. This approach continues for loans applied for a qualifying purpose before 1 August 1988. It was, however, considered unfair that two or more unmarried persons occupying a single property could each obtain relief for interest paid on maximum loans of £30,000, in contrast to a husband and wife who were limited to relief for interest on aggregate loans of £30,000 only. In the case of loans applied

22
JOINT OWNERS

On 12 July 1992, three unmarried friends, Peter, Paul and Mary borrowed £90,000 to purchase a house which they subsequently occupied as their only residence. Peter borrowed £40,000, Paul £30,000 and Mary £20,000. Interest of £8,100 (gross) paid in 1998–99 was shared in these proportions.

Although each individual has borrowed a different amount, the limit of £30,000 must be shared equally, namely £10,000 each. Therefore the relief available to each joint owner will be calculated as follows:

Interest attributable to £30,000:

$$\frac{30,000}{90,000} \times £8,100 = \underline{£2,700}$$

Each individual will obtain relief on:

$$1/3\text{rd} \times £2,700 = \underline{£900}$$

23
JOINT OWNERS – RESTRICTION

Adjusting the facts in Example 22, let it be assumed that Mary contributed a loan of £5,000, with Peter contributing £50,000 and Paul £35,000. Mary has been allocated interest relief on a loan of £10,000 but this must be limited to her actual contribution of £5,000. The balance of £5,000 will be re-allocated between Peter and Paul on the basis of their otherwise disallowed loans. This produces the following shares of the qualifying loan:

	£	£
Peter		
Basic allocation . . .	10,000	
Add		
$\frac{40,000}{65,000} \times £5,000$ . . .	3,077	13,077
Paul		
Basic allocation . .	10,000	
Add		
$\frac{25,000}{65,000} \times £5,000$ . . .	1,923	11,923
Mary		5,000
		£30,000

Relief for aggregate interest of £2,700 will be allocated on this basis also.

on and after 1 August 1988, this anomaly has been removed by restricting relief to £30,000 for all loans, or joint loans, affecting a single property. The maximum relief for interest on £30,000 will be shared equally between the two or more individuals

involved. However, where there are unequal contributions, with the result that the interest paid by one individual is less than his or her share of interest on £30,000, the balance may be transferred to other joint borrowers.

If the joint contributors include a husband and wife, each spouse counts as a separate share. These persons retain the ability to vary each other's shares, providing that the aggregate shares allocated to husband and wife collectively are not altered (see page 39).

Bridging loans

It has previously been pointed out that a property must be used for a qualifying purpose at the time interest is paid, be so used within a period of twelve months following the acquisition date or (see below) be temporarily unoccupied, before relief for interest will be forthcoming. This may give rise to difficulty where an individual moves from one property to another and delay arises in selling the old asset. As a result, interest may be payable both on the loan to acquire the old property and also on a new loan applied to acquire the new property. To reduce hardship, interest paid on the old loan may continue to qualify for relief for a period of twelve months, and perhaps longer, following the cessation of use. In such cases the upper limit of £30,000 will apply separately to both the old loan and the new loan. This provides the exception to the general rule that relief will be limited to interest on qualifying loans not exceeding in aggregate £30,000.

In earlier times it was a condition of the extended relief that the individual obtained a fresh loan to acquire the new home. The relief was not available for individuals who moved into rented accommodation or acquired a new home without the assistance of mortgage facilities. This restriction no longer applies and relief is now available to all those moving from their homes, provided the 'old' property is placed on the market for sale.

Temporary absence

Subject to the exceptions which apply where a home is acquired or sold, relief for interest paid on a loan applied to acquire a qualifying residence will only obtain relief if at the time of payment the residence is occupied for a qualifying purpose. In practice, however, there are a number of further exceptions to this general rule. Temporary absences from the property throughout a period not exceeding twelve months are disregarded. In addition, where an individual is required by reason of his or her employment to move from home to another place, either in the United Kingdom or overseas, for a period not expected to exceed four years, the original property can continue to be treated as a qualifying residence if it is to be occupied once more at a later date. Relief will not usually be given beyond the end of the four-year period. However, where property is re-occupied for a minimum period of three months a further four-year test can apply to future absences.

In those cases where an individual retains certain government appointments and is required to move his or her home abroad, any property being purchased in the United Kingdom which has previously been used as the only or main residence will continue to qualify if there is a reasonable expectation of re-occupation on return from the overseas posting.

It is possible that an individual may let his or her property during a qualifying period of absence. In those situations where the property is being purchased with the assistance of a qualifying loan the individual retains the option of obtaining relief under the MIRAS arrangement or including the interest paid in the calculation of income chargeable to income tax under Schedule A.

Two or more properties

Subject to the exception which applies on leaving property, and the withdrawal or restriction of relief for new loans applied after 5 April or 31 July 1988, relief can only be obtained for interest paid in relation to an only or main residence. Where an individual retains two or more residences, for example a town house used on weekdays and a country cottage occupied at weekends, it is not possible to choose the qualifying dwelling, as it only remains to determine which is 'the' main residence.

This selection may prove troublesome where a husband and wife are 'living together' and each owns a separate property as only one property can qualify. The selection can usually be made by agreement between the parties but where a husband uses, or intends to use, a property as his only or main residence and the wife uses, or intends to use, some other property for a similar purpose, the property first acquired will be identified as the qualifying residence.

Loans to directors and employees

Employees earning £8,500 or more and company directors who receive loans either interest-free or at a rate of interest falling below a commercial rate may be assessed to income tax on the benefit arising. However, where the notional interest creating the taxable benefit would produce relief by applying the above rules, if actually paid, a reduced liability to tax may arise (see page 69).

JOB-RELATED ACCOMMODATION

Some employees may be required to reside in living accommodation provided by their employer for the purpose of carrying out the obligations of employment. This accommodation will normally comprise the employee's only or main residence and prevent relief being obtained for interest paid on a loan applied to acquire some other property. However, relief will be forthcoming for interest paid on a loan applied to purchase land, a building, a caravan or a houseboat which is also used as a residence by such an employee, or is intended to be used as the only or main residence on some future occasion, perhaps following retirement, where a number of conditions are satisfied. Included in these conditions is the requirement that living accommodation provided by the employer must be job-related. Living accommodation will only be job-related:

a Where it is *necessary* for the proper performance of the duties of the employment that the employee should reside in that accommodation; or

b Where the accommodation is provided for the *better performance* of the duties of the employment, and it is one of the kinds of employment in the case of which it is *customary* for employers to provide living accommodation for employees; or

c Where, there being a special threat to the employee's security, special security arrangements are in force and the employee resides in the accommodation as part of those arrangements.

Most company directors are precluded from satisfying requirements **a** and **b**.

The availability of relief for interest paid by an employee occupying job-related accommodation is extended to certain self-employed individuals. These individuals must be carrying on a trade, profession or vocation and in this capacity be contractually bound to occupy living accommodation. This requirement will be satisfied if the taxpayer's spouse is similarly bound. Examples will include the proprietor of licensed premises required to reside in those premises under arrangements with brewers. The requirement cannot be satisfied where accommodation is supplied by certain persons closely related to or associated with the self-employed individual.

In the case of both employed and self-employed individuals, relief for interest paid remains governed by the ceiling of £30,000 and is given at the reduced rate of 10 per cent only for 1998–99.

LOANS TO PURCHASE LIFE ANNUITY
Where at least 90 per cent of monies borrowed are applied to purchase an annuity ending on death, and the borrower is at least 65 years of age, interest on the borrowings may qualify for limited relief. It is a condition that the loan is secured on land in the United Kingdom or the Republic of Ireland, and that either the borrower or the annuitant uses the land as his or her only or main residence. This requirement is relaxed where the individual leaves the property as relief will remain available for interest paid in the succeeding 12 month period, and perhaps longer. Should the borrowing exceed £30,000, only interest calculated on this figure will be allowable. Higher rate income tax relief cannot be obtained but relief is available at the basic rate of 23 per cent for 1998–99. It is not limited to the reduced rate of 10 per cent.

PARTNERSHIPS
Interest paid to finance the purchase of an interest in a trading or professional partnership will qualify for relief without limitation. This relief will also extend to interest paid on monies borrowed which are applied as a contribution towards capital or loans and made to the partnership for use in the business. Relief is confined to persons who are members of the partnership at the time any interest is paid.

Where a loan is taken out after 30 March 1994 as part of an arrangement to refinance borrowings by the partnership, there may be some restriction in the amount of relief which can be obtained. This restriction applies to partnerships commenced before 6 April 1994 and is imposed to prevent tax avoidance during the transitional change-over period affecting the taxation of partnership profits.

INDUSTRIAL CO-OPERATIVES
Interest on a loan obtained by an individual for the purpose of contributing capital to an industrial co-operative may be relieved in full.

EMPLOYEE-CONTROLLED COMPANIES
Interest paid on a loan used to acquire ordinary shares in an employee controlled company will usually qualify for relief where paid by an employee of that company. The company's shares must not be quoted on a stock exchange, and several further conditions require satisfaction before relief will be forthcoming.

CLOSE COMPANIES
Interest paid to finance the purchase of ordinary shares issued by a company retaining 'close company' status may often be relieved in full. This relief extends also to interest paid on monies which are reapplied in loaning funds to such a close company for use in its business. If the individual paying interest does not retain a significant shareholding, he or she must devote the greater part of their time to the company's affairs. Broadly, a company retains 'close company' status if it is under the control of five or fewer shareholders, or is controlled by its directors. No relief can be obtained under this heading if the cost of acquiring shares qualifies for enterprise investment scheme or business expansion scheme relief.

PLANT AND MACHINERY FOR USE IN AN EMPLOYMENT
Interest paid by an employee on a loan obtained to finance the acquisition of plant or machinery for use in his or her employment will qualify for relief in full.

PERSONAL REPRESENTATIVES
Relief is available for interest paid on a loan used by personal representatives of a deceased person to satisfy inheritance tax becoming payable on death. This relief is limited to interest on money borrowed for the payment of tax before the grant of representation, or the delivery of an account, and applies only to tax on personal property. In addition, relief is restricted to interest paid in a period of one year from the making of the loan.

Where, immediately before death, an individual could claim relief for interest paid on a loan applied to acquire land, buildings, a caravan or a houseboat used, or to be used, as an only or main residence, the obligation to satisfy future interest payments may be assumed by the personal representatives, or by trustees administering a settlement created by the deceased's will. These persons may continue to obtain relief for interest paid if the asset is used, or is intended to be used, by a surviving spouse of the deceased. Relief may also be available if the deceased died before 6 April 1988 and a dependent relative was in occupation of the property at that time.

COMMERCIAL PROPERTY
Previously any interest paid on a loan to finance the purchase of land, a building, a caravan or houseboat

which was not used as a qualifying residence, could only obtain relief if the property was let at a commercial rent. The property had to be so let for at least 26 weeks in a 52-week period and throughout the remainder of the time the property must have been either available for letting or undergoing repair or improvement. Any interest attributable to the acquisition of commercial property satisfying these requirements was set against rent received and not against income generally. If the interest paid exceeded the rent any surplus could be carried forward and set against rental income for future years.

A new system was introduced on 6 April 1995 for calculating income arising from property located in the United Kingdom. The new system enables interest paid to be treated as an expense when calculating profits or losses from a Schedule A business. With the introduction of this new system it is now unnecessary to consider separately the availability of relief for interest paid to acquire commercial property.

BUILDING SOCIETY INTEREST

Mortgage interest paid to a building society will usually relate to a loan made for the acquisition of an only or main residence. If the requirements outlined on the previous pages and which relate to such a residence are satisfied, relief for the interest paid will be forthcoming, although relief must be limited to the reduced rate of 10 per cent for 1998–99.

In some situations building society borrowings are made on the security of property, without being used to purchase that property. It then remains to establish whether the borrowings have been applied for some other qualifying purpose if relief is to be obtained for payments of interest.

OVERDRAFT INTEREST

Interest paid on a bank overdraft, or that which may be charged on the account of a person as the holder of a credit card cannot obtain relief in the manner outlined on the previous pages. Such interest can only be relieved if it is included in the calculation of profits or gains of a business.

OVERSEAS INTEREST

Interest paid to a person residing overseas may now entitle the payer to relief where the interest is paid on a loan applied for a qualifying purpose. Relief of this nature was not usually available for payments made before 6 April 1995.

In general, where land or buildings are situated outside the United Kingdom or the Republic of Ireland, for example, in the Channel Islands, the Isle of Man, France, Spain or Portugal, no relief for interest paid on a loan obtained to acquire the property will be forthcoming. This previously gave rise to an anomaly where the overseas property produced rental income as that income, less expenses, could be chargeable to United Kingdom taxation without relief being obtained for interest paid on a loan applied to acquire the property. However, the anomaly was removed for payments made after 5 April 1995 and it is now possible to subtract interest paid from rental income arising overseas when calculating the net sum chargeable to United Kingdom taxation.

HIRE-PURCHASE INTEREST

The so-called 'interest' payable under a hire-purchase agreement is not really interest but a 'hire charge'. No relief can be obtained for such a payment, unless the payer may treat it as a business expense in computing profits.

BUSINESS EXPENSES

The requirements outlined above, which must be satisfied before payments of interest made by an individual can qualify for tax relief, have no application to 'business' interest. An individual carrying on a trade, profession or vocation may include in the calculation of business profits or losses sums laid out 'wholly and exclusively' for the purposes of the business. For example, interest paid by a sole trader on a loan applied to acquire assets for use in the business, or to provide working capital, may usually be relieved in this manner without regard to the requirements outlined on the previous pages. However, relief for an interest payment cannot be obtained both as a deduction from business profits and also by reducing the amount of income tax payable. In some situations it may be advisable to consider which form of relief is to be preferred, if indeed any choice is available.

COMPANIES

The above rules governing relief for interest paid have little application to companies, as special provisions apply for the purpose of determining liability to corporation tax.

How to obtain relief for interest paid

MORTGAGE INTEREST – RESTRICTIONS ON RELIEF

Payments of interest made on a loan applied to acquire an only or main residence may obtain relief where the requirements outlined earlier are satisfied. This relief extends to interest paid on a loan used to acquire an only or main residence occupied by a dependent relative, a divorced or separated spouse, or to finance the improvement of property where the loan was obtained before 6 April 1988.

For payments of interest made before 6 April 1991 the payer could obtain relief at the basic rate and the higher rate also where income was sufficiently substantial. Subject to rare exceptions which have long ceased to be available, no higher rate relief could be obtained for interest payments made on and after 6 April 1991. The preservation of relief at the basic rate was relatively short-lived. Interest payments made after 5 April 1994 gave rise to relief at the reduced rate of 20 per cent only, with a further reduction to 15 per cent for payments after 5 April 1995. Yet a further adjustment has reduced relief to a mere 10 per cent for interest paid on and after 6 April 1998.

In contrast, relief remains available at the basic rate of 23 per cent for 1998–99 where interest is paid on loans applied by an individual over 65 to acquire an annuity secured on land.

The removal of relief at the higher rate and the introduction of a restriction to the reduced rate of 10 per cent does not extend to other payments of qualifying interest. These payments continue to support relief at the higher, basic or lower rate, where of course the income of the payer is sufficiently substantial.

MORTGAGE INTEREST — THE MIRAS DEDUCTION SCHEME

Relief for payments of qualifying mortgage interest could be given either by adjusting the PAYE tax deductions made from earnings paid to employed persons or by deducting the interest from income on which tax is directly chargeable. This would give rise to considerable administrative difficulties, particularly in the case of PAYE, when changes are made in the rate of mortgage interest payable.

To avoid these and other problems a mortgage interest relief at source scheme (MIRAS) is used. It must be emphasised that the purpose of the scheme is to provide a more efficient method of granting relief and it does not affect the net income tax liability of most individuals, although occasionally increased relief will be available to those having little or no liability to income tax. Not all payments of mortgage interest are brought within the scheme and any excluded qualifying interest will be relieved in the manner outlined later.

Reduced rate relief – 1998–99

The substance of the MIRAS scheme is that when payments of interest are made to a qualifying lender during 1998–99 the payer will deduct and retain income tax at the reduced rate of 10 per cent. There is a lengthy list of qualifying lenders, including building societies, banks, insurance companies, local authorities and others. The qualifying lender is obliged to allow the deduction of income tax and will recover the sums deducted from the Inland Revenue.

The MIRAS deduction scheme applies to mortgage interest payable on a loan made to acquire an only or main residence in the United Kingdom which satisfies the requirements shown on pages 32 to 35. It also extends to interest on a loan used to purchase other property by a person compelled to reside in job-related accommodation. Although MIRAS applies to interest on a loan used to purchase an annuity secured on land (see page 36), tax is deducted from such interest at the basic rate of 23 per cent for 1998–99 and not at the reduced rate of 10 per cent. Where the amount of any loan exceeds the £30,000 limit governing relief for interest paid, qualifying lenders will operate MIRAS on that part of the loan which does not exceed £30,000.

It is important that borrowers fully advise lenders of any other qualifying loans existing at the time of new borrowings as these other loans may affect the availability of relief under the MIRAS scheme. Notification must also be made where interest on a loan ceases to qualify for relief. This is a most significant matter as the Inland Revenue have often expressed concern that the MIRAS deduction scheme is being heavily abused. Responsibility for its operation rests primarily between the lender and the borrower. Once errors or maladministration have been detected, serious financial consequences will arise.

The MIRAS deduction scheme is limited to income tax at the reduced rate of 10 per cent for 1998–99. As the amount of tax deducted can be

————24———— RELIEF FOR INTEREST PAID – MIRAS

In 1982 David obtained a mortgage loan from a building society to purchase his own home. The loan was repayable by monthly instalments, including interest. The interest element in monthly instalments paid during 1998–99 aggregated £2,860, before deducting income tax at the reduced rate of 10 per cent. All interest paid qualified for tax relief.

The total amount of interest actually paid in the year will be:

		£
Gross interest		2,860
Less income tax deducted at 10 per cent		286
Payments actually made . . .		£2,574

The only income of David for 1998–99 comprised a salary of £31,000. The income tax payable on this salary, assuming the taxpayer is a married man entitled to the full basic married couple's allowance, will be:

		£
Total income		31,000
Less Personal allowance . . .		4,195
		£26,805

Tax payable:

		£
On first £4,300 at 20 per cent . .		860.00
On balance of £22,505 at 23 per cent .		5,176.15
		6,036.15
Less Married couple's allowance – £1,900 at 15 per cent		285.00
		£5,751.15

The net income tax burden is:

		£
Tax payable		5,751.15
Deduct tax retained by deduction . .		286.00
Net tax suffered		£5,465.15

retained, it is not also possible to subtract interest when calculating income chargeable to income tax. If the taxpayer has insufficient income to produce tax liability, for example where income is exceeded by allowances, income tax deducted can still be retained.

MORTGAGE INTEREST – RELIEF OUTSIDE THE MIRAS SCHEME

Not all payments of mortgage interest are brought within the MIRAS scheme; for example, where interest is paid to a person whose name does not appear on the list of qualifying lenders. In these circumstances interest will be paid gross, leaving the taxpayer to obtain relief either in the PAYE notice of coding or by deduction from direct assessment.

————25———— RELIEF FOR INTEREST PAID GROSS

Mark obtained a loan from a person who was not a qualifying lender within the MIRAS scheme. The loan was applied to acquire Mark's home. Interest amounting to £2,860 was paid gross in 1998–99 and qualified for relief. The only income of Mark, a married man, was a salary of £31,000. No election had been made to apportion the married couple's allowance.

Income tax payable for 1998–99 becomes:

		£
Total income		31,000
Less Personal allowance . . .		4,195
		£26,805

Tax payable:

		£
On first £4,300 at 20 per cent . .		860.00
On balance of £22,505 at 23 per cent .		5,176.15
		6,036.15

	£	£
Less		
Married couple's allowance – £1,900 at 15 per cent	285.00	
Interest on £2,860 at 10 per cent	286.00	571.00
		£5,465.15

It will be seen that the tax payable of £5,465.15 is identical to the net tax suffered by David in Example 24 opposite who paid interest falling within MIRAS. This illustrates that the purpose of MIRAS is to provide income tax relief by deduction at source, rather than when calculating the liability of the payer.

One disadvantage of this approach is that full relief will only be forthcoming where tax on net income calculated by disregarding interest, equals or exceeds interest relief at 10 per cent.

MORTGAGE INTEREST – HUSBAND AND WIFE

Where a husband and wife are 'living together' there can be only one qualifying residence between the parties collectively. Interest paid on a loan applied to acquire that residence will qualify for tax relief in the normal manner. This requires that where a husband and his wife jointly acquire a property the maximum loan ceiling of £30,000 will be divided equally, with each able to obtain relief for interest on £15,000. If the loan is made to one spouse only that individual will obtain relief for interest paid on a loan up to the maximum of £30,000.

However, it is possible to submit an 'allocation of interest' election. Where the election applies the interest paid by either, or both, parties to the

26
RELIEF FOR INTEREST PAID – HIGHER RATE

In 1984 Michael borrowed a substantial sum of money which he applied to acquire shares in a close company. Interest of £6,200 was paid gross on the borrowings in 1998–99 and qualified for relief. Michael was a married man entitled to the full basic married couple's allowance. His only income for the year comprised a salary of £51,000 from the company. Income tax payable will be:

	£	£
Total income		51,000
Less		
Personal allowance . . .	4,195	
Gross interest	6,200	10,395
		£40,605
Tax payable:		
Lower rate:		
On first £4,300 at 20 per cent . .		860.00
Basic rate:		
On next £22,800 at 23 per cent . .		5,244.00
Higher rate:		
On balance of £13,505 at 40 per cent .		5,402.00
		11,506.00
Less Married couple's allowance – £1,900		
at 15 per cent		285.00
		£11,221.00

The gross interest of £6,200 has reduced taxable income by the same amount and therefore obtained relief at the full higher rate of 40 per cent. As the interest is not payable on a loan to acquire an only or main residence no restriction to 10 per cent is necessary.

marriage can be allocated between them in whatever proportions they consider appropriate. The election may also allocate the collective interests held by husband and wife between the parties where there are one or more other individuals retaining interests in a single property and the £30,000 limit must be apportioned.

The election must be made jointly by husband and wife not later than 31 January falling some 22 months after the end of the year of assessment to which the election relates. The election will then apply not only for the year of assessment concerned but for all following years. However, either husband or wife may withdraw the election by giving notice not later than 31 January falling some 22 months following the end of the year of assessment to which the withdrawal relates. Once a valid withdrawal has been submitted the normal rules will apply, unless of course the parties submit a revised election.

At earlier times the election was widely used where one spouse incurred liability to income tax at the higher rate but the other spouse did not. There would usually be an advantage in all interest being treated as paid by the spouse with the higher income. With the removal of higher rate relief and the application of relief at the reduced rate of only 10 per cent, the 'allocation of interest' election has lost much of its former attraction. In limited situations it may still remain beneficial; for example, where:

a Interest is paid outside the MIRAS scheme and there is insufficient taxable income of one spouse to absorb the relief; or,

b Increased personal allowances and married couple's allowances are available to individuals over the age of 64.

OTHER INTEREST
Although most items of interest qualifying for relief and paid by an individual will comprise mortgage interest falling to be relieved in the manner outlined above there are other classes of interest which may also obtain relief for income tax purposes. This other interest will be paid gross without deduction of income tax unless, exceptionally, it is paid to a lender residing overseas. The payment will qualify for relief at the lower rate, the basic rate and the higher rate of tax where these rates are suffered by the payer.

OBTAINING RELIEF
Where MIRAS applies to payments of interest, relief will be obtained by making deductions at the rate of 10 per cent from sums paid to lenders. The required documentation will be completed when the loan giving rise to payments of interest is made.

Other qualifying payments of interest falling outside MIRAS will usually obtain relief by a claim being made in the income tax return. The amount of interest on which relief is forthcoming will then be subtracted when calculating the payer's liability to discharge income tax commitments.

Exceptions arise where interest can be included in the calculation of business profits or in the calculation of rental income assessable under Schedule A. Such payments merely comprise an ingredient in the calculation of profits and will be dealt with when recording the calculation on the tax return form.

Other reliefs

Business expansion scheme

THE AMOUNT of income tax payable by an individual may be reduced by a range of allowances and outgoings. Comments on the previous pages have examined such matters as personal and other allowances, together with relief for pension contributions and interest paid. A further deduction which was previously of considerable interest to some taxpayers involved relief for subscriptions made under the business expansion scheme. This scheme ceased to apply for transactions taking place after 31 December 1993, but as future events can lead to the retrospective withdrawal of relief a brief comment may be helpful.

Business expansion scheme relief was available to individuals who subscribed for eligible shares issued by a company. Relief was limited to a maximum of £40,000, representing subscriptions made in a year of assessment, although it was possible to relate some subscriptions made in a year back to the previous year. The relief was given by subtracting the amount of qualifying subscriptions from taxable income.

Business expansion scheme relief, once granted, could be withdrawn retrospectively if the individual, or indeed the company, ceased to satisfy numerous requirements at any time in a five-year or three-year period. There could also be the complete or partial withdrawal of relief should the individual dispose of his or her holding within a period of time, usually five years from the issue date. It is the possibility of this withdrawal which must not be overlooked for events taking place before the end of the maximum five-year anniversary on 31 December 1998.

No liability to capital gains tax arises on the subsequent disposal of shares issued after 18 March 1986 if the business expansion scheme relief has been obtained and not withdrawn.

Enterprise investment scheme

FOLLOWING THE DEMISE of the business expansion scheme, a new enterprise investment scheme was launched on 1 January 1994. This scheme retained many features similar to those used by its predecessor but there were significant differences. Although the enterprise investment scheme continues to confer substantial tax advantages, several important changes came into operation on 6 April 1998.

QUALIFYING SHARES
It is a feature of the enterprise investment scheme that tax advantages are confined to the cost of subscribing for eligible shares issued by a qualifying company. Most shares remain eligible, for this

purpose, unless they carry preferential or unusual rights. The scheme has no application to shares acquired from a previous owner as only the cost of subscribing for shares issued by a company can obtain relief.

INDIVIDUALS WHO QUALIFY

At the time of the share issue the individual subscriber must be either resident in the United Kingdom or, if not so resident, be liable to United Kingdom income tax. This may enable a non-resident individual to claim relief against his or her liability to United Kingdom taxation. An individual who is an employee or director of a company is usually precluded from obtaining relief when subscribing for shares issued by that company. However, this prohibition does not prevent an individual becoming a paid director if he or she was neither connected with the company or with the company's trading activities at any time before eligible shares were issued.

QUALIFYING COMPANIES

The company must be carrying on a qualifying trade in the United Kingdom. It is unnecessary for the company to be resident here as the only requirement is that there must be a trade carried on wholly, or mainly in the United Kingdom.

Most trades carried on by a company qualify for the purposes of the enterprise investment scheme but there are exceptions, including dealing in land and securities, the provision of accountancy services and most forms of leasing. In addition, the following trading activities have been disqualified where shares are issued on or after 17 March 1998:

a Farming and market gardening.
b Forestry and timber production.
c Property development.
d Operating or managing hotels or guesthouses.
e Operating or managing nursing or residential care homes.

The company must not have shares marketed on the Stock Exchange but this restriction does not extend to shares dealt in on the Alternative Investment Market. The maximum sum which most companies can raise under the scheme in a twelve-month period was previously limited to £1 million. However, this restriction was removed for shares issued after 5 April 1998 but replaced by a require-

ment that immediately before the issue the gross assets of the company must not exceed £10 million.

RELIEF FOR THE INVESTOR

Where the several requirements are satisfied an investment in shares under the enterprise investment scheme will qualify for income tax relief. This relief must be limited to the reduced rate of 20 per cent and is given as a deduction against income tax otherwise payable. It is not possible to obtain relief at the basic rate of 23 per cent or the higher rate of 40 per cent. In those situations where income tax otherwise payable is not sufficient to absorb the relief, the excess must be disregarded.

The maximum investment, or aggregate investments, which an individual can make during a year of assessment ending on 5 April 1998 was £100,000. This limit has been increased to £150,000 for years commencing on or after 6 April 1998.

27
ENTERPRISE INVESTMENT SCHEME – RELIEF

In 1998–99 Roger received a salary of £130,000. He was married and entitled to the entire married couple's allowance. During the year Roger subscribed £80,000 to acquire shares in an unquoted trading company. It was agreed that the investment qualified for enterprise investment scheme relief.

The tax payable for 1998–99 will be calculated as follows:

	£
Total income	130,000
Less Personal allowance . .	4,195
	£125,805

Tax payable:		
Lower rate:		
On first £4,300 at 20 per cent . .		860.00
Basic rate:		
On next £22,800 at 23 per cent . .		5,244.00
Higher rate:		
On balance of £98,705 at 40 per cent .		39,482.00
		45,586.00

	£		
Less			
Married couple's allowance – £1,900 at 15 per cent . .	285.00		
Enterprise investment scheme relief – £80,000 at 20 per cent . . .	16,000.00	16,285.00	
		£29,301.00	

The calculation of relief for a year of assessment will be primarily based on share subscriptions actually made in that year. However, where a qualifying investment is made not later than 5 October an amount not exceeding one-half of that investment may, at the taxpayer's option, be treated as made in the previous year of assessment ending on 5 April. The maximum subscription which can be related back to an earlier year was previously £15,000. This was increased to £25,000 for subscriptions made after 5 April 1998. Any amount related back in this manner cannot increase relief beyond the £150,000 (or £100,000) limit in the previous year.

Enterprise investment scheme relief may be withdrawn retrospectively should the individual subscriber or the underlying company cease to satisfy a range of requirements throughout a period of years.

Gains arising from the eventual disposal of qualifying shares will be exempt from capital gains tax if income tax relief once granted has not been withdrawn and shares have been held throughout a five-year period. However, should losses arise these may be relieved against capital gains on other assets, or perhaps relieved against income chargeable to income tax.

An additional attraction is the ability to defer capital gains tax arising on the disposal of other assets, where gains are matched with a subscription for shares under the enterprise investment scheme – see page 148 for further details.

HUSBAND AND WIFE
The annual limit of £150,000 (or £100,000) applies separately to a husband and wife, whether or not the couple are 'living together'.

Venture capital trusts

A FURTHER VEHICLE capable of conferring substantial tax advantages to investors became available during 1995. Not unexpectedly, several requirements must be satisfied before this vehicle, the venture capital trust, can be used to obtain those advantages.

THE TRUST
A venture capital trust is a company whose shares are listed on the Stock Exchange. It is not possible for an unlisted company to obtain recognition.

The trust's main function is to invest in unlisted trading companies. Some trading companies must be excluded by applying qualification rules similar to those which apply to investments under the enterprise investment scheme.

At least 70 per cent of all investments made by the trust must be in qualifying unlisted trading companies, with not more than 15 per cent of trust funds being invested in any one company. The investment in such a company may be in the form of shares, or perhaps loans with a minimum period of five years to maturity, but at least 30 per cent of the investments must be made in new ordinary shares. For trust investments taking place on and after 2 July 1997, certain guaranteed loans must be excluded and at least 10 per cent of the trust's total investment in any company must be held in the form of ordinary non-preference shares.

28
VENTURE CAPITAL TRUSTS RELIEF

James earned business profits of £95,000 which were assessable for 1998–99. He is married and entitled to the entire married couple's allowance. James invested £50,000 when subscribing for shares in a venture capital trust during 1998–99. The tax payable for 1998–99 will be calculated as follows:

			£
Total income			95,000
Less Personal allowance	.	.	4,195
			£90,805

Tax payable:		£
Lower rate:		
On first £4,300 at 20 per cent . .		860.00
Basic rate:		
On next £22,800 at 23 per cent . .		5,244.00
Higher rate:		
On balance of £63,705 at 40 per cent		25,482.00
		31,586.00
Less	£	
Married couple's allowance –		
£1,900 at 15 per cent .	285.00	
Venture capital trust relief –		
£50,000 at 20 per cent .	10,000.00	10,285.00
		£21,301.00

Trusts are given three years to satisfy the 70 per cent and other requirements. Should an unlisted company in which investments have been made become listed, those investments may continue to be held for a period without breaching the requirements.

It is necessary for a venture capital trust to be approved by the Inland Revenue. The purpose of this approval is to ensure that the several conditions conferring recognition for tax purposes are properly satisfied.

RELIEF FOR THE INVESTOR

Individuals may subscribe for ordinary shares in a venture capital trust and obtain substantial tax reliefs. No relief of this nature is available where shares are acquired from a previous holder as it is necessary for a subscription to take place.

Tax relief is limited to maximum investments of £100,000 in a year of assessment ending on 5 April. Subject to this upper limit, relief is given at the reduced rate of 20 per cent of the amount subscribed as a deduction from income tax otherwise payable. The relief may be withdrawn, in whole or in part, if shares are sold or otherwise disposed of within a five-year period.

Investors aged 18 years or more are exempt from income tax on dividends arising from qualifying shares in a venture capital trust. This exemption is limited to investments which satisfy the £100,000 limit and cannot apply to any 'extra' shares which may have been acquired. In addition, gains arising on the disposal of qualifying shares are exempt from capital gains tax if the many requirements remain satisfied at the time of disposal.

Like investments under the enterprise investment scheme, it is possible to defer gains on the disposal of other assets by matching those gains with the cost of acquiring shares in a venture capital trust. Further details are available on page 148.

The availability of relief for an investment in shares issued by a venture capital trust company, the exemption from income tax on dividends arising, freedom from capital gains tax and the ability to obtain deferment relief, collectively provide a considerable attraction. It will not, however, be overlooked that the underlying venture capital trust must invest heavily in unlisted companies. This does carry a measure of risk.

HUSBAND AND WIFE

The annual limit of £100,000 which governs qualifying investments applies separately to a husband and wife, whether or not the couple are 'living together'.

Life assurance premiums

TAX RELIEF may be available where premiums are paid on older qualifying life assurance and other policies. This relief applies only to premiums on policies made before 15 March 1984, and cannot be obtained for new policies entered into on or after that date. Changes to a pre-1984 policy which secure increased benefits may result in relief being withdrawn from the date of the change. Where relief is available this has no effect whatsoever on the policyholder's liability to income tax but merely reduces the amount of the premium.

When paying premiums on an approved pre-1984 policy the policyholder will deduct and retain income tax at the rate of 12.5 per cent. It is immaterial whether the individual is liable to income tax, or exempt on the grounds that his or her income is insufficient to justify liability. In all cases the deduction can be made. A restriction arises, however, where the premiums paid in any one year exceed £1,500, as relief will be limited to deductions of £1,500 or one-sixth of the individual's total income, whichever is the greater. If the amount deducted at the rate of 12.5 per cent exceeds these limits the policyholder will be required to refund the excess.

Separate calculations of total income must be prepared to establish whether premiums paid by a husband or his wife exceed the one-sixth limit.

Medical insurance premiums

FOR SEVERAL YEARS income tax relief could be obtained for premiums paid on private medical insurance contracts. However, this relief was limited to premiums paid on a policy for the benefit of an individual aged 60 years or over. In the case of husband and wife, only one spouse need have attained this age. Several conditions had to be satisfied before relief would be forthcoming. In particular, the policy had to be in a form approved by the Inland Revenue and limited to a period not exceeding twelve months in duration.

Qualifying premiums were discharged after

deducting income tax at the basic rate, with no relief available at the higher rate. The payments virtually fell outside the tax system and did not affect the availability of other allowances or reliefs.

With few exceptions, relief ceased to apply for premiums paid on insurance contracts made or renewed on or after 2 July 1997. The exceptions involved individuals who had made arrangements to obtain or renew cover before that date. These individuals could preserve relief throughout a maximum twelve-month period if contracts were entered into not later than 31 July 1997.

Vocational training

VOCATIONAL TRAINING relief is available for study and examination fees paid by an individual resident in the United Kingdom who undertakes a qualifying course of vocational training. Detailed arrangements have to be observed but to qualify for relief the training must lead to National Vocational Qualifications or Scottish Vocational Qualifications at levels 1 to 5. These are qualifications accredited by the National Council for Vocational Qualifications, which covers England, Wales and Northern Ireland, or by the Scottish Vocational Education Council. Levels 1 to 4 incorporate training up to middle management and supervisory skills. Level 5 extends to senior managerial and professional skills including degree-level qualifications. However, children under the age of 16 together with 16 to 18 year-olds in full-time education at a school must be excluded. In addition, training undertaken wholly or mainly for recreational purposes or as a leisure activity does not qualify.

The list of qualifying courses was widened to include a full-time course lasting more than four weeks which is wholly aimed at learning or practising knowledge or skills for gainful employment. To qualify under this heading the trainee must be 30 years of age or over. Relief was also extended by removing rules which prevented trainees obtaining Career Development Loans and access funding from qualifying.

When making qualifying payments of study and examination fees the payer will deduct income tax at the basic rate of 23 per cent for 1998–99. The tax deducted may be retained whether or not the payer is liable to income tax at that rate. Any payers who are liable to income tax at the higher rate may deduct their outgoings when calculating liability at

this rate also. Relief for payments made is not restricted to the reduced rate of 10 per cent which applies to MIRAS.

Persons providing training and who receive fees after deduction of income tax at the basic rate can obtain repayment of the tax deducted from the Inland Revenue.

National insurance contributions

NATIONAL INSURANCE contributions are payable by many employed and self-employed individuals. There are numerous exceptions and the level of contributions due will frequently be governed both by the amount of earnings and also by upper and lower thresholds. In summary form, the scope of the five contribution Classes is as follows:

Class 1 An employee pays primary contributions based on a percentage of earnings. A secondary contribution, also based on a percentage of an employee's earnings, is payable by the employer.

Class 1A Employers pay contributions where cars are supplied for use by employees and directors.

Class 2 Self-employed individuals pay a flat rate contribution.

Class 3 Some individuals may pay voluntary flat rate contributions for the purpose of securing social security benefits.

Class 4 In addition to Class 2 flat rate contributions, self-employed individuals suffer a percentage rate Class 4 contribution based on taxable profits.

Secondary Class 1 contributions and also Class 1A contributions paid by an employer may usually be deducted when calculating taxable profits of the employer's business, if the contributions are satisfied for an employee engaged in such a business. Subject to this, no relief is available in respect of national insurance contributions paid when calculating the contributor's liability to income tax.

An exception previously concerned Class 4 contributions paid by a self-employed individual. One-half of these contributions attributable to a year of assessment could be deducted from total income when arriving at liability to income tax for that year. No similar deduction was available for Class 2 flat rate contributions. However, the ability to obtain relief in this manner ceased to apply after 5 April 1996. As a result no relief for Class 4 contributions paid is now available.

The reason for the withdrawal of relief was to achieve some further simplification in the tax system in preparation for self-assessment. This was achieved by removing one element in the calculation of liability to income tax. To compensate for the loss of relief and the increased liability to income tax, the rate at which Class 4 contributions become payable after 5 April 1996 was reduced.

7

Employments

Pay As You Earn

PAYE is *not* a separate tax but a scheme whereby income tax on wages, salaries and other earnings is collected by deduction as and when the wages and salaries are paid. A 'receipts basis' governs the year of assessment into which earnings fall. The rules which determine the time of 'receipt' are discussed on page 54. Identical rules apply to establish the date of 'payment' for the purposes of PAYE.

Although all wages and salaries are taxable under Schedule E, circumstances occur where it is impractical to operate a PAYE scheme of tax deduction. For example, an individual employed abroad by a foreign employer may be liable to tax on his earnings but the employer could not operate PAYE, and in such a case the employee will be required to account for the tax due, usually by self-assessment. However, this approach cannot be used as a device to avoid the PAYE scheme where an employee is paid abroad, perhaps on secondment to a United Kingdom employer.

PAYE extends to all income tax payable on earnings or other income to which the scheme relates, including tax at the lower rate, the basic rate and the higher rate.

EMPLOYMENT OR SELF-EMPLOYMENT
In most situations it will be apparent whether an individual rendering services holds an office or employment to which the PAYE deduction scheme applies, or can be treated as self-employed and therefore outside the scheme unless the 'agency worker' approach, mentioned later, supports a different conclusion. There are, however, inevitably borderline cases where the distinction between employment and self-employment is not easy to resolve. No firm rules can be laid down to establish on which side of the borderline a particular engagement falls as each case must be governed by its own facts.

A long-running problem of widespread application concerns individuals working in the construction industry. In an attempt to provide assistance when establishing the status of these individuals, the Inland Revenue and the Social Security Contributions Agency jointly published a leaflet, 'Are Your Workers Employed or Self-Employed?' It was indicated that contractors would be given a reasonable time in which to review the status of their workers and to set up any PAYE arrangements considered necessary. This 'reasonable time' eventually expired on 5 April 1997. If, following that date, contrctors are found not to be accounting for PAYE and Class 1 national insurance contributions, where liability arises, that liability will be related back to 5 April 1997. It is unlikely that attempts will be made to recover deductions and contributions for earlier years, unless there is some evidence of evasion.

In theory, this approach did not support any change in the employment or self-employment status of individuals. The correct status is a matter which can only be established from a review of the available evidence. In practice, however, it is not unreasonable to assume that many sub-contractors and others providing services to the construction industry will be increasingly hard-pressed to resist an allegation that they are employed persons.

Some employers outside the construction industry may choose to disregard the distinction between employment and self-employment with the result that earnings are discharged without deducting PAYE. This is a most dangerous practice as subsequent detection by the Inland Revenue will have serious financial and other consequences.

However, certain individuals engaged in diving operations who could be correctly treated as employees may be regarded as self-employed and taken outside the PAYE scheme.

Agency workers

Many individuals whose services are supplied through agencies and who do not technically become employees of the person to whom services are supplied are regarded as 'employees' for income tax purposes. PAYE will be applied to any remuneration paid by the employer of such persons. This 'employer' will usually be the agency involved in the supply of services.

These agency requirements do not apply to services made available by an individual as an actor, singer, musician or other entertainer, or as a fashion, photographic or artist's model. Nor do they usually extend to services rendered wholly in the worker's own home. Previously, services made available by a self-employed sub-contractor were also excluded from the agency worker provisions but this exclusion ceased to apply to payments made for services rendered on or after 6 April 1998.

Extension of the PAYE scheme

The collection of tax on most jobfinders' benefits paid to the unemployed is brought within the PAYE deduction scheme. The scheme also applies to the collection of tax on social security maternity pay, payments of incapacity benefit, to many pensions paid under occupational schemes and to annuities paid under personal pension scheme arrangements.

CODE NUMBERS

Each employee should have a code number and this is arrived at by the tax office from the income tax return or other information disclosing details of allowances claimed. All the allowances are added together and if the employee has no other income

the total of his allowances, less the last figure, could fix his code number. However, some allowances, including the married couple's allowance, are given at the reduced rate of 15 per cent for 1998–99. The code number will then be adjusted to ensure that relief is only given at that rate when applying PAYE.

If the taxpayer has other income, for example, a retirement pension or income from property, the estimated amount of this income may be deducted from the total allowances to calculate the code number. Whilst this will increase the amount of tax deducted under PAYE, it will avoid the need to collect tax directly from the taxpayer for the purpose of recovering tax on that other income. Taxpayers wishing to arrange for tax to be collected in this manner, rather than by direct collection, should file tax returns not later than 30 September after the end of the year of assessment.

Tax on car and car fuel benefits enjoyed by directors and higher paid employees is also collected through the PAYE system. This is achieved by deducting the estimated benefits from total allowances when fixing the code number. However, where the deductions exceed the allowances a 'K' code procedure will be used (see page 50). PAYE may also be used to tax other notional earnings (see page 51).

No adjustment is usually made on the coding notice for contributions to an approved occupational pension scheme or superannuation fund as these will be deducted from earnings in arriving at the net earnings chargeable to tax. A number of special adjustments will be required to the code number where tax has been underpaid for earlier years, tax is being deducted from annual payments made, or liability arises at the higher rate.

The letters 'L', 'H', or 'T' will often appear at the end of the code number, e.g. Code Number 419L. The letter 'L' indicates that the individual concerned is entitled to the basic personal allowance and the letter 'H' that the married couple's allowance, or the additional personal allowance for single parent families, is available. The use of these letters enables the code to be adjusted quickly where there is any change in the rate at which relief is given.

The letters 'L' and 'H' do not indicate the remaining allowances or reliefs to which an employee may be entitled, but if the employee does not wish his or her employer to know which allowance is available the employee may request the Tax Office to replace the letter 'L' or 'H' with the letter 'T'. The letter 'T' will also be used where no personal allowance is available, for example, where an individual has two employments and the personal allowance and any other allowances have been applied in calculating the code number for the main employment only. Code numbers issued to elderly taxpayers entitled to claim the increased personal allowance or increased married couple's allowance have the letter 'P' to denote a single person and 'V' for a married man.

Although these are the main letters used, others apply in special circumstances. For example, BR indicates that tax is to be deducted at the basic rate and NT shows that no tax is to be deducted. D implies that tax will be deducted at the higher rate and F indicates that tax due on a social security pension or benefit is being collected from earnings or a pension from a previous employment. Social security retirement pensions and widows' benefits are paid gross, without deduction of income tax. This requires that where tax is due, recovery of that tax must be made by adjusting the PAYE code number of an employment or by direct collection from the taxpayer using self-assessment.

CHANGES IN THE CODE NUMBER

Should any change in the available allowances occur during the year the Tax Office must be notified immediately as this will enable the code number to be quickly altered. The need for an alteration may arise, for example, where a taxpayer marries and qualifies for the married couple's allowance, becomes entitled to the additional personal allowance for children or qualifies for the widow's bereavement allowance.

Individuals completing self-assessment income tax returns should include all claims in those returns. Where necessary these claims will lead to the insertion of adjusted figures in notices of coding.

Many employees will not receive income tax returns and must largely rely on the PAYE deduction scheme when making their contributions to income tax. It will often be found that entries made on a notice of coding for one year will be 'rolled over' and inserted on the notice for the following year. An exception obviously arises where the amount of any personal allowance or relief is adjusted but in other situations the 'rolled over' entry may not be correct and should be amended. In the absence of an Inland Revenue enquiry, a taxpayer's affairs will usually achieve finality on 31 January falling some twenty-two months after the end of a particular year of assessment. In the absence of some tax offence, matters relating to the particular year will not be re-opened at a later date.

29
NOTICE OF CODING

A notice of coding relating to the year 1998–99 and issued to Alan read as follows:

Tax allowances	£	Allowances taken away	£
Personal allowance	4,195	Allowance restriction	660
Married allowance	1,900	Car benefit	1,010
Job expenses	90	Part-time earnings	440
		Untaxed interest	120
	£6,185		£2,230

Tax code 395H

The explanation for these entries will be as follows:

Personal allowance
Alan receives the basic personal allowance of £4,195.

Married allowance
He is a married man entitled to the full married couple's allowance of £1,900.

Job expenses
Job expenses of £90 qualify for relief, perhaps on the basis of round sums agreed with a trade union.

Allowance restriction
The married couple's allowance of £1,900 is only available at the rate of 15 per cent. To achieve this, with liability at the basic rate of 23 per cent, the allowance must be reduced by £660.

Car benefit
Alan is taxable on £1,010, representing the benefit from the use of a motor car.

Part-time earnings
These arise from a second job and, like the car benefit of £1,010, are effectively taxed by reducing the net allowances brought into the calculation of PAYE.

Untaxed interest
Tax on this interest is also being collected by using £120 of the available allowances. However, interest is taxable at 20 per cent and not at the basic rate of 23 per cent. The actual figure of interest has therefore been reduced to avoid imposing too high a tax rate.

The difference between tax allowances of £6,185 and deductions of £2,230 is £3,955. By removing the last figure, a code number of 395 will be used – the letter H does no more than identify a code number which includes the married couple's allowance.

It is probable that the notice of coding will have been issued to Alan before the commencement of 1998–99. Therefore, entries for car benefits, part-time earnings and untaxed interest represent estimated figures. When the true figures are known, adjustments will be necessary to recognise tax overpaid or underpaid.

PAYE DEDUCTIONS AND REPAYMENTS

Tax tables are supplied to all employers (and others operating the PAYE scheme) so that the actual tax deductions can be calculated. The amount of the deduction in any particular case depends upon the code number, and the employer is advised of this number so that the correct amount of tax to be deducted can be ascertained from the tax tables. Employers are provided with official Deductions Working Sheets for each employee, unless the employer chooses to use a similar record of his or her own design. Details of payments made to employees are entered on these sheets together with information extracted from the tax tables. This enables the employer to calculate the amount of PAYE deductions which should be made from payments of earnings.

If current earnings are smaller than those for earlier weeks or months falling in the same tax year, it is possible that some tax will be repaid to the employee. This may happen if the tax paid for previous weeks or months is greater than the tax due up to the end of the week or month in respect of which the earnings are small. It may also occur where entitlement to some further allowance or relief arises. In these circumstances the employer will refund to the employee part, or perhaps all, of the tax deducted on earlier occasions.

Class 1 national insurance contributions are also entered on the Deductions Working Sheets. However, these contributions do not represent the payment of income tax and are only dealt with under the PAYE scheme for administrative reasons.

UNEMPLOYMENT

Unemployment benefit and income support for the unemployed have been replaced by jobseeker's allowance. Like its predecessors this allowance is taxable, although no deduction of tax will usually be made until the period of unemployment has ended.

On becoming unemployed an individual will be handed a leaving certificate, Form P45. If he or she claims jobseeker's allowance the form must be handed to the benefit office. On subsequently finding a new employment the individual will deliver a completed card UB40 to the benefit office. This office then issues the individual with an updated Form P45, including the amount of any taxable jobseeker allowance, and will make any repayment of PAYE deductions which may be due. The new employer uses the information shown on the P45 to make future deductions from earnings. If the period of unemployment extends beyond the following 5 April, the benefit office will make any repayment of PAYE which may arise.

It follows that where an individual becomes unemployed, no repayment of PAYE deductions can be obtained until the end of the tax year, or the end of the period of unemployment, whichever occurs first. Persons becoming unemployed by reason of strike action cannot obtain repayment of PAYE until the strike ends.

The purpose of withholding refunds during a period of unemployment, and refraining from deducting PAYE on allowances paid, is one of administrative convenience. In many cases the amount due to be refunded will be similar to the tax due on the taxable social security benefit.

THE 'K' CODE

The PAYE scheme is used to collect income tax by deduction when earnings are paid. Not all rewards chargeable to income tax are received in the form of cash payments. Examples include a large number of benefits in kind enjoyed by directors and employees (see page 64). It has long been the practice to collect tax indirectly on these non-cash sums by subtracting the estimated taxable benefits from allowances when arriving at the code number used to operate PAYE. However, this approach cannot be fully effective where the total non-cash items exceed the amount of the allowances as it is not possible to use a negative code number.

To resolve this problem a 'K' code procedure is used. This does not require any amendment to an existing code number. Instead, additions are made to the amount of taxable pay from which PAYE deductions must be subtracted. The additions, made at agreed rates, reflect the value of taxable benefits and enable income tax to be collected on those benefits through the PAYE system.

The 'K' codes may also apply to pensioners whose social security retirement pensions exceed the available allowances.

It may be found that by adding notional earnings, reflecting taxable benefits, to actual earnings the amount of PAYE to be deducted from payments made is excessively high, or may even exceed the amount of the actual payment. To avoid distortions of this nature a restriction is placed on the maximum deduction, which will not usually exceed 50 per cent of the actual pay. Subject to this modification, the existing PAYE procedure will apply generally to those taxpayers allocated 'K' codes.

30
THE 'K' CODE

When completing the 1998–99 notice of coding for Brian it was found that the only allowance comprised a personal allowance of £4,195. Amounts to be deducted from this allowance comprised:

	£
Car benefit	4,100
Car fuel benefit	1,280
Property income	1,525
	£6,905

The deductions of £6,905 exceed the personal allowance of £4,195 by £2,710. The 'K' code procedure will therefore be used to calculate the 'negative amount' of £2,710.

The tax code becomes K271, with the result that £2,710 will be added to earnings and the aggregate subjected to PAYE deductions.

NOTIONAL PAYMENTS

The insertion of notional earnings where 'K' code arrangements are in operation does not exhaust the list of special additions which must be made when accounting for PAYE deductions. Further adjustments may be required in recognition of arrangements for avoiding the PAYE deduction procedure by rewarding employees in gold bullion, coffee beans, and other commodities or assets. As rewards of this nature did not represent 'payments' the PAYE deduction scheme could not apply. It was unlikely that this achieved any permanent tax avoidance as the employee was directly charged to tax on the value of assets received. However, a considerable interval of time could elapse before tax was collected and paid in this manner, in contrast to the immediate liability where the PAYE deduction procedure applied.

To counter this form of avoidance employers are now required to account for PAYE when directors or employees are rewarded with a wide range of 'readily convertible assets' (previously termed 'tradeable assets'). Notional earnings, representing the cost of assets supplied, must be entered on the deductions working sheets for the month in which the supply of assets is made. Where earnings are sufficiently substantial to absorb the additional amount of PAYE this will be deducted. However, where earnings are not sufficient the employer must still account for the proper amount of PAYE deductions which ought to be made. Any tax accounted for in this manner will be treated as borne by the director or employee.

CHANGING JOBS AND NEW EMPLOYMENTS

If an individual changes jobs, he or she will receive from the old employer a leaving certificate, Form P45, which sets out the code number, the total pay to date and the total tax that has been deducted in the tax year.

Form P45 comprises four duplicate Parts. The old employer will submit Part 1 to the Tax Office. The employee will retain Part 1(a), and hand the remaining Parts 2 and 3 to the new employer, if any, who will then continue the deductions from the later earnings of the same tax year.

It is often found that delay occurs in obtaining a Form P45, and some individuals may fail to take proper care of the form handed to them. This causes considerable work, both for the new employer and also the Inland Revenue, as laborious steps must be taken to trace details relating to the tax affairs of the employee. Individuals should take great care of a Form P45 and hand it to the new employer at the earliest opportunity. If they do not, excessive PAYE deductions may be made by the new employer until a revised notice of coding is issued. To avoid problems of this nature a special procedure is used. This procedure, which applies where a Form P45 is not handed to the new employer promptly, requires the issue of a short questionnaire. The questionnaire urges the new employee to contact his old employer for the speedy production of Form P45 and also requires the provision of sufficient information for the Tax Office to compute a provisional code if there is further delay.

School leavers and others commencing employment for the first time should be placed on an emergency code until they have completed an income tax return which enables an accurate code to be issued. However, such persons will, after signing a simple declaration, be given a code number for a single person and no income tax return will be issued, unless requested by the taxpayer.

Taxpayers starting an additional job are placed on an emergency code, if their earnings are sufficiently substantial, or may have no tax deducted until the Tax Office issues a code number. Tax deductions made from earnings arising from the additional job are imposed at the basic rate of 23 per cent.

Where the 'K' code procedure outlined above applied to the old employment, this will be reviewed by the Inland Revenue to establish whether it should be continued by the new employer, if any.

ACCOUNTING FOR DEDUCTIONS

Most employers are required to pay over to the Collector of Taxes, not later than fourteen days after the end of each tax month, deductions made in the previous month. A tax month ends on the fifth day with the result that the employer's liability to account for deductions arises on the nineteenth of each month. A similar procedure applies to the discharge of Class 1 national insurance contributions.

However, a change in the accounting arrangements is available for small employers. If the average aggregate monthly payments of PAYE deductions and national insurance contributions fall below £600 the employer may adopt a quarterly, rather than a monthly, accounting basis. Payments will then fall due fourteen days after the end of each quarter terminating on 5 July, 5 October, 5 January and 5 April.

Contractors in the construction industry may also adopt a quarterly basis when accounting for deductions from payments to sub-contractors (see page 91) where the average aggregate monthly payments of PAYE, national insurance contributions and sub-contractors' deductions fall below £600.

OMISSION TO DEDUCT TAX

The purpose of the PAYE deduction scheme is to collect tax on earnings when emoluments are paid, or deemed to be paid, to an employee. However, the employer's obligation is not limited to the satisfaction of sums actually deducted but extends to the amount of deductions which ought to have been made, less repayments properly due to employees. Failure on the part of the employer to make the full deductions can therefore have serious consequences, as the Inland Revenue may demand payment of the full sums due. This situation often arises following an investigation of an employer's affairs and the allegation that the deduction procedure has not been properly applied.

In two situations the employer may be relieved from the obligation to account for deductions which have not been made. The first arises where the Collector of Taxes can be satisfied that the employer took reasonable care to comply with the PAYE regulations, and the under-deduction was due to an error made in good faith. In this situation the Collector may direct that the outstanding sum should be recovered from the employee or employees concerned. The effect of such a direction is to absolve the employer from further liability.

The second exception arises where the Commissioners of Inland Revenue (and not the Collector of Taxes) are of the opinion that an employee has received his emoluments knowing that the employer has wilfully failed to make the deductions required by the PAYE regulations. In these circumstances also the Commissioners may absolve the employer from liability to account for under-deductions and recover the proper amount of tax from the employee or employees.

The application of either approach is very much a matter for the discretion of the Inland Revenue, and no employer should anticipate that an appropriate direction will be issued. This merely serves to emphasise the obligation placed on employers to ensure that the proper PAYE deductions are made when paying emoluments to employees.

There are similar provisions which enable under-payments of national insurance contributions to be recovered.

RECOVERY OF TAX AND INTEREST

Some employers fail to account for PAYE deductions made, or indeed to operate the lawful requirements. HM Inspector of Taxes may then determine the amount thought to be due and issue an assessment. If the amount of such an assessment, known as a Regulation 49 determination, is to be disputed the employer must provide notice of appeal within a period of thirty days from the issue date. Failure to provide the required notice of appeal will result in the tax shown by the assessment falling due for payment. The amount of tax shown by a disputed assessment which is under appeal will often be settled by agreement between the parties, but where it is not, the appeal will be heard by a body of Commissioners. A liability to satisfy interest will usually arise where action is taken under Regulation 49 and an amount of tax falls due for payment.

Where PAYE deductions have not been paid over to the Collector of Taxes within fourteen days after the end of a year of assessment (namely, by 19 April) a general interest charge may be imposed. The charge was first applied to deductions made in 1992–93 where the amount deducted was not paid over by the employer by 19 April 1993, and it was continued for later years. The rate of interest imposed will vary in line with changes in the money market generally but is applied at rates identical to those which are used for late payments of tax (see page 141). It will not be overlooked that any interest commitment discharged in this manner cannot form an ingredient in the calculation of the employers profits chargeable to tax.

The interest charge is limited to sums remaining

outstanding fourteen days following the end of the year of assessment. It does not apply to late monthly or quarterly payments made during the year.

Similar interest procedures also apply to deductions made under the sub-contractors' scheme (see page 91) and to late payments of Class 1 national insurance contributions.

END OF YEAR RETURNS

Shortly following the end of the tax year on 5 April an employer must submit end of year returns to the Tax Office. These returns disclose details of earnings, PAYE deducted and also record Class 1 national insurance contributions for each employee. The returns must be filed not later than 19 May following the end of the year of assessment. Any return filed late will result in an automatic penalty being imposed. However, a few days period of grace is available for returns due to be filed on 19 May 1998 and this period can elapse before the automatic penalty accrues due.

The end of year returns will be checked by the Tax Office to establish whether the correct amount of tax has been suffered from the application of the PAYE deduction scheme. Subject to the tolerance levels outlined below, any underdeduction may be carried forward to the following year with increased tax being collected under the PAYE scheme for that year. Alternatively, where sums in excess of £1,000 are involved the underpayment will usually be collected directly from the taxpayer.

A finding that excessive tax has been suffered may result in a repayment being made to the taxpayer.

PAYMENT AND REPAYMENT TOLERANCE

It is apparent that the administrative cost of collecting small amounts of tax or repaying small sums can become considerable. This is recognised by the Inland Revenue who apply a tolerance of £30 below which the tax is not collected. In those cases where the tax payable exceeds the tolerance by a small amount all tax will be collected and not only the excess.

Widows and single women pensioners under the age of 65 years may receive social security pensions on which any tax due must be collected by direct assessment. No assessments will be raised on such persons to recover small amounts falling due within the limits of the tolerance.

In those cases where the end of year check carried out by the Tax Office discloses an overpayment not exceeding £10 the amount of that overpayment will not automatically be repaid to the taxpayer. However, if repayment is requested the entire amount will be refunded.

REQUEST FOR INFORMATION BY EMPLOYEES

Many end of year returns checked by the Tax Office will require no further action, either on the grounds that the correct amount of tax has been suffered by deduction or that the under or overpayment falls within the level of tolerance. However, within a period of five years from 31 October following the end of the year of assessment the taxpayer may apply to the Tax Office for the issue of a return. This return will disclose details of earnings and tax suffered.

EMPLOYER'S ADDITIONAL REQUIREMENTS

If an employee is to comply with the requirements of self-assessment and complete his or her own tax return the individual must be supplied with the necessary information. Part of this information will relate to the employment. It will therefore be necessary for the employer to provide each employee with the following information during the summer of 1998 in relation to 1997–98, namely the tax year ending on 5 April 1998:

a A Form P60 which is a certificate of pay and tax deductions for all employees who were working on 5 April. This form must be made available not later than 31 May 1998

b Details of taxable benefits and other related matters not later than 6 July 1998 in relation to the year ended on 5 April 1998 (Details of these requirements are shown on page 71.)

c Where the employer operates a Fixed Profit Car Scheme details of the scheme must be provided not later than 6 July 1998. (See page 58 for further details.)

Similar information must be supplied for 1998–99 and future years.

ALLOCATION OF EARNINGS

All earnings of directors and employees must be allocated to, and treated as income of, the year of assessment in which they are 'received'. There is no need to apportion bonuses and other lump sum payments between one year of assessment and another or to make an adjustment where earnings are received late. In all cases the date of 'receipt' will determine the year of assessment into which earnings fall.

DATE EARNINGS RECEIVED

For most employees, earnings will be treated as 'received':

a On the date emoluments are *paid*; or

b On the date an employee becomes *entitled* to those emoluments,

whichever event first occurs.

These rules apply also to company directors but for such individuals there are three further possible dates, namely:

c The date emoluments are *credited* in the accounts or records of the company;

d If emoluments for a period are *determined* before the end of that period – the last day of the period; or

e If emoluments for a period are *determined* after the end of that period – the date of determination.

In all cases it is the earliest of the possible dates which establishes the time of receipt. Particular caution must be exercised when dealing with remuneration payable to directors of family companies for the purpose of ensuring that the date of 'receipt' is not unduly advanced or delayed.

The 'receipt' date will also establish that on which earnings are treated as 'paid' for PAYE purposes. In addition, it may apply to determine the accounting period in which a deduction for earnings paid can be made when calculating profits of the employer.

OVERSEAS EMPLOYMENTS

Earnings from an office or employment are only capable of being charged to income tax under Schedule E and cannot be dealt with under any other Schedule. For this purpose it is immaterial whether duties are performed in the United Kingdom or in some territory overseas. However, the liability to United Kingdom taxation in respect of earnings from employments undertaken wholly or partly outside the United Kingdom will largely depend on the place where the employee is resident and also the place where duties are actually carried out.

Employees resident and ordinarily resident

If an employee is both resident and ordinarily resident in the United Kingdom all earnings, whether from duties carried out at home or overseas, are potentially liable to income tax. It may be possible to reduce the amount of taxable earnings by applying a 'foreign earnings deduction' where duties are performed overseas, but the application of this deduction is now severely limited.

A 'foreign earnings deduction' of 100 per cent may be available to an individual who works full-time overseas for a 'qualifying period' of 365 days or more. This would effectively reduce overseas earnings otherwise chargeable to United Kingdom taxation to nil. A period is treated as a 'qualifying period' unless during that period the employee is present in the United Kingdom:

a on more than 62 consecutive days; or

b for more than one-sixth of the total of days in the period.

The 'foreign earnings deduction' is limited to earnings for duties carried out overseas and cannot extend to duties performed in the United Kingdom, unless those duties are merely incidental to the overseas activities.

For seafarers the number of days in **a** is increased to 183 and the factor in **b** to one-half.

It seems that the foreign earnings deduction had been exploited by individuals involved in tax avoidance arrangements. With a single exception, it can no longer apply after 5 April 1998. The only exception is limited to seafarers who may continue to obtain the deduction in the normal manner.

Other employees

An individual who is either not resident or not ordinarily resident in the United Kingdom will be charged to tax on his earnings, if any, for work undertaken in the United Kingdom. This charge does not extend to earnings for work performed overseas.

Special rules apply to employees domiciled outside the United Kingdom and employed by non-resident employers. If these individuals perform the whole of their duties overseas only sums remitted to the United Kingdom will be chargeable to tax.

PROFIT-RELATED PAY

The calculation of earnings received by employees will sometimes be influenced by the level of profits achieved by the employer. To encourage arrangements of this nature part of an employee's earnings, identified as profit-related pay, can be exempted from liability to income tax, although the benefit of this exemption is being withdrawn.

To achieve a measure of exemption, profit-related pay must arise under a scheme approved by the Inland Revenue. The scheme enables employees to receive profit-related pay based on the employer's profits for a profit period, in addition to the employees' normal earnings. A profit-related pay scheme is applied to an 'employment unit' and need

—— 31 ——
PROFIT-RELATED PAY

Charles was a member of an approved profit-related pay scheme throughout the twelve-month profit period to 30 September 1997. On 15 January 1998, he received profit-related pay of £3,500 for that period. Normal pay received by Charles in the year ended 30 September 1997 was £12,000.

The profit-related pay of £3,500 comprises income for 1997–98. However, the exempt amount will be the smallest of:

						£
a actual profit-related pay	.	.	.	.	.	3,500
b 1/5 × (£3,500 + £12,000)	.	.	.	.	3,100
c maximum	.	.	.	.	.	4,000

Calculation **b** produces the smallest figure and £3,100 will be exempt from income tax. The taxable part of profit-related pay therefore becomes £400 (£3,500 less £3,100).

—— 32 ——
PROFIT-RELATED PAY
PHASING OUT

Adapting Example 31, let it be assumed that the profit period ended on 30 September 1999 and profit-related pay was received in the following January.

The profit period commenced on 1 October 1998, namely in the calendar year 1998. Profit-related pay received by Charles and exempt from income tax will now comprise the lowest of:

				£
a Actual profit-related pay	.	.	.	3,500
b 1/5 × (£3,500 + £12,000)	.	.	.	3,100
c Maximum	.	.	.	.	2,000

The smallest figure is that under **c**. Of actual profit-related pay amounting to £3,500, only £2,000 can be recognised as exempt from tax.

---

not necessarily extend to all business activities of the employer. At least 80 per cent of employees working in that employment unit must be members of the scheme, although new employees having less than three years of service may be excluded. The earlier requirement that part-time staff should be excluded no longer applies. Controlling directors must not be permitted to participate and the scheme is limited to employees in the private sector. A profit-related pay scheme can be for a single accounting period of twelve months in duration or extend throughout a longer period.

A participating employee will receive both normal earnings and profit-related pay. However, the profit-related pay may be wholly or partly exempt from income tax. The level of exemption has changed from time to time but for profit periods commencing not later than 31 December 1997, exemption has been limited to the lowest of:

a The actual profit-related pay;
b One-fifth of normal pay plus profit-related pay; and
c £4,000.

When applying the PAYE deduction scheme the employer will disregard the exempt profit-related pay and confine deductions to net earnings remaining. The exclusion of pay in this manner has no application to the calculation of national insurance contributions, which extends to the full earnings.

Applications to register a profit-related pay scheme may be submitted at any time, but the scheme must be registered before the com-

mencement of the employer's first profit period used to measure profit-related pay if the tax exemption is to be obtained.

Withdrawal of relief

The tax relief which employees may obtain by using profit-related pay schemes is being phased out over a period of years. This is achieved by progressively reducing the factor of £4,000 which is one of the three factors governing the amount of profit-related pay achieving tax exemption. There is no change in this factor of £4,000 for profit periods commencing before 1 January 1998 but subsequent factors are as follows:

Profit periods commencing		Factor
		£
Between 1 January 1998 and		
31 December 1998	. .	2,000
Between 1 January 1999 and		
31 December 1999	. .	1,000
On or after 1 January 2000 .	. .	NIL

PENSIONS

Any pension from an office or employment in the United Kingdom is assessable to income tax under Schedule E. In most cases the pension will be subject to deduction of tax under the PAYE scheme outlined above. By concession, any additional pension awarded due to injury, work related illness or war wounds is not charged to tax.

An exception arises where the pension is paid by

an overseas employer to a former employee resident in the United Kingdom, as in such a case PAYE will not usually apply. Overseas pensions are chargeable to tax under Schedule D but assessment is limited to 90 per cent of the pension, whether it is remitted to the United Kingdom or not. The remaining 10 per cent will escape liability.

EXPENSES

Disregarding the cost of travelling, any expenses which the holder of an office or employment is *obliged* to expend and which are incurred *wholly, exclusively and necessarily*, in the *performance of the duties of the office*, may be deducted from the earnings to be assessed. Before an expenses claim is admitted by the Inland Revenue the items of expenditure are closely scrutinised to establish whether the requirements have been satisfied.

When identifying those expenses which may obtain relief, a distinction must be drawn between expenses which are personal to an employee and those which would be incurred by any holder of the office. For example, an incapacitated employee may have to incur expenses by reason of his incapacity, for example, the maintenance of a guide dog by a blind person, but this expense would not be incurred by *any* holder of the office and it must be disallowed. Some expenditure relating to insurance and insurable risks may confer an entitlement to relief as shown on page 58.

An expenses claim should be structured by showing each individual item making up the total sum claimed. Vouchers and receipts must always be obtained when making payments and subsequently retained for possible examination by the Inland Revenue. Unless these details are presented and made available, if requested, the claim may well be rejected. Many trade unions have negotiated round sum allowances on behalf of their members. These allowances should be granted without further enquiry, although individual employees may attempt to establish increased relief if supporting evidence can be supplied.

Fees and subscriptions paid to a large number of professional bodies and learned societies may be deducted from earnings. The Inland Revenue retains a list of approved bodies and only subscriptions paid to a body or society whose name appears on the list can be deducted.

Costs of travelling

For many years employees and office holders have been entitled to somewhat limited relief for the cost of travelling. This relief was restricted to expenditure which the individual was necessarily obliged to incur when travelling in the performance of his or her duties. Clearly, the cost of travelling from home to the place of employment could not usually be admitted as travelling was not undertaken when performing the duties of the office but to place the individual in a position from which to carry out those duties. In contrast, once the place of employment had been reached the cost of any further business journeys would usually qualify for relief. Although this distinction was rigorously maintained, several practices developed which enabled some relief to be obtained. For example, where the employee travelled direct from home to the business premises of a client or customer (often referred to as 'triangular travel') relief was conferred at the lower of:

a the actual cost of the journey; and

b the cost which would have been incurred had the individual travelled from the normal workplace to the client or customer.

In addition, where the individual was required by his or her employer to perform duties at a temporary workplace for a period not exceeding twelve months in duration, the cost of travelling between home and that workplace was generally allowable.

The use and application of these and other practises was frequently criticised and new rules were introduced to provide a firmer basis for granting relief for the cost of travelling. Originally, new rules were due to come into operation on 6 April 1998. Whilst the date of introduction remains, the original rules were subsequently amended. The new rules which finally came into operation on 6 April 1998 are outlined below.

The old requirement that relief will be available where the holder of an office or employment is necessarily obliged to incur expense when travelling in the performance of duties remains. This provides relief for an employee who is required to travel from his employer's business premises for the purpose of delivering goods or supplying some service to a customer or client.

In addition, relief is now made available for expenses of travelling:

a which are not expenses of ordinary commuting but are

b attributable to the attendance of the individual at any place on an occasion where his or her attendance at that place is in the performance of the duties of the office or employment.

To establish the cost of 'ordinary commuting' which cannot be allowed, the permanent workplace of an individual must be determined. In most situations this workplace will represent the place where the individual regularly attends in the performance of his or her duties. The cost of travelling between the individual's home and the permanent workplace represents 'ordinary commuting', with that cost being excluded from any relief.

There will be situations where the permanent workplace does not identify the location of the employer's main business. For example, some employees are required by the terms of their engagement to work from home. This may establish the home address as the permanent workplace. In other situations, some employees may attend a party or other event held away from home. Travelling directly from the location of that event to the permanent workplace will be classed as ordinary commuting as no business travel is involved.

Some employees may be required by their employer to work at a temporary location, perhaps a branch or depot. Providing the period of attendance at such a location does not exceed twenty-four months, this will not identify the place of temporary working as the permanent workplace. Therefore the cost of travel undertaken directly from the individual's home to the temporary workplace may well be relieved.

The cost of travelling which may be included in an expenses claim will be restricted to travel undertaken for business purposes. It will not extend to private journeys or any other form of non-business travel. Subject to this, the cost of travelling may include:

a Travel by car, air, rail, bus or by any other conveyance.
b The cost of subsistence and perhaps the cost of overnight hotel accommodation.
c Car park and toll fees, to the extent that these are attributable to business.

The cost of travelling to be included in an expenses claim will reflect expenditure incurred by the employee or office holder. This may involve the receipt of mileage allowances and the application of authorised mileage rates used in Fixed Profit Car Scheme arrangements (see page 58).

Notwithstanding the introduction of revised rules on 6 April 1998, a number of practises continue to apply, notably those relating to working rule agreements concluded between industry representatives and the Inland Revenue.

33
COST OF TRAVELLING

Colin resides with his family at a house in Cambridge. His permanent workplace is the office premises of an employer in Peterborough and Colin normally travels between the two locations by car.

During 1998–99 Colin made frequent visits to his employer's customers in Oxford and Swansea. Some trips were made from the premises in Peterborough but often Colin travelled direct from his home in Cambridge.

For three months commencing on 1 October 1998 Colin was required to work exclusively at his employer's branch office in Edinburgh. He travelled directly from home to Edinburgh on Monday mornings and made the reverse journey on Friday afternoons.

All journeys were made by Colin in his own motor vehicle.

The permanent workplace is the employer's office premises in Peterborough. The cost incurred by Colin when travelling from his home in Cambridge to Peterborough represents ordinary commuting and cannot be included in an expenses claim.

Of the remaining travelling:

a Journeys made directly from office premises in Peterborough to Oxford and Swansea were undertaken in performance of the duties.

b Travelling directly from Colin's home in Cambridge to Oxford and Swansea was undertaken for the purpose of attending to the employer's business at those locations.

c The temporary assignment to Edinburgh was for less than twenty-four months in duration and therefore office premises in Peterborough remain the permanent workplace. The travel was not ordinary commuting.

The cost of travel under each of the three headings is eligible for inclusion in an expenses claim.

Employees performing services wholly outside the United Kingdom under the terms of a separate contract, may usually deduct the cost of travelling from, and returning to, the United Kingdom. These employees also are not affected by the new rules.

Examples of expenditure which can be included in an expenses claim:

a **Office Accommodation**, clerical assistance, stationery, and similar expenses where necessary to the employment.

b **Overalls, Clothing and Tools** where the employee must supply these items specially for his employment. Many trade unions have negotiated round sum allowances for these items on behalf of their members.

c **Class 1 and Class 1A** national insurance contributions paid by employees for assistants they employ, if the cost of that assistance can be included in a claim for relief.

d Professional Fees and Subscriptions paid to Societies with activities related to an employee's work.

e Rent and other outgoings incurred by clergymen and ministers of religion.

Examples of expenditure which cannot be included in an expenses claim:

a Travelling Expenses in travelling to and from the taxpayer's normal place of employment, unless the employment is carried out overseas.

b Instruction Fees and Cost of Books where incurred by the employee to enable him to qualify in his appointment or to put him in a position to carry out his employment. There may be some relief for expenditure incurred on approved vocational training (see page 45).

INSURABLE RISKS

Some directors and employees must increasingly contemplate taking out personal insurance cover against work-related risks. Others who have no or insufficient cover may be compelled to personally discharge uninsured liabilities. The outlay involved may be considerable and from 5 April 1995 the cost of obtaining insurance cover against work-related risks can be subtracted from income chargeable to tax. In addition, the cost of meeting uninsured work-related liabilities can also be relieved. This latter relief is limited to risks capable of being insured against and will not apply to other risks, for example, liabilities associated with criminal convictions.

Similar relief for both the cost of obtaining insurance cover and meeting uninsured liabilities will be available to a former director or employee. It is a condition that the expenditure is incurred within a period of six years following the end of the year of assessment in which the employment ended.

Where the employer discharges the cost of personal insurance cover or the cost of satisfying uninsured risks this previously created a benefit on which the director or employee was required to suffer income tax. However, tax commitments of this nature may now be avoided (see page 61).

MOTOR MILEAGE ALLOWANCES

Where an employee uses his or her own motor car for business purposes the employer will usually pay a motor mileage allowance. This allowance may be generous or austere, but any sum paid is strictly income chargeable to income tax, with PAYE deductions being imposed. Subject to the comments made later, it then remains for the employee to submit an expenses claim in an endeavour to obtain relief from income tax suffered.

The Fixed Profit Car Scheme

This is a cumbersome and time-consuming exercise and considerable administrative savings may be achieved by adopting the 'Fixed Profit Car Scheme', with the approval of the Inland Revenue. The broad effect of this scheme is that the Inland Revenue announce the maximum amount of mileage allowances (referred to as 'authorised mileage rates') which will not result in the employee becoming chargeable to income tax. Motor cars are graded into a number of bands for this purpose.

To the extent that mileage allowances paid exceed the authorised mileage rates, the excess will be treated as income chargeable to income tax without the benefit of any expenses claim.

The Fixed Profit Car Scheme is limited to mileage allowances paid for business motoring and has no application to other matters. Employees are not obliged to adopt the scheme and may choose to apply the statutory basis. Whilst consideration must be applied to individual circumstances, it is unlikely that the statutory basis will result in any increased exemption from taxation.

34
FIXED PROFIT CAR SCHEME

Throughout the year of assessment 1998–99 Sam used his own motor car when travelling on his employer's business. The vehicle was of 1,600cc cylinder capacity and 6,200 miles of business motoring were involved in the year. The employer paid a mileage allowance at the rate of 50p per mile and the Fixed Profit Car Scheme applied.

The tax-free mileage allowance for 1998–99 will be calculated as follows:

	£
First 4,000 miles at 45p	1,800.00
Next 2,200 miles at 25p	550.00
	£2,350.00

Total mileage allowances paid	
6,200 at 50p	£3,100.00

Sam will suffer income tax on £750 (£3,100 less £2,350). This tax should be imposed through the PAYE deduction scheme. There can be no expenses claim, or claim for capital allowances, on the cost of the motor car.

The authorised mileage rates used for the Fixed Profit Car Scheme take account of depreciation, insurance, road tax, fuel, services and repairs attributable to the business miles travelled. They do not include interest. It follows that any interest paid on a loan applied to acquire a motor car may enable the employee to obtain relief for the business proportion of that interest.

The rates used for the purposes of the Fixed Profit Car Scheme are identical for both 1997–98 and 1998–99 as shown by the following table.

FIXED PROFIT CAR SCHEME AUTHORISED MILEAGE RATES 1997–98 AND 1998–99		
Cylinder capacity (cc)	Up to 4,000 miles per mile (p)	Over 4,000 miles per mile (p)
Up to 1,000	28	17
1,001–1,500	35	20
1,501–2,000	45	25
2,001 and above	63	36

Employers operating a Fixed Profit Car Scheme and who pay mileage allowances not exceeding the 'tax-free' limits may apply to the Inland Revenue for a dispensation. If this dispensation is granted, details of mileage payments need not be reported. In other situations where the tax-free payments are exceeded the employer must insert details on Form P11D (see page 71). These forms must be supplied to the Inland Revenue not later than 6 July following the end of the tax year to which they relate, with copies being made available to employees.

Employees not in the scheme

Where an employer does not operate a Fixed Profit Car Scheme but individual employees use their own motor vehicles for business travel, those employees may submit expenses claims. Previously these claims had to be based on the actual cost incurred, which frequently gave rise to uncertainty. For 1996–97 and future years, however, employees may use the authorised mileage rates when calculating expenses to be set against earnings. It is immaterial whether the employer provides mileage allowances or the employee must finance travel entirely from his or her own resources. If mileage allowances are paid these will be compared with the authorised mileage rates to establish whether any excess sums are chargeable to tax, or further relief for expenses should be obtained.

There is no obligation to use the authorised mileage rates but many car owners will select this route on the grounds of simplicity.

Other uses

Although the authorised mileage rates are primarily used by employees providing their own motor vehicles for business travel, the use of those rates has been extended to others.

Self-employed taxpayers with a turnover which does not exceed the VAT registration threshold may use the authorised mileage rates as an alternative to keeping detailed records. The registration threshold was increased to £50,000 on 1 April 1998. Individuals who drive for voluntary organisations and receive mileage allowances may incorporate figures taken from the authorised mileage rates when calculating profits chargeable to income tax.

8

Benefits in kind

ALL EMPLOYEES

Assessment under Schedule E extends to 'emoluments' arising from an office or employment. The expression 'emoluments' is defined to include 'all salaries, fees, wages, perquisites and profits whatsoever'. This definition will embrace most 'rewards' received by an employee but some advantages may be enjoyed which are not necessarily subject to tax, including earnings arising under a profit-related pay scheme. As a general rule, any advantages which can be turned into money will be taxed but those which cannot may escape liability. For example, an employee may enjoy the use of a company car but as such an advantage cannot be converted into money no liability will arise. This remains subject to the special rules, discussed on page 65, which apply to company directors and many employees.

In those cases where an employee receives 'money's worth' which is chargeable to tax, liability will arise on the market value of the benefit and not necessarily on the cost to the employer of providing that benefit, but there are many exceptions. An employee who is provided with a voucher, by reason of his or her office or employment, will be taxed on the cost to the employer in providing the voucher and not on the value of goods for which that voucher can be exchanged. Advantages which arise from the provision of season tickets financed by an employer, or the use of an employer's credit card, incur liability to income tax. Payments made to an employee during a period of sickness or disability are taxable, except to the extent that the payments are funded from contributions made by the employee. This is in addition to the tax imposed on statutory short term sickness benefit paid by an employer. The first 15p in value of a luncheon voucher is exempt but the excess is not. Travel vouchers, warrants and allowances made available to members of the armed forces when going on, or returning from, leave are not chargeable to tax.

Where an employer satisfies a personal obligation of an employee the amount involved will be assessable. An illustration may involve the employer who satisfies the council tax payable by an employee, unless the tax is attributable to property occupied by the employee as part of his or her employment. Liability may, however, be avoided on the reimbursement of expenditure relating to insurable risks, as explained on the following page.

In practice, the Inland Revenue do not seek to charge tax in respect of awards made to directors and employees as testimonials to mark long service where the period of service is not less than twenty years and no similar award has been made to the recipient within the previous ten years. This concession is usually limited to tangible articles, for example a watch or television set, having a cost or value not exceeding £20 for each year of service but may also include the provision of shares in the employing company. Also by concession, rewards paid under a genuine suggestion scheme, the reimbursement of expenses where an employee has been required to make alternative travelling or accommodation arrangements due to industrial disputes, the cost of late night journeys where an employee is occasionally required to work late and the provision of financial assistance to severely disabled employees when travelling from home to work are among the arrangements which do not create a liability to income tax. Nor will liability arise where an employee is reimbursed the cost of car parking at or near the place of work.

Some employees receive gifts from third parties. The value of these gifts will not be taxed if they are neither solicited nor provided by arrangement with the employer. It is a requirement that gifts received from the same source do not exceed £150 in any year and the exemption does not extend to cash gifts or tips. If the gift exceeds £150 tax will be due on the entire sum. However, a payment made to an individual as an inducement to take up employment, sometimes referred to as a 'Golden Hello', is likely to be fully taxable.

Where an employee is working wholly abroad the reimbursement of travelling and hotel expenses by the employer will not create an emolument assessable to income tax. A similar exemption applies where the employer bears the cost of travel incurred by an employee's spouse and children. It is a necessary requirement that the family travel to and from the country where the employee is working and the United Kingdom. Expenses incurred by, or reimbursed to, a non-domiciled individual when travelling to the United Kingdom for employment purposes are also exempt, but this extends only to travelling within a period of five years from the initial date of arrival in this territory.

Employees who stay away from home overnight on business will often incur incidental expenses of a personal nature. These expenses may include the cost of newspapers, personal telephone calls and laundry. Where, as will frequently be the case, expenditure of this nature is borne by the employer a taxable benefit will arise. However, the creation of this benefit may be avoided where the amount borne by the employer does not exceed £5 per night whilst in the United Kingdom or £10 per night overseas. Should these limits be exceeded the entire amount borne by the employer will be treated as a taxable benefit accruing to the employee.

RELOCATION PACKAGES

An employee may need to move home on being relocated by his or her employer to some other area. A move may also be necessary where an employee takes up a new job. In circumstances such as these the employee may receive cash payments or other benefits from the employer which could become chargeable to income tax. However, no liability will arise if those items form part of a qualifying relocation package which satisfies the following conditions:

a The employee must change his or her main residence as the result of a change in the duties of an existing employment, a change in the location of that employment or commencing a new employment;

b The new main residence must be within reasonable daily travelling distance of the new normal place of work;

c The old residence must not be within reasonable daily travelling distance of the new normal place of work; and

d The expenses must be incurred, or the benefits provided, before the end of the year of assessment following the one in which the employee commences the new task. The date on which the actual move from one residence to the other takes place is not material. The time limit may be extended at the discretion of the Inland Revenue.

Where these several requirements are satisfied, eligible expenses and benefits may fall within six broad categories, namely:

a Matters attributable to the disposal, or intended disposal, of the old residence.

b Matters attributable to the acquisition, or intended acquisition, of a new residence.

c The provision of transportation and storage of domestic belongings.

d Travelling and subsistence for the employee and members of the employee's family.

e The replacement of domestic goods for use in the new property.

f Interest on certain bridging loans which would otherwise create taxable benefits (see page 69).

These headings include not only expenses actually incurred but also the provision of taxable benefits, for example, the use of living accommodation. It is a requirement that exemption is confined to an aggregate of £8,000, representing both expenditure and benefits.

INSURABLE RISKS

It is sometimes necessary for an employee or company director to obtain personal insurance cover against work-related risks. If the cost of obtaining this cover is borne by the employer the amount involved could create a benefit in kind on which the individual must suffer income tax. In the absence of any, or sufficient, insurance cover an employer may fund the cost of meeting an employee's uninsured liabilities. Here also the amount involved may well create a taxable benefit. However, the creation of most forms of potential tax liability under this heading may be avoided if a number of conditions are satisfied. In the case of insurance premiums it must be shown that the liability is work-related. Where uninsured liabilities are involved these must identify matters capable of being insured against. Commonly this will comprise legal costs and the payment of damages but it will not extend to other liabilities, including criminal matters.

Tax liability is avoided by enabling qualifying expenditure to be included in a Schedule E expenses claim (see page 58). Therefore, although a taxable benefit may arise it is offset by subtracting the expense deemed to have been incurred.

PROVISION OF LIVING ACCOMMODATION

An additional liability to income tax may arise where an employee is provided with living accommodation by reason of his or her employment. This liability also applies where such accommodation is provided for use by the employee's wife or husband, son or daughter, son-in-law, daughter-in-law, parent, servant, dependant or guest. There are, however, exceptions and no liability will accrue where the employer is an individual and the accommodation is made available in the normal course of a domestic, family or personal relationship. Nor will it apply to most accommodation used by employees of a local authority. In addition, no liability will arise on the provision of living accommodation for an employee:

a Where it is necessary for the proper performance of the employee's duties that he or she should reside in the accommodation, or
b Where the accommodation is provided for the better performance of the duties of employment, and this is one of the kinds of employment in the case of which it is customary for employers to provide living accommodation for employees, or
c Where, there being a threat to the employee's security, special security arrangements are in force and the employee resides in the accommodation as part of those arrangements.

The exclusions under a and b have little application to most company directors.

Where liability does arise, the employee is treated as receiving an additional emolument taxable under Schedule E. This emolument will comprise an amount equal to:

a The value of the accommodation for the period of availability in each year of assessment; less
b Contributions, if any, made by the employee.

It will be clear that no additional emolument will arise where the employee pays a rent which equals or exceeds the value under a.

--- 35 ---

PROVISION OF ACCOMMODATION

In 1989 Company A purchased a residential property in Surrey having a gross rateable value of £2,500. Basil is an employee of the company and throughout the year ending on 5 April 1999 he occupied the property as his private home. No rent was paid in return for the provision of living accommodation.

The emolument on which Basil will suffer income tax for 1998–99 must be calculated as follows:

	£
Value of accommodation – gross rateable value	2,500
Less contribution	NIL
Emolument 1998–99	£2,500

For properties in the United Kingdom, the value of the accommodation will comprise the gross rateable value used for rating purposes or, if it is greater, any rent paid by the person providing accommodation. To eliminate distortions in Scotland where properties were uprated, the former rateable value continues to be used. Although general rates were replaced in Great Britain by the community charge, which in turn was replaced by yet another system, the council tax, rateable values continue to be used as a 'measure' for income tax purposes. In the case of new properties it will be necessary to estimate a comparable rateable value.

Two or more employees may each use a unit of accommodation at the same time. In theory each could incur liability to income tax on a full year's benefit. This possibility is avoided by a concession which enables the full charge to be apportioned between those individuals occupying accommodation simultaneously. Limitations must also be imposed where accommodation is provided for part only of a year.

Expensive accommodation

A further liability to income tax may arise where an employer provides an employee with 'expensive' living accommodation. This is in addition to the liability mentioned above and remains subject to the exclusions and exemptions referred to earlier.

The further liability is confined to living accommodation obtained at a cost exceeding £75,000, and can have no application where cost falls below this figure. 'Cost' includes not only expenditure laid out to acquire accommodation but includes any further outgoings on carrying out improvements, where those outgoings have been incurred before the commencement of the year of assessment concerned. In some situations, where property has been retained for more than six years before the employee enters into occupation, 'cost' may be replaced by 'market value'.

Where the cost, or market value if appropriate, of providing living accommodation does exceed £75,000, the excess over this figure must be established. The further emolument then represents 'the additional value of the accommodation', which is calculated by applying the official rate of interest at the beginning of the tax year to the excess. This

---

36
PROVISION OF EXPENSIVE ACCOMMODATION

Using the facts of Example 35, let it be assumed that Company A paid £150,000 to acquire the residential property in 1989. Further expenditure of £40,000 was incurred before 6 April 1998 in carrying out improvements to the property. It will be assumed that the official rate of interest on 6 April 1998 was 7.25 per cent per annum. On this basis the emoluments arising to Basil for 1998–99 become:

			£
a Emolument as calculated in Example 35 .			2,500
b Additional emolument:			
Cost of providing			
accommodation:		£	
Cost of acquisition	.	150,000	
Improvements .	.	40,000	
Aggregate cost .	.	190,000	
Less to be excluded	.	75,000	
Excess . .	.	£115,000	
Emolument:			
£115,000 × 7.25 per cent .	.	.	8,337
Total emoluments from living			
accommodation .	.	.	£10,837

---

rate is altered from time to time, but on 6 August 1997 was increased to 7.25 per cent per annum.

If the employee provides rent, or makes some other contribution for the use of living accommodation, this may be subtracted from the additional emolument, but only to the extent that it exceeds the gross rateable value of the property, or rent paid by the employer, whichever is the higher.

Therefore, for 1998–99 two different emoluments may arise where expensive living accommodation is made available. This combined liability affects all employees and is not confined to directors and the higher-paid.

SHARE SCHEMES

There are a number of approved tax efficient arrangements which may enable employees to acquire shares on terms which avoid liability to income tax. However, gains arising on the ultimate disposal of shares may well be chargeable to capital gains tax if the amounts involved are sufficiently substantial. Brief details of the approved schemes are outlined below.

Savings-related share option schemes

Under the terms of an approved savings-related share option scheme (or Save-As-You-Earn scheme) employees are provided with options to purchase shares at a fixed price in three, five or seven years' time. To generate sufficient funds employees pay monthly contributions throughout a three-or five-year period. The minimum contribution is £5 and the maximum £250. At the end of the term contributions are repaid, together with a tax-free bonus. The sums repaid are then available to be applied in the purchase of shares. No income tax should be payable on the grant or exercise of the option to acquire shares.

Profit-sharing schemes

An approved profit-sharing scheme requires shares to be allocated to employees. The shares are placed in trust for an initial period and must remain in the hands of trustees throughout a minimum period of two years. If shares are withdrawn from the trust within the succeeding twelve months a liability to income tax may arise. No income tax should be imposed once the twelve-month period has elapsed.

Share option schemes

Approved share option schemes require the grant of an option to purchase shares at a fixed price. The option must not be capable of being exercised within the initial three-year period or more than ten years from the date of the grant. Subject to this and the satisfaction of numerous other requirements, no liability to income tax arises on either the grant of option rights or the exercise of those rights.

Before 17 July 1995 shares retaining a substantial value could be brought within a share option scheme. However, this relaxation was withdrawn and only applies to option rights granted on or before 17 July 1995 or where a written offer or invitation to apply for options was made on or before that date.

In the case of option rights granted subsequently a limit of £30,000 is placed on the value of the options. With the exception of some transitional provisions which have long expired, options granted in excess of this sum will not be exempt from income tax.

The need for approval

The three share schemes or arrangements outlined above only apply to attract income tax advantages if those arrangements are approved by the Inland Revenue. A lengthy list of requirements must be fully discharged before approval will be forthcoming.

Valuation of shares

The value of shares issued by an unlisted company may frequently become a matter of uncertainty and debate. This could inhibit the grant of option rights as both company representatives and the potential grantee may require to determine tax commitments before proceeding. However, it is possible to agree the value of unlisted shares with the Shares Valuation Division of the Capital Taxes Office before making any grant. This is a most important advantage as it introduces certainty which would otherwise be notable by its absence.

EMPLOYEES EARNING £8,500 OR MORE AND DIRECTORS

The assessment of fringe benefits is broadened considerably for most company directors and many employees. The persons affected are employees earning £8,500 or more and company directors, an approach which incorporates:

a All directors, except certain individuals earning less than £8,500 per annum and who do not, either on their own or with certain members of their family, retain a substantial shareholding interest in the company. This exception is limited to full-time working directors and directors of non-profit making companies or charitable bodies; and

b All employees earning £8,500 or more per annum.

For the purpose of establishing whether a director or employee earns £8,500 or more per annum and is therefore subject to the additional liabilities discussed below, his or her actual earnings must be increased by:

a Adding the value of any benefits mentioned on the previous pages;

b Adding the value of any benefits referred to below;

c Ignoring any expenses which may be deducted from earnings.

This implies that many employees earning less than £8,500 per annum may become assessable on 'fringe benefits', once the adjustments have been made to the calculation of their notional income. Once it is recognised that the figure of £8,500 falls very substantially below average full-time earnings, the significance and widespread application of the following comments becomes apparent.

Assessment of benefits

The assessment of benefits is not limited to facilities and advantages made available to a director or employee personally but extends also to benefits provided for that person's spouse, his sons and daughters and their spouses, his parents, servants, dependants and guests.

Where an employer pays a sum representing 'expenses' to a director or employee this sum will comprise an additional emolument and it remains for the director or employee to submit an acceptable expenses claim if additional liability to income tax is not to arise. In many cases this formality can be avoided by obtaining a dispensation from HM Inspector of Taxes. In those cases where an employee provides his or her own motor car for business travel and receives a mileage allowance, the Fixed Profit Car Scheme outlined on page 58 may also be used to avoid the formality of a claim for expenses. This scheme will not always be available for a director.

Should an employer incur expense in providing some facility or advantage for the benefit of a director or employee the cost incurred by the employer, referred to as the 'cash equivalent', is treated as additional remuneration unless, or to the extent that, the cost is made good by the recipient. For example, should an employer purchase a television set for, say, £600 and immediately transfer the ownership of that set to a qualifying director or employee for no consideration, a benefit of £600 will be chargeable to income tax. If the individual provides consideration of, say, £150, the taxable benefit becomes £450.

The calculation of the cash equivalent could give rise to uncertainty where an employer makes facilities available to employees on advantageous terms. This may affect employees whose children are educated at a reduced fee at private schools and employees of transport undertakings able to travel at a price lower than that charged to full fare paying customers. However, the Inland Revenue accept it is only the *additional* cost incurred by the employer in making these facilities available which represents the 'cash equivalent' and not the *average* cost for all children or customers.

Liability will not extend to the cost of providing meals in a canteen where those meals are available to all employees, to certain accommodation provided for an employee who is required as a condition of his employment to use the accommodation, or to the cost of providing future pensions under an approved scheme. An employer will often incur expenses in providing a Christmas party, annual dinner dance or similar function for the benefit of employees. In practice, no taxable benefit will arise on those attending when the cost does not exceed £75 per head. This figure is determined by dividing the entire cost of the function, including transport and accommodation, by the numbers attending. Should the limit be exceeded the entire benefit will be taxable. No liability will accrue from the provision of most in-house sports facilities provided by the employer.

A taxable benefit may be provided by some person other than the recipient's employer. However, where entertainment is made available for a director or employee by a third party no benefit will arise unless the advantage arose under an arrangement with the employee's own employer or was given in return for some service or anticipated service. 'Entertainment' may also include the provision of seats at a sporting or cultural event.

Scholarship awards

The employer of a director or employee may sometimes finance the cost of scholarships awarded to a child of that individual. This is frequently achieved by a company contributing funds to the trustees of an educational trust who provide the award to selected children. Arrangements of this nature will result in the parent being assessed on the cost involved.

Workplace nurseries

Benefits arising from a limited range of child care facilities are not assessable on those earning £8,500 or more. Exemption extends to nurseries run at the workplace or elsewhere by the employer. It will also extend to nurseries run by employers jointly with other employers, voluntary bodies or local authorities, and include facilities made available for older children after school or during school holidays. A condition for obtaining exemption requires that the child care facilities must comply with any registration requirement imposed by the appropriate local authority. No exemption will be forthcoming if the child care facilities are made available in domestic premises.

The exemption will not extend to the provision of cash allowances for child care or the payment by an employer of an employee's bills. Nor will it be available where the employer provides vouchers which can be used by the employee to discharge child care expenses.

USE OF ASSETS

Many items of expenditure incurred, or deemed to have been incurred, by an employer will not result in the transfer of any asset to the director or employee. However, where the asset is used by, or made available to, such a person, detailed rules must be applied to calculate the benefit assessable to income tax. For this purpose a distinction is drawn between the provision of motor cars, fuel for private motoring, mobile telephones, vans, loan facilities, and other assets or advantages. The application of these special rules is discussed below.

MOTOR CARS

Where a motor car is made available for private motoring a substantial taxable benefit may arise. For this purpose a distinction must be drawn between 'private motoring' and 'business travel'. From 6 April 1998 'business travel' represents any travelling, the cost of which would entitle a director or employee to tax relief in the manner outlined on page 56.

However, where the vehicle is used for private motoring, or indeed made available for such a purpose, the amount of business travel, if any, may have some effect on the calculation of the taxable benefit. Subject to the amount of business mileage, it must be emphasised that it is the availability of a motor car for private motoring which produces a benefit and not the actual use to which the vehicle is applied.

37
PROVISION OF MOTOR CAR

A company purchased a new motor car at an inclusive cost of £22,000 on 17 June 1997. The vehicle was first registered on that date and on the previous day had a 'list price', as calculated for tax purposes, of £26,000. The company had negotiated a substantial fleet discount when purchasing the vehicle from a local dealer. Immediately following purchase the car was used by a director who continued this use throughout 1998–99. There were 12,000 miles of business motoring in the year in addition to private motoring.

The list price of £26,000, and not the purchase price of £22,000, must be used to calculate the taxable benefit. This gives rise to the following basic benefit:

35 per cent × £26,000 . . . . £9,100

As there were more than 2,500 miles, but less than 18,000 miles, of business motoring the taxable benefit may be reduced as follows:

	£
Basic benefit	9,100
Less one-third	3,033
Taxable benefit 1998–99	£6,067

Following changes which came into operation on 6 April 1994 the taxable benefit arising from the availability of a motor car for private motoring is now governed by the list price of the vehicle.

Calculating the list price
The list price of a motor car will usually comprise the aggregate of:

a The manufacturer's, importer's or distributor's list price of the vehicle on the day before the date of its first registration;

b Value added tax and car tax attributable to the supply;

c Delivery charges, including value added tax;

d The list price of any accessory, including value added tax, which was fitted before the car was first made available to the employee (this will include delivery and fitting charges); and

e The list price of any accessory over £100, including value added tax, fitting and delivery costs, fitted after the car was first made available to the employee. This applies only to accessories fitted after 31 July 1993.

A motor car may require conversion to suit the needs of a disabled driver. This will usually involve the installation of 'accessories', an action which increases the list price of the vehicle. However, the cost of installing accessories specifically for use by a disabled driver can be ignored when calculating the list price. This includes automatic transmission and power steering where the employee is an orange badge holder and needs that accessory by reason of disability.

Steps may be taken to convert an existing motor car to run on road fuel gases, namely compressed natural gas or liquid petroleum gas. The cost of conversion will not be treated as an accessory when establishing the list price which applies for 1999–2000. In addition, where a motor car is designed to run on road fuel gases from new, that part of the purchase price which is solely attributable to equipment necessary to allow the car to perform in this manner will be ignored when establishing the list price for 1999–2000 and following years.

For classic cars more than fifteen years old and having a market value exceeding £15,000 the list price is replaced by market value.

It is possible that an employee may provide a contribution towards the cost of acquiring a motor car or fitted accessories. Any contribution of this nature, up to a maximum of £5,000, may be deducted from the list price or market value. It is then only the net figure remaining which represents the adjusted list price.

The maximum list price or market value is limited to £80,000. Any sum in excess of this amount is disregarded.

Calculating the benefit – 1998–99
The basic taxable benefit for 1998–99 will comprise 35 per cent of the list price (or market value). This figure will be reduced:

a By one-third if the annual business mileage exceeds 2,500 miles; and

b By two-thirds if business mileage is 18,000 miles or more.

Vehicles which are four years of age or more on the last day of the income tax year will attract a further reduction of one-third when calculating the taxable benefit.

In those situations where a director or employee has more than one motor car available for his or her use, only one vehicle can be identified when establishing the deductions under **a** and **b** above. This will be the vehicle which is the subject of the greater business mileage.

No benefit will usually arise from the use of a vehicle forming part of a 'pool' provided that:

a The vehicle is actually used by two or more employees;

b Any private use by an employee is merely incidental to business use; and

c The vehicle is not normally kept overnight in or near the vicinity of the employee's home.

Whether private use is 'merely incidental to' business use frequently gives rise to uncertainty. The Inland Revenue consider that where private use of a motor vehicle is independent of the employee's business use the 'merely incidental' requirement is unlikely to be satisfied. In contrast, where private use follows from business use, perhaps whilst absent from home on a business trip, that use is likely to be 'merely incidental'.

38
MOTOR CAR –
THE ALTERNATIVES

Example 37 illustrates the taxable benefit arising from the availability of a motor car less than 4 years of age, with a list price of £26,000 and used for more than 2,500 miles of business motoring. There is a basic benefit of £9,100.

Using the same basic benefit, the possible taxable benefits are as follows:

	Age of vehicle	
	Under	Over
Business Mileage	4 years	4 years
	£	£
Not exceeding 2,500 miles	9,100	6,067
Between 2,500 and 18,000 miles	6,067	4,045
18,000 miles or more	3,033	2,022

The amount of any taxable benefit will be reduced where a vehicle is available for part only of a full year. There will also be an adjustment where the car user contributes towards the cost of private motoring.

No additional benefit will arise from the availability of a motor car unless the employer provides a chauffeur. Where a chauffeur is provided his wages and any other expenses will represent a further benefit derived by the director or employee. The provision of a car parking space at or near the place of work will not be treated as producing a taxable benefit. The availability of a car telephone will give rise to a separate benefit (see next page).

The collection of tax on car benefits is usually achieved by using 'K' codes. The function of these codes is reviewed on page 50.

FUEL SUPPLIED FOR PRIVATE MOTORING

The calculations which apply to create a taxable benefit where a motor car is provided for private motoring during 1998–99 will not necessarily exhaust all liability for the same year. There may be additional fuel benefit charges. These potential fuel benefits arise whenever a motor car is made available to a director or employee (including members of those individuals' families and households) for private motoring. Therefore, where a car benefit arises from the availability of a motor car (as discussed above), a car fuel benefit may also arise.

Car fuel benefits are measured by reference to scale charges. The scale charges for both 1997–98

CAR FUEL SCALE BENEFITS 1997–98
Cars having a recognised cylinder capacity

PETROL FUEL	Annual benefit
Cylinder capacity (cc):	£
1,400 or under	800
1,401 to 2,000	1,010
2,001 or more	1,490

DIESEL FUEL	Annual benefit
Cylinder capacity (cc):	£
2,000 or under	740
2,001 or more	940

Cars without a cylinder capacity

Any car	1,490

CAR FUEL SCALE BENEFITS 1998–99
Cars having a recognised cylinder capacity

PETROL FUEL	Annual benefit
Cylinder capacity (cc):	£
1,400 or under	1,010
1,401 to 2,000	1,280
2,001 or more	1,890

DIESEL FUEL	Annual benefit
Cylinder capacity (cc):	£
2,000 or under	1,280
2,001 or more	1,890

Cars without a cylinder capacity

Any car	1,890

39
MOTOR CAR AND FUEL BENEFITS

A company purchased a new petrol driven 1,600 cc motor car in August 1997. The list price of the vehicle was £17,500. It was established that the car had been used by a director for both business and private travel throughout 1998–99 and 8,000 miles of business mileage was involved. All petrol used for both business travel and private motoring was supplied by the company. No contribution was made by the director.

The taxable benefits for 1998–99 will be calculated as follows:

	£
Availability of motor car	
List price – £17,500	
Basic benefit 35 per cent of £17,500	6,125
Less one-third – mileage exceeding 2,500 miles	2,042
Taxable benefit	£4,083
Fuel for private motoring	
Scale charge – taxable benefit	£1,280
Total taxable benefits	£5,363

and 1998–99 are shown in the previous tables. It is now the practice to impose annual increases in fuel scale charges by an amount substantially greater than the actual increase in prices. In addition the 1998–99 scale used for diesel fuel has been increased considerably to remove the differential with petrol.

When applying the scale charges no distinction is drawn between substantial and insubstantial use, nor is the age of the car significant.

Should a vehicle be available for part only of the year, or a vehicle falling within one scale be replaced by a vehicle falling within a different scale, the calculation of benefit must be suitably adjusted.

There will be no scale charge if the employer only provides petrol or other fuel for business travel. Contributions towards the cost of fuel supplied for private motoring will only be recognised to eliminate the scale charge if:

a The director or employee is *required* to make good the whole of the expense incurred when providing fuel for private motoring;

b The *whole* cost is actually satisfied; and

c The individual makes good the saving in fuel costs on ordinary commuting achieved by undertaking business travel.

Arrangements for collecting income tax on car fuel benefits through the PAYE system are similar to those for motor car benefits.

NATIONAL INSURANCE CONTRIBUTIONS

Where a director or higher-paid employee has the use of a motor car for private motoring the income tax benefit calculations are also used to establish earnings for the purpose of Class 1A national insurance contributions. A similar approach is applied to the supply of fuel for private motoring, with the income tax scale charges being used. This does not require the satisfaction of primary Class 1 contributions by the employee but the employer must discharge Class 1A contributions. The amount of contributions arising under this heading is calculated after the end of each year of assessment and accounted for in the following June.

MOBILE TELEPHONES

A standard taxable benefit is created where a mobile telephone, whether fitted to a motor car or not, is made available for private use. The standard annual charge comprises £200 for each mobile telephone. The taxable benefit will only be avoided if there is either no private use whatsoever or, where private use does arise, the employee is required to make good the whole cost, including an appropriate proportion of subscriber and other standing charges.

VANS

A taxable benefit may arise where a van is made available for private motoring. Here also, 'private motoring' must be distinguished from 'business travel', using the approach outlined on page 56, from 6 April 1998. The word 'van' identifies a vehicle built primarily to carry goods or other loads with a gross vehicle weight not exceeding 3,500 kilograms.

Where a van is made available for non-business travel, a standard benefit of £500 arises for 1998–99. This is reduced to £350 for vehicles more than four years old at the end of the tax year. In those cases where the use of a van is shared between two or more employees the standard charge of £500, or £350, must be suitably apportioned. It is possible that the allocation of the standard charge for shared vans may result in more than £500, or £350, being allocated to an individual where two or more vans are involved. However, the allocation is restricted to ensure that no individual has aggregate taxable benefits from the use of shared vans exceeding the limit of £500 or £350.

The standard charge will be reduced pro rata for vans which become, or cease to be, available or are incapable of being used for thirty or more consecutive days during the year. In the rather unusual situation where an employee has more than two vans available simultaneously, a standard charge will arise in respect of each vehicle. No taxable benefit will arise in the case of pooled vans unless the vehicle is normally kept at or near the homes of the employees who share the van or private use is not 'merely incidental' to business use. There will be no additional charge for the provision of petrol or diesel fuel.

The standard charge for vans has no application to vehicles having a gross weight in excess of 3,500 kilograms. Nor does it extend to the private use of vehicles built primarily for the carriage of passengers, namely cars and mini-buses.

The standard charge of £500, £350 or a proportion of those amounts where vehicles are shared, will be reduced by any contribution made towards non-business use.

LOAN FACILITIES

Loans made available for the benefit of a director or employee may frequently be interest-free or carry a rate of interest falling below a commercial level. Where these facilities are obtained the director or employee may be treated as receiving a taxable benefit representing the difference between the official rate of interest and the actual interest paid, if any. The official rate is changed from time to time but was increased from 6.75 per cent to 7.25 per cent per annum on 6 August 1997. Different official rates apply to some loans made in overseas currencies.

There are alternative methods of calculating the taxable benefit using the official rate. One, 'the normal method', is to take the average rate of interest and the average amount of the loan for the entire year, or the period of the loan, if shorter. The other, 'the alternative method', which either the employee or HM Inspector of Taxes can require, calculates notional interest on the actual loan on a day-to-day basis. The average official rate for 1997–98, namely the year ending on 5 April 1998 was 7.08 per cent for United Kingdom loans.

Whichever method is used, the first step requires the calculation of the difference between interest paid, if any, and the official rate. However, the next step in the calculation of income tax liability will be governed by the facts of each individual case.

One possibility is that if interest had actually become payable on the loan that interest would, in whole or in part, have qualified for income tax relief.

40
LOAN USED FOR QUALIFYING PURPOSE

Albert, a married man whose only income for 1998–99 was a salary of £27,000, received an interest-free loan of £40,000 from his employers in 1991. The entire loan was applied to purchase the home occupied by Albert and his family and remained outstanding throughout 1998–99. It will be assumed that an average official rate of, say, 7.5 per cent applied throughout that year.

On the assumption that Albert is a married man entitled to the entire married couple's allowance, the tax payable for 1998–99 will be calculated as follows:

Taxable benefit:

	£
£40,000 × 7.5 per cent . . .	3,000
Less interest actually paid . . .	NIL
Taxable benefit . . .	£3,000
Tax relief limited to £30,000 × 7.5 per cent	£2,250

Total income:

	£
Salary	27,000
Taxable benefit . . .	3,000
	30,000
Less personal allowance . .	4,195
	£25,805

Tax payable:

On first £4,300 at 20 per cent . .	860.00
On balance of £21,505 at 23 per cent	4,946.15
	5,806.15

Less	£	
Married couple's allowance –		
£1,900 at 15 per cent .	285.00	
Interest – £2,250 at 10 per cent . . .	225.00	510.00
		£5,296.15

Notes:
(1) Although tax is payable on 'interest forgone' on the loan of £40,000, relief is only available for interest on £30,000.
(2) It will be seen that whilst the benefit of £3,000 has been taxed at Albert's top rate of 23 per cent, relief for notional interest of £2,250 has only been given at the reduced rate of 10 per cent.

This will frequently be the case where a loan is applied to acquire an individual's home. In a situation of this nature:

a The benefit arising will be treated as income chargeable to income tax; but

41
EXEMPT LOANS

Susan received two interest-free loans aggregating £4,750 from her employers. Both loans were outstanding throughout 1998–99. The loans do not exceed in aggregate £5,000 and no taxable benefit will arise.

John received a loan of £2,000 from his employers to finance the purchase of an annual season ticket. He also received a loan of £17,500 to purchase his home. On the assumption that any interest, if actually paid, on the loan of £17,500 would qualify for tax relief, no taxable benefit will accrue by reason of the further loan amounting to £2,000. However, liability will arise for interest forgone on the larger loan of £17,500 in a manner similar to that illustrated by Example 40.

---

b Relief will be available at the appropriate rate on the amount of interest which, if paid, would qualify for that relief.

This two-part adjustment is necessary as whilst income of an individual may be taxable at the rate of 20 per cent, 23 per cent or 40 per cent for 1998–99, relief for some payments of interest, notably mortgage interest, is limited to 10 per cent.

No taxable benefit will arise if all loans made to an employee do not exceed £5,000. Exemption from liability is also available if all loans, excluding loans which qualify for tax relief, do not exceed £5,000. In the latter case tax will be due for 'interest forgone' on the loan qualifying for relief.

Nor will liability arise for 'interest forgone' on loans made to employees on commercial terms by employers who lend to the general public. This deals with the situation where the official rate, which is altered rather infrequently, actually exceeds the commercial rate of interest charged.

It may also be possible to avoid tax on benefits in kind attributable to loans where these facilities form part of a relocation package (see page 61).

Where a loan provided for a director or employee is subsequently released or written off, in whole or in part, the amount involved will be treated as part of the individual's remuneration. No liability will, however, arise where the release or writing off occurs on or after the borrower's death.

Directors or employees may sometimes be permitted to acquire shares for a consideration falling below market value. Arrangements of this nature may produce liability to income tax under several headings, including the possibility that the advantage may be treated as representing a notional loan creating a benefit in the manner discussed above.

OTHER ASSETS

Where an employer provides a director or higher-paid employee with the use of an asset which is neither living accommodation, a motor car, fuel used for private motoring, a van, a mobile telephone nor a loan of money, the annual benefit assessable to tax will comprise the aggregate of:

a The annual value, and
b The expense incurred by the employer in providing the use.

If the employer rents or hires an asset made available for use by the director or employee the rental paid will be substituted for the annual value, should this produce a higher taxable benefit.

For land, including dwelling-houses, located in the United Kingdom the annual value will usually represent the gross annual value used for rating purposes, notwithstanding the successive replacement of rating by the community charge and the council tax. This will not apply to the provision of living accommodation, which is dealt with under a separate heading (see page 62). In other cases the annual value will be 20 per cent of the asset's value when it was first made available for use by the director or employee.

Should the ownership of such an asset subsequently be transferred to the director or employee, an additional benefit may arise. This will represent the difference, if any, between the market value of the asset when it was first made available and the aggregate of:

a The consideration given by the director or employee to acquire the asset, and
b The amount of taxable benefits arising during the employer's period of ownership.

This basis only applies if it produces a greater taxable benefit than the excess of current market value, at the time of acquisition by the director or employee, over the price paid by him or her.

SETTLEMENT AGREEMENTS

The requirement to tax small amounts of benefit may well involve a great deal of time and effort on the part of both the employer and the Inland Revenue. Typically, these items may involve the reimbursement of telephone expenses and the provision of late night taxis home. Problems may also arise when attempting to apportion the cost of providing a single benefit between a large number of employees. In recognition of these problems the

Inland Revenue have long been prepared to enter into 'annual voluntary settlements'. By their nature, these settlements were voluntary and although fairly widely used had no statutory force. However, this anomaly has now been removed by providing statutory recognition for the re-named 'PAYE settlement agreement'. The underlying purpose of the revised agreements remains as an arrangement enabling employers to settle, in a single payment, the income tax liability on largely minor benefits in kind.

There are a range of detailed requirements but where benefits and outgoings are brought within the arrangements the amount involved must be calculated. It is then necessary to establish the income tax due on that amount by reference to the personal tax rates suffered by employees to whom benefits and advantages have been provided. Employees may, of course, suffer different rates of tax. For example, some may incur liability at the basic rate of 23 per cent and others at the higher rate of 40 per cent. Where this situation arises each group must be separated and the amounts of income tax calculated at the appropriate rate, namely 23 per cent for one group and 40 per cent for the other. Once this calculation has been completed the amount of income tax must be 'grossed up' using the rates of 23 per cent or 40 per cent as required.

The employer will then pay to the Inland Revenue a sum representing the grossed-up equivalent calculated under the terms of the PAYE settlement agreement.

The advantage of this arrangement is considerable. There will be no need to calculate benefits and other matters attributable to individual employees. No Forms P11D, or Forms P9D for other benefits, need completion. Employees brought within the settlement are not required to include their share on personal income tax returns.

Similar arrangements are available for collecting amounts due on Class 1 national insurance contributions.

It needs to be emphasised that the use of settlement agreements does have limitations. The agreements cannot be used to account for cash payments of wages, salaries or bonuses, including those paid to casual employees. Nor are they available for major benefits provided for use by an individual, namely a company car, car fuel for private motoring, accommodation and beneficial loans.

EMPLOYERS' OBLIGATIONS

With the introduction of self-assessment on 6 April 1996 and the need of both directors and employees to obtain information for the completion of tax returns, employers incur an obligation to provide details. Two requirements have been mentioned earlier in relation to 1997–98, the year ending on 5 April 1998, namely:

a The provision of Forms P60 showing pay and PAYE deductions not later than 19 May 1998 for the tax year 1997–98

b The provision of details of any Fixed Profit Car Scheme not later than 6 July 1998, also for the year 1997–98.

These details will be supplied to the Inland Revenue and also made available to directors and employees. In addition employees must be made aware of any benefits included in a PAYE Settlement Agreement.

However, this does not exhaust the employer's mounting obligations. For many years employers have been required to complete Forms P11D showing benefits made available to directors and employees. This task continues for 1997–98 with forms reaching the Inland Revenue not later than 6 July 1998. The information to be recorded on Forms P11D will comprise:

a Details of each benefit

b A calculation of the cash equivalent attributable to each benefit

c Details of expenses payments made for business entertainment

d Where the employer arranges for a third party to provide benefits, details of those benefits.

Where two or more beneficial loans are made available, or are deemed to be made available, to the same employee the cash equivalent of each loan may be reported separately. However, closely controlled companies may exercise an option to report only the aggregate figure if this is more convenient.

Expenditure on business entertaining is not generally allowable when calculating tax commitments. However, in the situation recorded under heading c above if the employer does not obtain a deduction when calculating business profits it may be possible for the employee to include the expenditure in his or her own expenses claim.

Many employers may obtain dispensations from the Inland Revenue where expenses and benefits otherwise chargeable to tax are matched with deductions in calculating liabilities. One effect of these dispensations is to relieve the employer from including details on Form P11D.

The information recorded on Forms P11D must be made available to directors and employees not later than 6 July 1998 where this relates to the year of assessment 1997–98. This obligation is confined to those in employment on 5 April 1998, namely the last day of the year of assessment. Individuals who left employment during 1997–98 may apply to their former employer for the supply of information. Unless a request is received there is no obligation on the part of the former employer to proceed, although many employers may well supply the information on a voluntary basis.

Although the above comments are of application to the completion and supply of information on forms P11D, those comments may also be extended to forms P9D. These latter forms apply to taxable benefits supplied to employees earning less than £8,500.

In a limited range of situations third parties may provide benefits to others without entering into any 'arrangement' with the true employer. There is no obligation on the part of the third party to record details to the Inland Revenue but this third party must supply information to the director or employee on a basis identical to that required from the true employer.

Future years
The above comments have identified action to be taken shortly after the end of the income tax year on 5 April 1998. Similar action will be necessary in future years and it only remains to advance the dates given to the particular year involved.

9

Redundancy payments

REDUNDANCY AND LOSS of employment are matters of great concern to those affected. An outgoing director or employee may be entitled to benefit from, or to pursue, several statutory rights which are outside the scope of the present work. The individual may also receive certain payments as a result of redundancy or dismissal and the taxation liability of these sums is discussed below.

STATUTORY REDUNDANCY PAYMENTS
On leaving an employment a director or employee may be entitled to receive a statutory redundancy payment. The amount of this payment is tax-free and will not involve the recipient in any liability to taxation.

PAYMENTS DUE BY AGREEMENT
In addition to the statutory redundancy payment, if any, an outgoing director or employee may also receive other terminal payments, often described as 'golden handshakes', from his or her former employer. The treatment of these additional sums will be governed by the circumstances in which they are paid. For example, some service agreements or arrangements contain a provision that, in the event of premature termination, a lump sum will be payable to the employee. Payments of this nature will usually represent rewards arising from the contract of service and become assessable to income tax under Schedule E, although occasionally it may be possible to avoid liability on the grounds of genuine redundancy.

Problems of identification may arise where a payment linked with the termination of an office or employment is described as 'in lieu of notice'. This description is not significant for taxation purposes as it remains to establish the nature of the arrangements governing payment. Reference has already been made to an entitlement arising under the terms of a service agreement or arrangement. This may apply to treat the payment 'in lieu of notice' as assessable as earnings from the office or employment. A second possibility is that the relationship of employee or office holder will remain but the individual will not be required to perform any duties. In this situation, sometimes described as 'gardening leave', the absence of duties is unlikely to be material with the payment 'in lieu of notice' remaining chargeable to income tax under Schedule E. A third possibility is that the sum paid 'in lieu of notice' is not attributable to the office or employment but reflects either a breach of contract by the employer or a gratuitous payment which avoids liability under Schedule E.

OTHER TERMINAL PAYMENTS
Many lump sum payments made by an employer to an outgoing director or employee on the termination of an office or employment will avoid assessment under the normal Schedule E rules, either on the grounds that they do not relate to services rendered or do not arise from the office or employment. The treatment of these terminal payments will then be governed by a numer of complex rules.

First, an ex gratia payment made solely by reason of death or disablement by accident will not be directly assessable to income tax. Nor will severance payments made on redundancy or loss of office be assessable if they do not exceed the £30,000 limit mentioned later.

Secondly, lump sum payments made under the terms of an approved occupational pension scheme will not be treated as income.

Thirdly, other lump sum payments which are not made under the terms of an approved scheme may be exempt from tax if:

a There is only one lump sum payable to the director or employee;

b The individual is not a member of an approved scheme conferring benefits other than those attributable to death in service; and

c The lump sum payment does not exceed the limit placed on lump sums payable from approved schemes.

Fourthly, other ex gratia payments made on or in connection with an individual's death or retirement may well be chargeable to income tax under Schedule E, unless those payments are made on the grounds of redundancy.

Finally, those lump sum payments which are made solely on the grounds of genuine redundancy and for no other reason should be subject to the £30,000 exemption rule outlined below.

In addition to making lump sum payments, an employer may fund the cost of providing counselling services for employees who have become, or are about to become, redundant. These counselling costs can be included in the redundancy package giving rise to the £30,000 exemption.

The £30,000 exemption

It remains to examine the treatment of ex gratia or other terminal payments which are neither treated as income and chargeable to income tax nor made exempt from tax under the terms of an approved occupational pension scheme. This will broadly extend to payments made to an employee on severance of an employment due to redundancy or loss of office, or because of death or disability due to accident.

The first £30,000 received is usually exempt from income tax, with any excess remaining fully chargeable. Restrictions may arise where two or more employments held with 'associated employers' terminate at the same time, or payments arising from a single termination are payable by instalments. When calculating the amount, if any, by which the terminal payment, or payments, exceed £30,000,

---

————— 42 —————
TERMINAL PAYMENT

Joe became redundant on 30 September 1998 and received a statutory redundancy payment of £4,250. In addition he received a golden handshake of £60,000 solely on the grounds of redundancy.
The amount taxable for 1998–99 then becomes:

	£
Statutory redundancy payment . .	4,250
Golden handshake	60,000
Total terminal payments . . .	64,250
Less exempt amount . . .	30,000
Taxable	£34,250

Assuming Joe is below the age of 65, a married man living with his wife, entitled to the entire married couple's allowance and in receipt of other income amounting to £40,000 for 1998–99, the tax payable becomes:

Total income:	£
Other income . . .	40,000
Golden handshake	34,250
	74,250
Less Personal allowance	4,195
	£70,055

Tax payable:	
Lower rate:	£
On first £4,300 at 20 per cent . .	860.00
Basic rate:	
On next £22,800 at 23 per cent .	5,244.00
Higher rate:	
On balance of £42,955 at 40 per cent .	17,182.00
	23,286.00
Less Married couple's allowance – £1,900	
at 15 per cent	285.00
	£23,001.00

---

the statutory redundancy receipt must be included, although it is not subject to tax.

Late payments and benefits

Some terminal arrangements require cash payments to be discharged by instalments spread over two or more different years. In addition, those arrangements may confer on the outgoing director or employee a right to receive future benefits, perhaps the use of a company car.

A strict approach requires that where cash sums are received in a year following the year of termination, the Inland Revenue must be advised and will raise an appropriate assessment. However, this assessment is related back to the year of termination and does not take into consideration income, allowances and other matters for the year of receipt. In contrast, the strict approach requires that the right to receive future benefits must be valued at the time of termination and added to other terminal sums.

This treatment of the right to receive benefits created numerous problems. For example, the valuation process may be far from straightforward. Further, the outgoing director or employee suffers tax on a notional sum which may or may not reflect the true value of benefits subsequently enjoyed. In recognition of these problems an alternative approach could be adopted by an individual whose employment ceased in 1996–97 or 1997–98. This approach avoided the need to value the right to receive benefits. In substitution, the actual value of benefits received in each future year had to be determined. It then remained for the amount of the benefit to be related back to the year of termination.

Both the original strict basis and the optional approach no longer apply where the termination occurs on or after 6 April 1998. In future both cash instalments received and the value of benefits actually enjoyed in years following the year of termination will be assessed in each future year and not related back to the year the employment ceased.

Those taxpayers whose employments terminated in 1996–97 or 1997–98, and who adopted the alternative basis may also use the new approach for cash sums received or benefits enjoyed on and after 6 April 1998.

Whichever approach is applied, whether the old strict basis, the alternative basis or the new basis, the first £30,000 of aggregate cash and benefits continues to be exempt from income tax.

Other matters

Some terminal payments arising by reason of death, injury or disability, together with those arising under superannuation scheme arrangements or for services rendered outside the United Kingdom, are immune from liability, notwithstanding the sums involved may exceed £30,000.

It will often be found that where an outgoing director or employee fails to obtain alternative employment, some repayment of income tax suffered under PAYE will become available for the year of assessment in which redundancy occurs. However, the ability to obtain immediate repayment during a period of unemployment may be limited (see page 50).

10

Businesses and professions

INTRODUCTION

Profits earned by an individual from carrying on a business in his or her capacity as sole proprietor or member of a partnership are assessable to income tax. As tax is charged on profits for a year of assessment ending on 5 April the basis used to measure those profits is an important factor. This particularly affects businesses which do not prepare accounts to 5 April annually.

For many years the allocation of profits to a year of assessment was achieved by applying the 'preceding year' basis. However, the complex rules required to administer this basis have recently been replaced by a new 'current year' basis of assessment. It must be emphasised that the change did not significantly affect the *calculation* of profits but only the *allocation* of those profits to different tax years.

The new current year basis applies to all businesses commenced after 5 April 1994. Businesses which were begun on or before that date continued to apply the preceding year basis until entering the current year basis of assessment in 1997–98, with special rules to determine taxable profits for the transitional year, 1996–97.

To avoid distortion or exploitation, further rules may apply where a business commenced before 6 April 1994 is discontinued between 6 April 1997 and 5 April 1999.

It is therefore necessary to examine separately the assessment of profits for:

a Businesses commenced before 6 April 1994 and which ceased not later than 5 April 1997;

b Businesses which commenced before 6 April 1994 and continued beyond 5 April 1997;

c Businesses which commenced on or after 6 April 1994; and

d Businesses which commenced before 6 April 1994 and which ceased between 6 April 1997 and 5 April 1999.

When approaching this matter it is very important to distinguish between the commencement and cessation dates. Both dates must be accurately identified if the correct basis of assessment is to be established.

BUSINESSES COMMENCED BEFORE 6 APRIL 1994

Established businesses

Profits of an established business commenced before 6 April 1994 are assessed on a preceding year basis. This requires that profits for an accounting year ending in the previous year of assessment will be taxed in the following year. For example, if accounts of a business are made up to 31 December annually the results for the year ended 31 December 1994 will form the basis of assessment for 1995–96, commencing on 6 April 1995. Special rules, which are reviewed later, then deal with the assessment for 1996–97 which identifies the transition to the new current year basis of assessment, if the business continues beyond 5 April 1997.

New businesses

Clearly, the preceding year basis cannot apply in the first year of a new business as there was no preceding

43
DISCONTINUED BUSINESS
OLD RULES

Clive closes down his long-established business on 30 June 1996. Profits, as computed for income tax purposes, have been:

				£
Year to 30 September 1993	.	.	.	13,500
Year to 30 September 1994	.	.	.	15,000
Year to 30 September 1995	.	.	.	16,500
Nine months to 30 June 1996	.	.	.	12,600

The business ceased in 1996–97 and the assessment for that year will be based on the actual profits, namely:

3/9ths of £12,600   .   .   .   .   **£4,200**

Applying the preceding year basis the assessments for the two previous years become:

1995–96 (year to 30 September 1994)	15,000
1994–95 (year to 30 September 1993)	13,500

However, the actual profits of the two previous years were:

1995–96 (year to 5 April 1996)	£	£
6/12ths × £16,500 . .	8,250	
6/9ths × £12,600 . .	8,400	
		16,650
1994–95 (year to 5 April 1995)		
6/12ths × £15,000 . .	7,500	
6/12ths × £16,500 . .	8,250	
		15,750
		£32,400

As the figure of £32,400 exceeds the original aggregate assessments of £28,500 (£13,500 + £15,000) for 1994–95 and 1995–96, the assessments for these two years will be adjusted to:

1994–95	.	.	.	.	.	**£15,750**
1995–96	.	.	.	.	.	**£16,650**

The business was discontinued before 6 April 1997. As a result, the transitional rules for 1996–97, which are considered later, do not apply.

year on which to base the assessment. The rules which must be followed for a new business commenced before 6 April 1994 are then modified as follows:

a For the first tax year in which the business is commenced, use profits from the date of commencement to the following 5 April

b For the second tax year use the profits for a period of twelve months from the commencement date

c For the third tax year it is usual to base the assessment on profits for the period of twelve months ending on the last business accounting date preceding the commencement of the tax year

d For later years the normal preceding year basis applies, unless or until this is replaced by the current year basis or the business comes to an end.

The application of **b** and **c** in the early years of a new business will sometimes result in an injustice to the taxpayer. To avoid this an election may be made at any time within seven years from the end of the second tax year in which the business is carried on to have the assessment for the second and third years (but not one year only) based on the actual profits of those years ending on 5 April. If the taxpayer wishes he or she may withdraw the election within a period of six years from the end of the third year.

Discontinued business
Special provisions apply for determining the assessments which must be raised in the closing years of a business which commenced before 6 April 1994 but is discontinued or changes hands before 6 April 1997. These are as follows:

a For the final period of a business the assessment will be based on the actual profits of the period from the beginning of the tax year on 6 April to the date when the business closes down or changes hands

44
PARTNERSHIP CHANGES
OLD RULES

Sarah and Janet commenced to carry on business in partnership on 1 July 1989. On 1 July 1996 Betty was admitted as a member of the partnership. The enlarged partnership continued beyond 5 April 1997.

The basis on which assessments will be raised is as follows:

Continuation election made
a 1995–96 and earlier years – preceding year basis.
b 1996–97 – special transitional basis.
c 1997–98 and future years – current year basis.

No continuation election made
a Discontinuance of preceding year basis on 30 June 1996.
b Preceding year basis for 1996–97 (part) and earlier years.
c No special transitional basis for 1996–97.
d Commencement of current year basis from 1 July 1996.
e New business current year provisions apply.

b For each of the two previous tax years the normal basis of assessment is the profits of each preceding year. The Inland Revenue have power, however, to decide that the assessments may be based on the actual profits to 5 April for each of those years (but not one year only) if those assessments produce a higher aggregate tax liability.

It is to be assumed that this power will be exercised if the tax payable is thereby increased.

Partnerships

The above rules governing the assessment of profits where a business was commenced before 6 April 1994 are of general application to partnerships. However, the assessment to be raised where a new business is commenced or an existing business closes down during a period affected by the preceding year basis of assessment may require modification to recognise changes among the partners. These changes will occur where a sole trader admits a second individual or individuals into partnership, an individual joins or leaves an existing partnership, or a business carried on in partnership reverts to a sole trader. Special adjustments and elections may apply if at least one individual continues to be involved in the business both before and after the change.

Where a change occurs after 5 April 1994 but before 6 April 1997 in a business commenced before the earlier date there are two possibilities. Firstly, all individuals affected by the change may file a written notice to treat the business as continuing. The normal preceding year basis of assessment will then apply to determine the profits for each year of assessment until the subsequent introduction of the current year basis.

If no continuation election is made for a change taking place after 5 April 1994 but before 6 April 1997, the discontinuance rules outlined above must be applied. However, immediately following the change the current year basis of assessment discussed later and which applies to a new business must be used. In the absence of a continuation election it is not possible for members of a partnership to retain the application of the preceding year basis.

These rules apply only to changes in the persons carrying on business in partnership where those changes occurred after 5 April 1994 and before 6 April 1997. A finding that such a change occurred on or before the earlier date would preserve the preceding year basis, although several special rules applied which have no application subsequently.

45
PARTNERSHIP ASSESSMENT OLD RULES

John, Paul and Christopher commenced to carry on business in partnership during 1989, sharing profits equally, with accounts being prepared to 31 December annually. Taxable profits for the year ending 31 December 1994 were £60,000, assessable for 1995–96. On 1 January 1995 the profit share of John was reduced to one-fifth and that of the two other partners increased to two-fifths. The partnership continues.

The actual share of profits taken by each partner in the year to 31 December 1994 was:

1/3 × £60,000 =   £20,000

However, these profits were assessed in 1995–96, with the assessment being allocated by reference to the profit-sharing ratios for that year, namely:

						£
John	1/5 × £60,000	.	.	.	.	12,000
Paul	2/5 × £60,000	.	.	.	.	24,000
Christopher	2/5 × £60,000	.	.	.	.	24,000
						£60,000

As a result, John's share of taxable profits is less than the share actually received. Both Paul and Christopher bear tax on an increased share of profits.

Where the preceding year basis of assessment does apply, profits of the partnership are shared between individual partners by reference to their profit-sharing ratios in the year of assessment. These ratios may be different from those which applied when profits were actually earned. A single assessment is raised in the partnership name and all partners have a joint liability to discharge income tax becoming due.

OLD BUSINESSES – TRANSITION TO THE CURRENT YEAR BASIS

Businesses which commenced before 6 April 1994 and continue beyond 5 April 1997 must abandon the old preceding year basis and become involved with the new current year basis when determining profits chargeable to income tax. This involves a transition from the old to the new with a special adjustment for the transitional year 1996–97. A number of modifications may be required if such a business ceases on or before 5 April 1999, but these are examined later.

46

TRANSITIONAL ASSESSMENT 1996–97

Anne commenced business in 1985 and prepares accounts for the year to 31 October annually. The business is continuing and it is to be assumed that profits were:

	£
Year to 31 October 1994 . . .	20,000
Year to 31 October 1995 . . .	24,000
Year to 31 October 1996 . . .	18,000
Year to 31 October 1997 . . .	27,000

The assessment of these profits will be as follows:

	£
1995–96 – Last year of preceding year basis	
Year to 31 October 1994 . .	20,000
1997–98 – First year of current year basis	
Year to 31 October 1997 . .	27,000
1996–97 – Transitional year	
Period 1 November 1994 to 31 October 1996 = 24 months	
Profit for period £24,000 + £18,000 = £42,000	
Taxable:	
12/24ths × £42,000 . . .	21,000

Assessment for 1997–98 and 1998–99

The current year basis requires that profits for an accounting year or period ending in a year of assessment will comprise the taxable profits for that year. No other allocation is required in the case of a continuing business and it is immaterial whether the accounting year ends on 30 April, 31 December, 31 March or any other date.

For example, the profits assessable in 1998–99, where accounts are prepared to, say, 31 December, will represent profits for the twelve-month period ending on 31 December 1998.

Assessment for 1996–97 – the transitional year

There are two special transitional adjustments for businesses which commenced before 6 April 1994 and continue beyond 5 April 1997. The first adjustment is used to calculate the profits chargeable for the transitional year 1996–97. The calculation of taxable profit will usually proceed as follows:

a There must be identified the period from the end of the basis period for 1995–96 (end of the preceding year basis) to the commencement of the basis period for 1997–98 (first year of the current year basis). Where accounts are prepared to the same date annually this period will extend throughout exactly twenty-four months

47

TRANSITIONAL OVERLAP RELIEF

Anne in the previous example had profits of £27,000 assessed in 1997–98. These profits arose in the twelve-month period to 31 October 1997. Overlap relief is available on that proportion of the profits falling before 6 April 1997, namely (calculated in months):

5/12ths × £27,000 . . . . . £11,250

This relief may be set against future profits as explained later. It cannot affect the assessment of profits for 1997–98.

b There must then be established the result of the following calculation:

$$\frac{365 \text{ days}}{\text{number of days in period}} \times \text{profits for the period}$$

c The result will comprise the amount of profits taxable in 1996–97. If the period arising under a is exactly two years the calculation will produce a figure representing one-half of the profits for this period, which will represent the amount taxable for 1996–97. The remaining one-half escapes assessment entirely.

Strictly the calculation should be made in days. As 1996 was a leap year containing 366 days a small variation may arise. For reasons of simplicity calculations in the examples have been made in months.

It may be necessary to calculate profits for the period in two parts if one part produces losses.

Overlap relief

The second transitional adjustment recognises that part of the profits assessed on the current year basis for 1997–98 will have been earned before 6 April 1997. The part identified in this manner will represent 'overlap relief' which can be set against profits at some later date. However, the ability to utilise overlap relief is restricted and relief will only be available against profits for the year of assessment in which a business comes to an end, or where there is a change in the accounting date which results in a basis period of more than 12 months.

Avoidance

It will be apparent that steps could be taken to exploit the special arrangements for 1996–97 by artificially increasing profits. Similar steps might be taken to increase profits chargeable in 1997–98 to correspondingly increase the amount of transitional overlap relief. These increases could be achieved by a variety of methods, including the transfer of receipts and payments between different accounting periods. However, a range of special rules have been introduced to frustrate avoidance of this nature.

Partnerships

A similar approach applies to the assessment of partnership profits where a partnership which commenced before 6 April 1994 continues beyond 5 April 1997. However, the assessment of partnership profits for 1996–97 is imposed on the partnership and not on individual partners. Income tax became payable on two dates, namely 1 January 1997 and 1 July in the same year. It remains for each partner to return his or her share of partnership profits on personal income tax returns. Although those profits then become chargeable on individual partners, each receives a credit for his or her share of partnership income tax.

Once the preceding year basis and the transitional adjustments for 1996–97 have ceased to apply, the taxation of partnership profits will proceed in the manner discussed later.

NEW BUSINESSES COMMENCED AFTER 5 APRIL 1994

Businesses commenced after 5 April 1994 immediately become subject to the current year basis from the date of commencement. Those businesses are not affected by the preceding year basis, nor are they in any way concerned with the special transitional rules for 1996–97 or the calculation of overlap relief for an accounting period overlapping 6 April 1997. The rules which apply to the current year basis generally are outlined below.

New businesses

Where a new business is commenced after 5 April 1994 the profits are assessable as follows:

a For the first tax year in which the business is carried on, use profits from the date of commencement to the following 5 April

b For the second tax year the basis period will usually be twelve months to the date on which accounts are made up in the second year. If this date is less than twelve months from the commencement of the business, profits for the first twelve months must be used.

c For the third and subsequent years, profits for the accounting year or period ending in the year of assessment will be used.

48
NEW BUSINESS NEW RULES

David commenced business on 1 August 1995, subsequently preparing accounts to 31 July annually. Profits for the opening years of the business were as follows:

	£
Year to 31 July 1996	15,000
Year to 31 July 1997	21,000
Year to 31 July 1998	18,000
Year to 31 July 1999	24,000

Assuming the business is continuing, the amounts chargeable to tax will be:

	£
1995–96 Period to 5 April 1996 8/12ths × £15,000	10,000
1996–97 – Year to 31 July 1996	15,000
1997–98 – Year to 31 July 1997	21,000
1998–99 – Year to 31 July 1998	18,000
1999–2000 – Year to 31 July 1999	24,000

It will be seen that of the profits for the year to 31 July 1996, £10,000 has been assessed twice. Therefore overlap relief becomes £10,000 which is available for future use.

As David commenced his business after 5 April 1994 none of the transitional provisions apply.

Overlap relief

The basis used in the early years of a new business will often require that some profits are assessed more than once. No relief will be immediately available but overlap relief should be forthcoming. This relief will comprise the amount of profits which have been doubly assessed.

49
USING OVERLAP RELIEF

Let it be assumed that Elaine in the previous example had unused transitional overlap relief of £18,500 brought forward. The profits chargeable for 2000–2001 would then be adjusted as follows:

	£
Original profits	36,000
Less overlap relief	18,500
Revised profits	£17,500

Overlap relief may occasionally be set against future profits where there is a change in the date to which accounts are prepared. In most situations, however, this relief will only be offset against profits, or perhaps used to create losses, for the year of assessment in which the business is discontinued.

Established businesses

Where the new business and discontinuance rules do not affect the assessment of profits, the allocation of those profits to a year of assessment is straight-forward. If there is only one annual accounting date profits for the year ending in the year of assessment will comprise the amount of profits chargeable to income tax for that year. Occasionally there may be two or possibly more accounting periods ending in a single year of assessment. The date on which the most recent of these periods ends will establish the accounting date to which profits for that year must be measured. There may be some departure from this approach where there is a change in the annual accounting date to which profits are prepared as a number of requirements must be satisfied if the change is to be recognised for income tax purposes.

Discontinuance

On a business being discontinued the basis period for the year in which discontinuance occurs commences immediately following the end of the basis period for the previous year and ends on the date of discontinuance. This may establish a basis period for the final year of some considerable length. In the extreme case the profits for the final year may incorporate figures extending throughout nearly twenty-four months.

To some extent the disproportionately high level of profits assessable in the final year may be reduced by overlap relief, if of course that relief has not been used on an earlier occasion. Although the prospect of a large assessment in the final year of a business may seem unduly harsh, the theory of the current year basis of assessment is that throughout

51
PARTNERSHIP PROFITS NEW RULES

Jack and Rachael had been carrying on business in partnership for many years, preparing accounts to 30 September annually and sharing profits equally. Peter was admitted to the partnership on 1 October 2001 and acquired a one-quarter share of profits. Jack's profit share was reduced to one-quarter but Rachael's share remained one-half.

Taxable profits for the year to 30 September 2002 were £80,000, allocated as follows:

	£
Jack 1/4 × £80,000	20,000
Rachael 1/2 × £80,000	40,000
Peter 1/4 × £80,000	20,000
	£80,000

The business is continuing and taxable profits of Jack and Rachael for 2002–2003 (basis period 12 months to 30 September 2002) become:

	£
Jack	20,000
Rachael	40,000

These represent the actual share of profits. Apart from the change in profit shares, the calculations are unaffected by the admission of Peter.

Peter's liability will be established by applying the new business rules, namely:

	£
2001–2002 – actual share 1/2 × £20,000	10,000
2002–2003 – 12 months to 30 September 2002	20,000

Overlap relief of £10,000 will be due, as this amount has been assessed twice over.

50
DISCONTINUED BUSINESS NEW RULES

Elaine had carried on business for many years, preparing accounts annually to 30 April. The business ceased on 31 March 2001. Profits in the more recent years were as follows:

	£
Year to 30 April 1999	24,000
Year to 30 April 2000	21,000
Period to 31 March 2001	15,000

The business ceased in 2000–2001. The previous year was 1999–2000. Profits chargeable for this previous year will be those for the twelve months ended on 30 April 1999, namely, £24,000. The final basis period therefore commences on the following day, 1 May 1999, and ends on 31 March 2001 when the business ceased. As a result the charge for 2000–2001 will be based on profits for this period, namely:

	£
12 months to 30 April 2000	21,000
11 months to 31 March 2001	15,000
	£36,000

Profits of twenty-three months and amounting to £36,000 must therefore be assessed in a single year. These profits may be reduced by any overlap relief which has not previously been used, as shown by the following example.

the lifetime of a business all profits are assessed in total once only.

Partnerships

The introduction of the current year basis of assessment profoundly affects partnerships. Once this basis applies it remains necessary to calculate partnership profits on the basis of a single entity. However, those profits must then be shared between the partners in accordance with the ratios used when profits were actually earned. There will be no assessment on the partnership as such and no joint liability. In substitution, each member of the partnership will be charged to tax as a 'sole proprietor'. It follows that where a new partner joins a partnership his share of profits chargeable to tax will be calculated by reference to the new business rules. When a partner leaves his taxable profits must be determined by reference to the discontinuance rules. This treatment will have no effect whatsoever on the remaining partners, who will be charged on a continuing basis.

OLD BUSINESSES – CESSATION BETWEEN 6 APRIL 1997 AND 5 APRIL 1999

Although a business which commenced before 6 April 1994 and continued beyond 5 April 1997 will be subject to the current year basis of assessment for 1997–98 and later years, there are two possible modifications which are designed to prevent undue advantages arising from the transitional rules. These modifications deal with the situation where a business which commenced before 6 April 1994 is discontinued in either:

a The year ended 5 April 1998; or
b The year ended on 5 April 1999.

It must be emphasised that these modifications have no application whatsoever to new businesses commenced after 5 April 1994.

Discontinuance in 1997–98

Where the discontinuance of such a business occurs in 1997–98 (year ending on 5 April 1998) the Inland Revenue have the right to direct that the current year basis for calculating taxable profits will not apply. Should a direction be made, the old preceding year basis will be used, with the following results:

a For 1997–98 the assessment will be based on the actual profits for the period from 6 April 1997 to the date of discontinuance.

52
OLD BUSINESS DISCONTINUED IN 1997–98

Let it be assumed that Anne in Examples 46 and 47 ceased business on 31 December 1997. Her profits for the two-month period to the cessation date were £2,000.

In the absence of any Inland Revenue direction assessments for the last three years of the business become:

		£
1995–96 – as previously	. . . .	20,000
1996–97 – as previously	. . . .	21,000
1997–98 – £27,000 plus £2,000	£	
Less overlap relief – as	29,000	17,750
previously . . .	11,250	

However, should the Inland Revenue make a direction, the 'old' preceding year discontinuance rules apply, with the following results:

		£
1997–98 – Profit 6.4.97 to 31.12.97	. .	
7/12 × £27,000 + £2,000		17,750
1996–97 – Year to 31.10.95	. . .	24,000
1995–96 – Year to 31.10.94	. . .	20,000

The actual profits of these two earlier years were:

	£	£
1996–97 – year to 5 April 1997		
5/12 × £27,000	11,250	
7/12 × £18,000	10,500	21,750
1995–96 – year to 5 April 1996		
5/12 × £18,000	7,500	
7/12 × £24,000	14,000	21,500
		£43,250

As the figure of £43,250 does not exceed the aggregate of £24,000 plus £20,000 (£44,000) no adjustment is required for these two years.

The assessments for the three final years, should the Inland Revenue issue a direction, will be:

		£
1997–98	. . . . . .	17,500
1996–97	. . . . . .	24,000
1995–96	. . . . . .	20,000

No overlap relief can be obtained as the current year basis does not apply.

---

b For both 1996–97 and 1995–96 the old preceding year basis must be used. The Inland Revenue have the power, however, to decide that the assessments may be based on the actual profits to 5 April for each of these years (but not one year only) if those assessments produce a higher aggregate tax liability.
c As the current year basis does not apply, there can be no overlap relief.

It must be assumed that a direction will only be made if this increases the tax payable for 1995–96 to 1997–98 inclusive.

Discontinuance in 1998–99

Should the discontinuance of the business occur in 1998–99 (year to 5 April 1999), calculations based on the transition from the preceding year basis to the current year basis will continue to be made. However, it then becomes necessary to compare:

a The sum assessed for 1996–97, calculated by applying the transitional rules; and

b The actual profits for the twelve months ended on 5 April 1997.

If the component under **b** exceeds that calculated under **a** the Inland Revenue have the right to direct that the assessment for 1996–97 should be amended to reflect the actual profits for the twelve months ended on 5 April 1997.

Interest

Self-assessment requires that interest will be charged where tax is underpaid. It is clear that as the result of discontinuing an 'old' business in 1997–98 or 1998–99, assessments for earlier years may be increased. Although this increase may well indicate an underpayment of income tax for those earlier years, no interest commitment will arise by reason of that adjustment if the increased liability is discharged at an early date.

LOSSES – CONTINUING BUSINESSES

The calculation of business results will not invariably disclose profits and inevitably losses may sometimes arise. Where such a loss was incurred in a continuing trade or profession and the old 'preceding year' basis applied, no income tax liability would arise in the following year as the assessment for that year had to be based on the profits, if any, of the previous base year. A number of adjustments were required if the calculation was affected by the new business or discontinued business rules.

A rather different approach applies from the use of the 'new' current year basis as the results of an accounting year ending in the year of assessment will usually establish the profits assessable in that year. Where the results disclose a loss there will be no profits to assess.

It must be emphasised that the loss is calculated by reference to the results for the basis period. It does not reflect the actual results for the tax year ending on 5 April, unless of course this is also the accounting date. For example, where accounts are

53
OFFSETTING LOSSES

A dealer sustains a trading loss of £23,000, in an old-established business, during the accounting year to 31 March 1999.

He has income for the year of assessment 1998–99 of £17,000 arising from investments, on which he has suffered income tax by deduction.

The taxpayer may claim to set the loss against investment income of £17,000, with tax suffered on that income being repaid. If such a claim is agreed, the balance of the loss (£6,000) may be carried forward and set against future trading profits arising from the same trade, used in a similar loss claim for 1997–98 or perhaps set against capital gains in 1998–99.

---

prepared annually to 31 December in the case of a continuing business, the results for the twelve months ended 31 December 1998 will be used to calculate the loss, if any, for the tax year 1998–99.

Subject to any adjustments which may be required, losses arising from carrying on a business may be utilised in several different ways.

One method, which requires the submission of a claim, is to offset the loss against the individual's income for the year of assessment in which the loss arose. Where income for the year of loss is insufficient, any unused part of the loss may usually be set against income of a different year. In the case of continuing businesses established before 6 April 1994, any unused part of the loss arising in 1995–96 and earlier years could be set against income for the year of assessment immediately following the year of loss. However, for new businesses commenced after 5 April 1994, and in the case of all businesses for 1996–97 and future years, a loss can be set against income for the year of loss or offset against income for the previous (and not following) year.

This method of obtaining loss relief will frequently result in a repayment of income tax suffered on investment income. It may also result in tax payable on business profits for the previous year being recovered in whole or in part. However, a successful claimant must show that the loss arose from a trade or business being undertaken on a commercial basis and with a view to the realisation of profits. If there is any balance of loss in respect of which tax cannot be repaid, this may be carried forward and set against future profits of the same business.

In those cases where losses have been incurred in farming or market gardening for five consecutive

54
CARRYING LOSSES FORWARD

A trader preparing accounts to 31 October annually has the following profits and losses, as adjusted for income tax purposes:

		£
Year ended 31 October 1997	Loss	10,000
Year ended 31 October 1998	Profit	6,400
Year ended 31 October 1999	Profit	22,100

If the loss of £10,000 is carried forward the results become:

	£	Taxable profit £
Year ended 31 October 1997		NIL
Year ended 31 October 1998 –		
Profit	6,400	
Less loss brought forward (part)	6,400	NIL
Year ended 31 October 1999 –		
Profit	22,100	
Less loss brought forward (balance)	3,600	18,500

years the ability to offset future losses against income will be restricted.

A second method may be available where there is insufficient income to absorb the loss under the first method. This enables the unused business loss for a year of assessment to be set against chargeable gains otherwise assessable to capital gains tax in the same year.

A third method is to carry the loss forward year by year and offset it against subsequent profits arising from the same business. This process continues until the loss has been fully used or the business ends. Losses can only be carried forward to the extent that they have not been relieved under methods one and two above.

LOSSES – NEW BUSINESSES
Where a loss arises in the first year of assessment during which a new business is carried on, or in any of the three following years, a claim may be made to set that loss against income for the three years preceding the year in which the loss arose. This claim provides a further alternative to methods one, two and three outlined above. The replacement of the preceding year basis by the current year basis has not significantly affected claims of this nature, although the method used to calculate losses for a year of assessment has changed. These calculations are now based on the results for the accounting

55
CARRYING LOSSES BACKWARDS

An individual commenced a manufacturing business on 1 July 1996. The actual results attributable to the first four years of assessment, ending on 5 April, were as follows:

	£
1996–97 Loss	7,100
1997–98 Loss	3,400
1998–99 Profit	9,200
1999–2000 Profit	15,400

If a claim is made the loss of £7,100 arising in 1996–97 may be carried back and set against income in the following order:

a Income for 1993–94
b Income for 1994–95
c Income for 1995–96

Should a separate claim be made for the loss of £3,400 arising in 1997–98 this will be set against income in the following order, except to the extent that income has not been offset by the loss arising in 1996–97:

a Income for 1994–95
b Income for 1995–96
c Income for 1996–97

No relief is available for the two most recent years as both 1998–99 and 1999–2000 disclosed profits.

period, or basis period, ending in the year of assessment and not on the actual results for the full tax year ending on 5 April.

56
FARMERS AND AVERAGING

For several years Paul has carried on the business of farming. His profits for 1996–97 and 1997–98 were as follows:

	£
1996–97	40,000
1997–98	15,000

In the absence of any claim for averaging, these profits are chargeable to tax in the normal manner. However, if a claim is made the results for the two years may be averaged as follows:

	£
Profit for 2 years (£40,000 + £15,000)	55,000
1996–97 – one-half	27,500
1997–98 – one-half	27,500

FARMERS AND MARKET GARDENERS

The rules for allocating profits, and indeed losses, to a year of assessment apply also to individuals who carry on the trade of farming or market gardening. However, these individuals may claim to average the results of two consecutive years of assessment if the difference between the profits of each year is at least 30 per cent, or one year produces a loss. The claim must be submitted not later than 31 January falling some 22 months after the end of the second year and cannot apply to the first year of a new business or the last year of a discontinued business. A limited claim may also be available if the difference in profits between the two years is a little less than 30 per cent.

CALCULATION OF BUSINESS RESULTS

Proper accounts are essential if business profits are to be correctly calculated and the results inserted on a tax return form. Similar comments apply where the business results disclose a loss as losses can usually be included in a claim or claims for relief. The absence of proper accounts recording the correct results of a business may lead to an overcharge or perhaps an undercharge to tax which may later have serious consequences because failure to disclose the full profits assessable to tax or to overinflate a loss relief claim can involve a potential liability to interest and penalties. Many business proprietors use the services of qualified accountants who are expert in this work. They will prepare accounts and advise on the most favourable treatment which the law permits.

The general approach to the calculation of business profits initially requires the application of approved accountancy principles. Profits calculated on this basis will be accepted for income tax purposes unless there is a statutory provision indicating some different approach. There are a number of such provisions, notably the need to demonstrate that expenditure has been incurred 'wholly and exclusively' for the purposes of the business.

It follows that some items which commonly appear as expenses in the accounts are not allowable for tax purposes. These have to be added to the profits shown. On the other hand, there are occasionally receipts included in the accounts which should not be taxed as business profits or are chargeable under some other heading. These must be deducted from the profits shown.

It should be emphasised that the recent transition from the preceding year basis to the current year basis has had little effect on the calculation of profits or losses. The real significance of the change is the manner in which those profits are assessed to tax or losses are relieved. One change which has taken place involves the use of capital allowances arising on business assets. Previously, these allowances did not affect the calculation of profits but where the current year basis applies they are included as an expense.

EXPENDITURE NOT ALLOWED

The following list provides an illustration of some items of expenditure which may appear in the financial accounts of a business, but which are *not* allowed in computing income tax liability and therefore have to be added to profits, or deducted from losses, disclosed by the accounts to arrive at the profit or loss for income tax purposes.

a Expenses not wholly and exclusively laid out for the purpose of the business.

b Expenses for domestic or private purposes.

c The cost of business entertaining, including many gifts. Certain gifts made to charity may be allowed (see pages 125 and 126).

d The rent of property which is not used for business purposes. The deduction allowed in respect of any dwelling-house or domestic office is not normally to exceed two-thirds of the rent, but a larger proportion may be given for hotels, boarding houses and other establishments.

e Provisions for the repair of premises occupied for the business or for implements or utensils, unless sums have actually been, or are to be, expended.

f Any capital sums used in or withdrawn from the business.

g The cost of improvements to premises.

h Debts, other than bad debts or those estimated to be doubtful.

i Any royalty or other sum paid for the use of a patent, where tax is deducted from the payment.

j Income tax, capital gains tax, capital transfer tax or inheritance tax paid.

k Depreciation (capital allowances will usually be available, however – see page 93).

l Withdrawals by proprietors.

m Penalties for breaking the law and legal expenses in connection with the wrongdoing.

n Reserves (except for discounts or for *specific* doubtful debts).

o Payments which constitute the commission of a criminal offence by the payer.

p Payments made in response to threats, menaces, blackmail and other forms of extortion.

EXPENDITURE WHICH IS ALLOWED

Any sums expended wholly and exclusively for the purpose of the business may usually be included in the computation of profits, unless the outlay is of a capital nature. Among the deductions allowable are the following:

a Advertising expenditure (but *not* the original cost of permanent signs).

b Bad and doubtful debts.

c Costs of raising business loan finance.

d Interest incurred for business purposes.

e Insurance for business purposes. Note that recoveries under the policies must usually be included in the calculation of profits.

f Legal expenses for recovering debts or incurred in connection with other non-capital business matters.

g National insurance contributions paid in respect of employees.

h Reasonable payments for the hire of assets. Some restriction may be necessary for the cost of hiring motor cars having a retail price exceeding £12,000 when new.

i Redundancy payments made to former employees.

j Rent of business premises. (A restriction may be necessary as shown under head d on the previous page where domestic premises are involved.)

k Repairs to premises, excluding improvements and alterations.

l Subscriptions and donations; where the society to which payment is made has agreed with the Inland Revenue to pay tax on its profits; where purely to maintain the business; or where the staff of the business benefit.

m Wages, salaries and pensions paid to employees and past employees or their dependants (but note the time limit within which payments must be made – see below).

The above list is not intended to be comprehensive but is indicative of the type of expenditure which may be charged against business results to arrive at the profits on which income tax will be imposed or the losses qualifying for relief.

TRADING STOCK AND WORK IN PROGRESS

Unsold trading stock or work in progress retained at the end of an accounting period is usually valued at the lower of original cost or market value and included as a receipt in the financial accounts. Un-less the value has fallen, this will effectively eliminate the cost and transfer that cost to the next accounting period in which individual items are sold. If market value has fallen when compared with original cost, the fall will reduce the profits of the business.

Where a business comes to an end, or is sold, trading stock will frequently be transferred to another trader. The consideration received for the transfer must be included in the calculation of the transferor's profits or losses for the final period of the business. However, an adjustment may be necessary where the business is discontinued. Should trading stock be transferred between persons who are 'connected', namely under common control or closely related to each other, market value may be substituted for the transfer price. It is possible that this figure of market value may exceed both the consideration received by the transferor and the original cost incurred by the transferor when acquiring trading stock. In circumstances such as these, both parties to the transaction may elect to substitute the higher of these two figures in place of market value.

In those cases where unsold trading stock remaining on the discontinuance of a business is not transferred to another trader, it is treated as having been sold for a consideration representing market value.

REMUNERATION

Remuneration paid to directors and employees may usually be included in the calculation of business results where the 'wholly and exclusively' requirements outlined above are satisfied. However, remuneration attributable to a period for which accounts are made up may only be deducted if it is 'paid' within nine months following the end of that period. The date on which 'payment' is treated as taking place will be identical to that which governs the time of 'receipt' (see page 54). Although any remuneration paid after the expiration of the nine-month period will be deductible in arriving at the profits of a later period in which 'payment' takes place, this can result in the taxable profits of the earlier period being unnecessarily inflated.

Should accounts and supporting tax computations for earlier years be submitted to the Inland Revenue, or profit figures be included in a tax return in years affected by self assessment, before remuneration is paid and in advance of the nine-month deadline, the remuneration cannot be deducted. However, if the remuneration is subsequently paid before the dead-line is reached, the remuneration can be restored as a deduction, but only if a special claim is made.

CASH BASIS – THE WITHDRAWAL

It has long been customary for many sole practitioners, professional partnerships and barristers to prepare accounts on a 'cash basis'. This might involve the inclusion of only receipts and payments, to the exclusion of entries for outstanding debtors, outstanding creditors and work in progress. In some situations one or more of these ingredients could be included but the approach would still fall short of the full earnings basis adopted by many businesses.

The ability to adopt or continue a cash basis approach is being withdrawn. Once the withdrawal has been completed the results of all businesses will be prepared on a full earnings basis which reflects accounting standards.

The last accounts which practitioners and others may prepare using the cash basis will be those made up to a date falling in the year of assessment 1999–2000. All future accounts must be drawn on an earnings basis. For example, a practitioner who adopts 30 September as the annual accounting date and prepares accounts on a cash basis will use that basis for the year ended 30 September 1999. The accounts for the following year, ending on 30 September 2000, will be drawn on a full earnings basis.

The catching up charge

It will usually be found that the opening entries inserted in the accounts for the first year of the full earnings basis will include debtors, creditors and work in progress. As some or all of these items will have been omitted from the last cash basis accounts, a balance of profits effectively becomes immune from taxation. Unfortunately for those affected, these excluded profits will become subject to a 'catching up' charge.

The catching up charge will be spread over 1999–2000 and the next nine years. The charge imposed for the year of assessment 1999–2000, will represent 10 per cent of the catching up charge. This amount may be reduced if it exceeds 10 per cent of 'normal profits' or increased at the taxpayer's option. A similar approach is then adopted for each of the next eight years, with any outstanding balance of the catching up charge being assessed in the tenth year, 2008–2009.

The 'normal profit', which may be used to limit the catching up charge in each of the first nine

57

WITHDRAWAL OF CASH BASIS

Bruce is a solicitor who has practised on his own for many years. Accounts are consistently prepared to 31 July annually, using the cash basis. The use of this basis continued up to and including the year ended 31 July 1999. Accounts for the following year to 31 July 2000, were then prepared on a full earnings basis.

It was found that the opening figures on 1 August 1999 included debtors and work in progress, less outstanding creditors, amounting to a net sum of £45,000 which was not brought into the accounts for the period to 31 July 1999. Therefore a catching up charge arises on £45,000.

The catching up charge imposed under Case VI of Schedule D for 1999–2000 will be £4,500 (10 per cent of £45,000). This may be reduced to a figure representing 10 per cent of normal profits for the year to 31 July 1999, (which forms the basis of assessment for 1999–2000) or increased at Bruce's option. A similar approach will apply for 2000–2001 and the next seven years. In the tenth year, 2008–2009, the balance of £45,000 remaining, if any, will fall due.

---

years, represents the amount of business profits for the tax year to which the charge relates. Profits are calculated by disregarding the catching up charge and before making adjustments for capital allowances.

The catching up charge is imposed under Case VI of Schedule D and does not form part of professional or other profits assessed under Case II of the same Schedule. Nor is the charge liable to Class 4 national insurance contributions. However, Schedule D, Case II, losses may be offset against the charge and it is treated as 'net relevant earnings' for pension contribution purposes.

Should the individual cease to carry on business before the full ten-year period has elapsed the charge continues without any limitation based on 'normal profits'.

Barristers

New barristers, including advocates in Scotland, may remain on the cash basis until the seventh anniversary of their commencement in practice. Once this seventh anniversary is reached the above adjustments dealing with the catching up charge will commence to apply.

Partnerships

In the case of partnerships the 10 per cent limits for each of the first nine years will apply to the partnership as a unit, leaving the net Case VI charge to be allocated between the partners.

The Case VI charge for the first year, normally

1999–2000, will be allocated between persons who were members of the partnership during the twelve months ending on the date the catching up charge is calculated. This allocation will recognise profit-sharing arrangements for that twelve-month period.

A similar approach will be adopted when allocating the catching up charge in subsequent years. However, the allocation will proceed by reference to twelve-month periods ending on the anniversary of the catching up charge date, notwithstanding a change in the date to which partnership accounts are prepared.

Each partner remains liable for his or her share of the catching up charge for the period up to the date on which the individual leaves the partnership. Individuals joining the partnership in the ten-year period become liable for the share of the charge allocated to them from the date of joining.

Should the partnership business entirely cease, individuals who were partners in the period immediately prior to the cessation date continue to be liable for the charge throughout the remaining balance of the ten-year spreading period. As the business will have ceased there can no longer be any restriction based on 'normal profits'.

All partners must provide notice if increased payments are to be made in discharge of the catching up charge.

POST-CESSATION EXPENSES

Once a trade or profession has been discontinued and final accounts of the business properly prepared, subsequent events arising directly or indirectly out of the business will have little effect for taxation purposes. An exception concerns 'post-cessation receipts', namely, receipts which arise after the discontinuance date but which cannot be related back to the financial accounts of the business. These receipts are chargeable to income tax, usually under Case VI of Schedule D. Only limited relief is available for expenses and other outgoings when calculating the amount chargeable to tax in this manner.

However, a different form of relief is available where certain payments are made following the discontinuance of a business. To obtain this relief it is necessary to show that the payments have been made wholly and exclusively:

a In remedying defective work done, goods supplied or services rendered by the previous business;

b In defraying legal and other expenses in connection with claims for that work done, goods supplied or services rendered;

c In insuring against liabilities arising out of such claims or the incurring of such expenses; or

d For the purpose of collecting a debt taken into account in computing the profits or gains of the discontinued business.

Relief is also available for a debt which was previously included in the calculation of business profits but which has subsequently become bad. If relief is obtained for this bad debt and all or any part of that debt is later recovered the amount recovered must be charged to tax.

One further adjustment which must be noted concerns expenses which entered into the calculation of business results but which remain unpaid. The amount of these unpaid expenses must be subtracted from the expenditure for which relief is claimed.

Claims are limited to qualifying payments made, or bad debts arising, within a period of seven years following the discontinuance of the business. The amount of any claim is offset against income chargeable to income tax for the year of assessment during which payment takes place. Should income be insufficient for this purpose, any excess can be treated as an allowable loss for the same year and offset against chargeable gains assessable to capital gains tax.

ENTERPRISE ALLOWANCE

To provide some encouragement for unemployed individuals to set up in business, an enterprise allowance may be claimed. This is provided at a weekly rate throughout the initial twelve months of the business. Although the allowance is taxable it does not enter into the calculation of business results. The recipient is separately taxed under Case VI of Schedule D by reference to the amount arising in each year of assessment.

RETURN OF BUSINESS RESULTS

Before the introduction of self-assessment most proprietors of businesses, including a business carried on by individuals in partnership, were required to submit proper accounts to the Inland Revenue in support of tax computations. It then remained for the Inland Revenue to issue the appropriate assessment, or perhaps to dispute the accuracy of profits or losses disclosed by the computations. An exception arose in the case of businesses where the annual turnover did not exceed £15,000. No accounts were required and it was sufficient to indicate the amount of turnover on a tax return.

The recently introduced self-assessment tax return

58
BUSINESS RESULTS
SPECIMEN ENTRY

Matthew had been carrying on business for many years and prepares accounts to 31 May annually. His tax return form for 1997–98 contained the following summary of business results for the year to 31 May 1997.

	Disallowable Expenses £	Total Expenses £	£
Sales/business income (turnover)			494,151
Less:			
Cost of sales	–	247,519	
Construction industry sub-contractor costs	–	–	
Other direct costs	–	62,417	309,936
Gross profit/(loss)			184,215
Other income/profits			653
			184,868
Less:			
Employee costs	–	82,000	
Premises costs	–	15,400	
Repairs	–	1,075	
General administrative expenses	250	1,894	
Motor expenses	–	4,690	
Travel and subsistence	478	1,376	
Advertising, promotion and entertainment	300	2,149	
Legal and professional costs	1,091	2,581	
Bad debts	–	2,500	
Interest	–	1,985	
Other finance charges	–	3,168	
Depreciation and loss/(profit) on sale	4,500	4,500	
Other expenses	–	2,157	125,475
	£6,619		
Net profit/(loss)			59,393
Additions to net profit (deduct from loss):			
Disallowable expenses		6,619	
Goods for private use/other adjustments		1,472	8,091
Deductions from net profit (add to loss):			–
Net profit for tax purposes			£67,484

form retains the exemption where business turnover does not exceed £15,000. In this situation it is sufficient to record the following information:

Turnover, other business receipts and goods, etc. taken for personal use . A
Less expenses allowable for tax . . B
Net profit or loss C

Many businesses will have an annual turnover substantially in excess of £15,000. When completing their tax return forms, proprietors of such businesses

must provide substantially more information. However, the requirement that financial accounts should be submitted to the Inland Revenue has been abandoned, except in the case of very large partnerships.

In substitution for these accounts, business proprietors will be required to complete a summarised version of business results. This version will record receipts of the business, expenses deducted, disallowable expenses and other matters required to adjust the profit or loss disclosed by the financial

—————59—————
BUSINESS BALANCE SHEET
SPECIMEN ENTRY

Matthew in the previous example prepares a Balance Sheet at 31 May 1997. A summarised version of this duly entered on the tax return was as follows:

Assets:

	£	£
Plant, machinery and motor vehicles	21,400	
Other fixed assets (premises, goodwill, investments, etc.)	49,431	
Stock and work in progress	52,148	
Debtors/prepayments/other current assets	97,160	
Bank/building society balances	–	
Cash in hand	174	220,313
Less liabilities:		
Trade creditors/accruals	84,079	
Loans and overdrawn bank accounts	37,201	
Other liabilities	–	121,280
		£99,033

Net business assets represented by:		
Capital Account:	£	
Balance at start of period	72,140	
Net profit/(loss)	59,393	
Capital introduced	–	
Drawings	32,500	
Balance at end of period		£99,033

statements to the figure which must be used for income tax purposes. A specimen completed summary is shown in Example 58.

A separate part of the tax return will summarise the available capital allowances, including the claims which must be made. These allowances must then be subtracted in the calculation of business profits, with any balancing charges being added to those profits.

Most business proprietors will have a balance sheet. Details of this balance sheet also must be summarised on the tax return. A specimen balance sheet which has been completed by the insertion of assumed figures appears in Example 59.

Space is available for any additional information which the taxpayer may care to insert. Suitable comments should be made where there are matters

relating to the inserted summaries which could prove contentious and perhaps lead to demands for interest and penalties if detected by the Inland Revenue on some later occasion.

Although many business proprietors no longer need to forward accounts, this does not imply that such accounts will fail to be examined by the Inland Revenue. Should a notice of enquiry into a tax return be issued this may well be followed by a demand for detailed financial accounts in support of entries inserted on the return.

OVERSEAS ENTERTAINERS AND SPORTSMEN

A large number of non-resident entertainers and sportsmen visit the United Kingdom each year, to undertake performances or to compete at a sporting event. These individuals include pop and film stars, actors, musicians, tennis players, football players, golfers, boxers and motor racing drivers, among others. Whether sums arising from performances and other activities in the United Kingdom become liable to taxation will be governed by the personal circumstances of each individual and perhaps by the terms of a Double Taxation Agreement concluded between the United Kingdom and some overseas territory. However, there may well be liability to United Kingdom tax which the Inland Revenue experience some difficulty in collecting.

To resolve this problem special collection rules apply. These require that when making certain payments to a non-resident entertainer or sportsman for services performed in the United Kingdom the promoter or other person will deduct income tax at the basic rate of 23 per cent which applies for 1998–99. Deductions will also extend to associated income from sponsorship, advertising and endorsements. There will be no deductions for payments arising from record sales, nor will the deduction procedure usually apply to payments not exceeding £1,000. Any deductions made from payments must be accounted for to the Inland Revenue. The requirement to deduct income tax at the basic rate is not affected by the 20 per cent lower rate band.

Deductions made at the basic rate will not necessarily fully exhaust liability to United Kingdom income tax. Any additional liability arising at the higher rate must be recovered by direct assessment on the individual concerned.

The above rules have no application to entertainers and sportsmen who are resident in the United Kingdom for taxation purposes. Those rules are confined to non-residents, which will include both nationals of overseas territories and nationals of the United Kingdom also, if they are not resident in this territory.

SUB-CONTRACTORS

The PAYE scheme of tax deduction applies to emoluments paid to the holder of an office or employment. In addition, certain workers employed by agencies are treated as holding an office or employment and the PAYE scheme is of application to emoluments paid to such persons.

The distinction between employment and self-employment is not always easy to apply. Situations also emerge where the parties to an arrangement for the supply of services choose to disregard the distinction and treat the supplier as self-employed. On earlier occasions representatives of the Inland Revenue and the Department of Social Security discussed the application of the distinction with contractors engaged in the construction industry. As a result, contractors were given a 'reasonable time' to review the status of workers supplying services. This review had to be completed not later than 5 April 1997, with PAYE deductions and national insurance contributions being applied subsequently where those supplying services were treated as employees. It does need to be emphasised that the distinction between employment and self-employment is a matter which can only be determined from a review of the relationship between the parties. Neither the Inland Revenue nor the Department of Social Security can impose an 'employment status' where that status does not exist.

In other situations where there is no office or employment and the agency arrangements outlined on page 48 do not apply, the PAYE scheme must be disregarded. This could result in some loss of tax as the Inland Revenue may experience difficulty in tracing the persons to whom payments are made for the supply of services and in collecting tax from those persons.

To avoid this potential loss a wide-ranging tax deduction scheme is in operation for persons engaged in the construction industry. This scheme applies where a contractor makes a payment to a self-employed sub-contractor under a contract relating to construction operations.

The expression 'contractor' is widely defined and incorporates any person carrying on a business which includes construction operations, a local authority, a development corporation or New Town Commission and certain other persons. Private householders having work done on their own premises are not contractors and a business which is not normally involved in construction operations is unlikely to be treated as carried on by a contractor. A 'sub-contractor' includes any person engaged in carrying out construction operations for a business or a public body which is a contractor, and includes companies, individuals and partnerships.

'Construction operations' extend to almost anything that is done to a permanent or temporary building, structure, civil engineering work or installation. This includes site preparation, construction, alteration, many forms of repair, dismantling and demolition, but excludes some forms of installation.

Sub-contractors may apply to the Inland Revenue for a tax certificate. There are three types of certificate, namely the C certificate which is for certain companies, the P certificate which is for other companies and partnerships and the I certificate which is for use by individuals trading on their own account. Certificates are only issued to individuals, partnerships and companies who satisfy a lengthy list of requirements.

Before making any payment to a sub-contractor, the contractor must establish whether a current tax certificate is held. If a suitable certificate can be produced by the sub-contractor, the contractor will make the payment in full. In the absence of a certificate the contractor is obliged to deduct income tax at the rate of 23 per cent when making payments in 1998–99. The deduction rate is unaffected by the 20 per cent lower rate band.

Deductions are made from the full amount of the payment, less the direct cost of materials used, or to be used, in carrying out the construction operations to which the contract relates. This effectively confines the deduction scheme to payments for the provision of labour.

Income tax deducted by a contractor must be paid over to the Inland Revenue. Payment usually falls due fourteen days after the end of each income tax month. Therefore deductions made for the period ending on the fifth of a month should be accounted for to the Inland Revenue by the nineteenth of that month. However, some contractors are permitted to account for deductions on a quarterly basis. If this basis is to be used it must be shown that the aggregate of PAYE, national insurance contributions and deductions made from payments to sub-contractors do not exceed, on average, £600 per month. Where the quarterly procedure applies the contractor must account for his deductions fourteen days following 5 July, 5 October, 5 January and 5 April respectively. Failure on the part of the contractor to operate correctly the sub-contractors' deduction scheme can have serious repercussions and perhaps lead to the commencement of criminal proceedings. There may also be a liability to discharge interest where payment is made more than fourteen days following the end of the year of assessment in which the deductions were made.

At the end of each year of assessment the sub-contractor will calculate the total amount of income tax deductions made from payments received by him. This total amount will then be compared with the sub-contractor's liability to income tax and Class 4 contributions for the same year. Should the sums deducted exceed the liability, the surplus can be reclaimed from the Inland Revenue. Where the deductions fall below the full liability the sub-contractor must discharge the excess in the normal manner.

Sub-contractors able to claim a refund of excess tax suffered may make a claim by inserting details on the tax return form. However, it is not necessary to await the normal filing dates of 30 September or 31 January before taking action of this nature. Tax return forms incorporating the repayment claim may be submitted at any earlier date. In addition, it may be possible to submit repayment claims in advance of filing an income tax return, or indeed before the end of the year of assessment concerned. Clearly, no repayment will be made by the Inland Revenue until steps have been taken to verify the accuracy of any claim. Should tax be outstanding for previous years the repayment will be set against that tax due and only the balance, if any, returned to the sub-contractor.

Future developments
The number of sub-contractors remaining unaffected by PAYE deductions and the obligation to account for Class 1 national insurance contributions was considerably reduced following the review of business relationships generated by the Inland Revenue. This crystallised on 6 April 1997 and the extension of the agency workers' scheme came into operation one year later. However, for self-employed sub-contractors remaining, the sub-contractor scheme is being substantially revised on 1 August 1999.

From that date increased compliance requirements must be satisfied before a sub-contractor's certificate will be issued. In particular, it will be necessary to demonstrate that the applicant's turnover exceeds specified thresholds. However, for the purpose of certain parts of the turnover test income from all construction contracts may be included, whether or not they are within the sub-contractors' scheme.

Sub-contractors who are unable to obtain gross payment certificates will require a special registration card. This card will have to be produced before an initial payment is made by a contractor to the recipient sub-contractor.

Housing associations, development corporations and others are deemed to be 'contractors' for the purpose of the sub-contractors' scheme. In future, this approach will only apply to those organisations with an average annual expenditure on construction operations which exceeds £1 million.

By concession, payments under small contracts which do not exceed £250 are exempted from the sub-contractors' arrangements. This exemption will be made statutory from 1 August 1999 and the contract limit increased to £1,000.

The deduction scheme is being computerised and this will enable a new form of tax deduction voucher to be issued.

It will be apparent that the sub-contractors' deduction scheme in operation immediately before 1 August 1999 will be very substantially amended on the following day.

VOLUNTEER DRIVERS – MILEAGE ALLOWANCES
Individuals who drive for the hospital car service and other volunteer organisations usually receive mileage allowances. Any 'profit element' in these allowances will be treated as income chargeable to income tax. The profit may be calculated, at the individual's option, by:

a Using figures taken from the Inland Revenue approved mileage rates (see page 58) together with mileage receipts; or
b Taking the actual mileage receipts and the actual expenses.

COMPANIES
Profits, gains and income accruing to companies are chargeable to corporation tax. The assessment of companies to this tax is briefly dealt with on page 158.

11

Capital expenditure

CAPITAL EXPENDITURE incurred by an individual carrying on a trade, profession or vocation assessable under Schedule D cannot usually be subtracted when calculating business profits. However, many items of capital expenditure enable the individual to obtain capital allowances which are set against business profits, included in the calculation of business profits or perhaps absorbed against other income. Similar allowances are available to others not carrying on business, or to those receiving rental income assessable under Schedule A, but the ability to utilise such allowances may be somewhat limited.

The system of granting capital allowances has been drastically amended in recent years. At earlier times substantial initial allowances or first-year allowances were granted immediately many items of expenditure were incurred, leaving only limited, or perhaps no, annual allowances to be obtained subsequently. These accelerated allowances were largely withdrawn throughout a two-year transitional period and, with very few exceptions, ceased to apply entirely for expenditure incurred after 31 March 1986. However, following an interval in excess of six years both initial and first-year allowances were reintroduced for expenditure incurred between 1 November 1992 and 31 October 1993. First year allowances were again reintroduced for a limited range of expenditure incurred in the two year period commencing on 2 July 1997.

The nature and application of capital allowances and the assets to which those allowances apply is discussed below.

APPLICATION OF CAPITAL ALLOWANCES

Although the calculation of capital allowances is not significantly affected by the change from the preceding year basis to the current year basis, the method used for giving effect to those allowances has been changed. It may be helpful to compare the approach which must be made under each heading where allowances are available for assets used in a business assessable under Schedule D.

Preceding year basis

Where the preceding year basis applies capital allowances are given for a year of assessment. The factors used to calculate the allowances are those taking place in the basis year. For example, if a long-established business commenced before 6 April 1994 and continuing beyond 5 April 1997 prepares accounts to, say, 30 September annually the profits of the year ended on 30 September 1994 will be assessed for 1995–96. Capital allowances, and indeed any balancing adjustments, for 1995–96 will be based on events taking place in the period of account ending on 30 September 1994.

Capital allowances are not subtracted when calculating profits. The allowances are given against those profits assessed to income tax.

Current year basis

In contrast, where the current year basis of assessment applies, profits for a period of account ending in a year of assessment will be taxed in that year. Capital allowances are not given for a year of assessment but form an ingredient in the calculation of business profits. It follows that the allowances to be included in the profit calculation for a period of account will reflect events taking place in that period. For example, the results of an established business for a twelve month period of account ending on 30 September 1998 will form the basis of assessment for 1998–99. The calculation of capital allowances will reflect events taking place during the period of account and not those in the full year of assessment. A further adjustment must be made if the period of account is longer or shorter than twelve months in duration. The normal annual allowance must then be proportionately increased or reduced to correspond with the length of the period of account.

The years of change

In the case of a business commenced after 5 April 1994 the new current year procedure will apply from the inception of that business.

Businesses established on or before 5 April 1994 and continuing after 5 April 1997 will use the old preceding year basis for 1995–96 and earlier years. Special rules affect the transitional year 1996–97 with the result that capital allowances are not included in the calculation of profits but set against the profits chargeable to tax. The new current year basis will then apply for 1997–98 and future years.

Business proprietors seeking to obtain capital allowances will usually include the relevant claim when completing a tax return.

PLANT AND MACHINERY

Capital allowances are available for the capital cost of providing plant and machinery wholly and exclusively for the purposes of a business. These assets comprise many items commonly used for trading or other activities, including industrial equipment, tractors, motor cars, typewriters, desks, chairs and machinery, among others. They also include most items of computer software. Buildings and structures cannot be treated as plant for expenditure incurred after 29 November 1993, although few items of this nature would be so treated for expenditure incurred earlier.

Also from 29 November 1993, claims must be made within a period of two years from the end of the tax year in which the expenditure is incurred and to which it should be related. Late claims may still be made to obtain allowances but this will result in relief being available at a later date or year.

First-year allowances

After being withdrawn in 1986 the first-year allowance was reintroduced for expenditure incurred in the twelve-month period commencing on 1 November 1992, and ending on 31 October 1993. Most items of plant and machinery qualified for the allowance, with the notable exception of many ordinary motor cars. The allowance was given at the rate of 40 per cent although it remained possible to disclaim part of that allowance.

The first-year allowance was again reintroduced for expenditure incurred during the two-year period commencing on 2 July 1997 and ending on 1 July 1999. Not all persons incurring expenditure will qualify for first-year allowances. These allowances are confined to 'a small company or small business'.

The expression 'small company' identifies a company which is small- or medium-sized within the meaning of section 247, Companies Act 1985, or the Northern Ireland equivalent. To achieve this status two of the three following conditions must be satisfied:

a Annual turnover not more than £11.2m.

b Balance sheet recording gross assets of not more than £5.6m.

c Not more than 250 employees.

Where a company is a member of a large group, the entire group taken as a whole, must satisfy these conditions.

An identical approach is applied to establish whether individuals and partnerships comprise a 'small business'. Curiously, it is therefore necessary, for identification purposes, to apply the provisions of the Companies Acts to the affairs of individuals and partnerships who are clearly not companies. However, the three conditions indicate the existence of a substantial business and it seems apparent that very few sole traders and practitioners, together with individuals carrying on business in partnership, will fail to satisfy the 'small' requirement.

Most expenditure incurred on plant and machinery within the required time limits will qualify for the first-year allowance, with the exception of:

a Ordinary motor cars not comprising taxis, vehicles used for short-term hire or mobility allowance vehicles for the disabled.

b Ships and railway assets.

c Most leased assets.

The first-year allowance is generally given at the rate of 50 per cent for expenditure incurred in the twelve month period ending on 1 July 1998, although a reduced rate of only 12 per cent is available for

60
FIRST-YEAR ALLOWANCES

For many years Keith had been a sole trader, preparing accounts to 30 September annually. After subtracting capital allowances for 1996–97 the unused balance of expenditure in the pool was £18,000. On 17 August 1997 £7,000 was incurred when acquiring plant and the full first-year allowance claimed. No other acquisitions or disposals took place until after 30 September 1998.

Assuming no election was made to exclude the acquisition from the pool, the calculation of capital allowances is as follows:

	£	Pool £
Balance brought forward		18,000
Addition – August 1997	7,000	
Year to 30 September 1997		
First year allowance 50% × £7,000	3,500	
	3,500	
Writing-down allowance 25% × £18,000		4,500
		13,500
Balance of expenditure	3,500	3,500
		17,000
Year to 30 September 1998		4,250
Writing-down allowance 25% × £17,000		
Balance carried forward		£12,750

61
WRITING-DOWN ALLOWANCES PRECEDING YEAR BASIS

A manufacturer who commenced business in 1970, prepares accounts to 31 March annually. The balance of expenditure remaining in the pool of plant and machinery on 31 March 1994 was £14,000. He incurred expenditure of £12,500 when acquiring new plant on 24 September 1994, and further expenditure of £10,000 was incurred on 19 February 1995. £6,500 was received from the sale of obsolete plant on 12 December 1994.

Results for the twelve months ended 31 March 1995 showed profits of £80,000.

Profits of £80,000 for the year ended 31 March 1995 will be assessed in 1995–96. Capital allowances which may be set against those profits will be calculated as follows:

	£	Pool £
Balance brought forward		14,000
Additions:		
September 1994	12,500	
February 1995	10,000	22,500
		36,500
Less sales		6,500
		30,000
Writing-down allowance 1995–96:		
25 per cent of £30,000		7,500
Balance carried forward		£22,500

long life assets. The allowance falls from 50 to 40 per cent where expenditure is incurred in the following twelve month period ending on 1 July 1999, with no allowance for long-life assets. It is possible to disclaim part of the allowance. However, where a first-year allowance is claimed, or is available, for a year of assessment no annual writing-down allowance will be forthcoming for the same year.

Annual writing-down allowances

An annual writing-down allowance is available for expenditure incurred when acquiring plant and machinery. This allowance, usually given at the rate of 25 per cent, is calculated on the reduced balance of unrelieved expenditure remaining after subtracting allowances for earlier years.

In those cases where the first-year allowance is obtained for expenditure incurred in the two year period ending on 1 July 1999, no writing-down allowance will be available for that expenditure in the same year. The balance of the expenditure, usually representing 50 (or 60) per cent of the outlay,

remains available for the 25 per cent writing-down allowance in the second and succeeding years.

Although the annual writing-down allowance is normally given at the rate of 25 per cent, there is one exception. This concerns certain assets acquired after 25 November 1996 which have a working life of twenty-five years or more. Expenditure incurred on these assets attracts a reduced annual writing-down allowance of 6 per cent. However, few assets will be affected as those acquired at a cost falling below £100,000 are excluded. Where the first year allowance is available for expenditure incurred on these long life assets in the twelve month period ending on 1 July 1998, the allowance is given at the rate of 12 per cent only.

Pooling

Most items of plant and machinery, with the exception of motor cars and long-life assets acquired after 25 November 1996, enter into a 'pool'. Adjustments must be made to the expenditure remaining in this pool where a new asset is added or an existing asset

—62— WRITING-DOWN ALLOWANCES CURRENT YEAR BASIS

As the business in Example 61 commenced before 6 April 1994 it is clear that the current year basis of assessment cannot apply to the facts in that example. However, if each of the dates used was advanced by five years the calculation would be as follows:

Capital allowances	£	Pool £
Balance brought forward		14,000
Additions:		
September 1999 . .	12,500	
February 2000 . . .	10,000	22,500
		36,500
Less sales		6,500
		30,000
Writing-down allowance – year to 31 March 2000:		
25 per cent of £30,000		7,500
Balance carried forward		£22,500

Profits – Year to 31 March 2000 – Assessable 1999–2000:	
Original calculation	80,000
Less writing-down allowance . .	7,500
Adjusted profits	£72,500

Notes:
It will be seen when contrasted with Example 61:

a The allowances are given one tax year earlier; and
b The allowances directly affect the calculation of profits.

The example assumes that first year allowances will not be extended to include expenditure incurred after 1 July 1999.

—63— ELECTION FOR NON-POOLING

Let it be assumed that the manufacturer in Example 62 also acquired a further asset at a cost of £30,000 on 5 October 1999. An election was made to exclude this asset from the common pool. The asset realised £4,000 when sold on 15 March 2002.

Capital allowances confined to this asset only are calculated as follows:

	£
Cost	30,000
Writing-down allowance – year to 31 March 2000:	
25 per cent of £30,000	7,500
	22,500
Writing-down allowance – year to 31 March 2001:	
25 per cent of £22,500	5,625
	16,875
Sale proceeds 15 March 2002 . . .	4,000
Balancing allowance – Year to 31 March 2002 .	£12,875

If the asset had been included in the common pool the aggregate allowances for the year to 31 March 2002 would be considerably smaller than £12,875.

sold. The 25 per cent annual writing-down allowance is applied to the 'pool' as a whole and it is unnecessary to identify each separate asset. Should the sale, or other proceeds, of an asset exceed the balance of unrelieved expenditure remaining in the pool, a balancing charge will be imposed to recoup allowances obtained in earlier periods. Any balancing charge will be allocated to a year of assessment or profit period on a basis identical to that used for the annual writing-down allowance.

This 'pooling' approach is available where capital allowances can be claimed for a Schedule A business producing rental income.

Election for non-pooling

The 25 per cent reducing balance approach enables some 90 per cent of the cost of an asset to be relieved throughout a period of approximately eight years. Many items of plant and machinery have a lifespan falling below eight years and where assets acquired have a limited life expectation the taxpayer may elect to exclude these assets from the common pool. The advantage of the election is that when the excluded asset is sold a balancing adjustment will arise which is not distorted by entries in the common pool.

In those cases where plant and machinery is used only partly for business purposes, a suitable restriction in the allowances granted must be made.

The introduction of a first year allowance at the rate of 50 or 40 per cent will write off the cost of an asset more quickly. This may reduce the attraction of submitting an election to exclude expenditure from the common pool, as reduced allowances will be available for later years.

Motor cars

Writing-down allowances are available at the rate of 25 per cent for the cost of acquiring motor cars, where the vehicles are used for business purposes. However, a restriction must be imposed for motor cars costing more than £12,000, as the annual allowance is not to exceed £3,000 on these vehicles. This restriction does not extend to taxis, short-term

64
MOTOR CARS

A doctor, who had been in practice since 1982, purchased a motor car for use in his practice on 9 May 1997 at a cost of £23,500. Assuming the vehicle is used exclusively for business purposes and that accounts are made up to 31 October annually, the calculation of capital allowances will proceed as follows:

	£
Cost	23,500
Writing-down allowance – Year to 31 October 1997:	
25 per cent of £23,500 – but restricted to	3,000
	20,500
Writing-down allowance – Year to 31 October 1998:	
25 per cent of £20,500 – but restricted to	3,000
	17,500
Writing-down allowance – Year to 31 October 1999:	
25 per cent of £17,500 – but restricted to	3,000
	14,500
Writing-down allowance – Year to 31 October 2000:	
25 per cent of £14,500 – but restricted to	3,000
	11,500
Writing-down allowance – Year to 31 October 2001:	
25 per cent of £11,500 (no restriction necessary)	2,875
Available for future writing-down allowances	£8,625

hire cars and mobility allowance vehicles for the disabled.

Where the current year basis of assessment applies and a period of account exceeds or falls below twelve months in duration, the annual allowance, as restricted, will be increased or reduced proportionately.

Should a car costing more than £12,000 when new be leased to a business proprietor, the lessee may suffer some restriction in the hire or rental charge which can be deducted when calculating profits assessable to tax.

Only part of the available allowance may be obtained where a car is used partly for business and partly for private motoring.

Fixtures in buildings

Special rules apply to calculate capital allowances for expenditure on fixtures installed in buildings. Allowances are not available for assets installed in dwelling-houses although this exclusion does not extend to installations in hospitals, prisons and university halls of residence. Subject to this, the rules recognise the problems which may arise where a building changes hands as it will usually be necessary to apportion the consideration passing between the building and the fixtures.

INDUSTRIAL BUILDINGS

Allowances are available for expenditure incurred on the construction of buildings or structures used, or to be used, for industrial purposes. These include buildings or structures used for the purpose of the following, among others:

a   A trade carried on in a mill, factory or similar premises;

b   A transport, dock, inland navigation, water, electricity, or hydraulic undertaking;

c   A tunnel undertaking;

d   A bridge undertaking;

e   A highway undertaking;

f   A trade consisting of the manufacture of goods or materials, or the subjection of goods to a process;

g   A trade which consists in the storage of certain goods;

h   A trade which consists in the catching or taking of fish or shell fish;

i   A trade which consists in the repairing and servicing of goods.

The allowances do not apply to expenditure on retail shops, offices and other non-industrial buildings.

Where part of a building is, and some other part is not, used for a qualifying purpose, allowances must usually be restricted to the cost of constructing the qualifying part. Some relaxation in this approach is, however, available where the cost of constructing the non-qualifying part does not exceed 25 per cent of the cost of constructing the entire building. In this situation, allowances may be obtained on the aggregate cost.

Initial allowances

At earlier times initial allowances were available for expenditure incurred on the construction of a qualifying building. These allowances ceased to apply in 1986 but were briefly reintroduced at the rate of 20 per cent for expenditure incurred on the construction of a building under a contract entered into between 1 November 1992 and 31 October 1993. It remained a requirement that the building was brought into use for the purposes of a qualifying trade not later than 31 December 1994. The initial allowance could also be obtained for existing unused buildings completed, or in course of construction, before 1 November 1992, if they were acquired

65
INDUSTRIAL BUILDINGS

On 27 February 1998, a manufacturer entered into a contract for the construction of an industrial building. The cost was £200,000 and the completed building was first used in November of the same year. Accounts are prepared to 31 December annually and the allowances available are as follows:

	£
Cost (during accounting year to 31 December 1998)	200,000
Writing-down allowance: year to 31 December 1998:	
4 per cent of £200,000	8,000
	192,000
Writing-down allowance: year to 31 December 1999:	
4 per cent of £200,000	8,000
	£184,000

Annual writing-down allowances of £8,000 will continue until the expenditure has been exhausted, unless the building is sold or ceases to be used for a qualifying purpose.

under a contract entered into during the year ended 31 October 1993 and brought into use by the end of 1994. The first year allowance which is available for expenditure incurred on plant and machinery after 1 July 1997 has no application to industrial buildings.

Annual writing-down allowances
An annual writing-down allowance of 4 per cent is available for qualifying construction expenditure. This allowance will be given for the first year in which the building is brought into use. It is therefore possible that the 20 per cent initial allowance and the first annual allowance of 4 per cent may have been available in the same year, although in many cases there was an interval between the two allowances.

In the absence of any initial allowance, the annual writing-down allowance of 4 per cent will exhaust all construction costs once a period of twenty-five years has elapsed. This period will be shortened where a 20 per cent initial allowance has been obtained, as the aggregate of initial and writing-down allowances cannot exceed the construction cost.

Where an industrial building, for which allowances have been obtained, is sold, a balancing charge may arise. This will represent the difference between the written-down tax value of the expenditure and the disposal proceeds. However, any balancing charge cannot exceed the aggregate allowances previously granted. No balancing charge will arise should the sale take place more than twenty-five years, or fifty years for older buildings, following the date expenditure was incurred.

A balancing allowance may arise should the sale proceeds fall below the written-down tax value.

A person who acquires an existing building from the previous owner cannot base annual writing-down allowances on the price paid, unless the building is bought unused. However, some future annual writing-down allowances will usually be available, based on the previous owner's 'residue of expenditure', namely the written-down tax value increased by any balancing charge or reduced by any balancing allowance.

HOTELS
Expenditure incurred on the construction, extension or improvement of hotels may qualify for capital allowances. It is a necessary requirement that the hotel has at least ten letting bedrooms, is not normally in the same occupation for more than one month, regularly provides guests with breakfast and evening meals and is open for at least four months between April and October. Additionally, all sleeping accommodation offered at the hotel must consist wholly or mainly of letting bedrooms. Any expenditure on that part of the premises occupied by the proprietor or his family must be disregarded but accommodation used by employees may usually be included.

Like other items of capital expenditure, that incurred on hotels previously attracted an initial allowance. This ceased to apply in 1986. In addition an annual writing-down allowance could be obtained at the rate of 4 per cent until the expenditure had been entirely written off.

An initial allowance at the rate of 20 per cent was reintroduced for expenditure incurred between 1 November 1992 and 31 October 1993. The annual writing-down allowance may also be obtained until the expenditure is exhausted. No initial allowance will be forthcoming for expenditure incurred subsequently. Nor will any first year allowance be available for expenditure incurred after 1 July 1997.

Should an hotel for which allowances have been obtained be sold, the vendor may be taxed on a balancing charge, or receive relief for a balancing allowance, and the purchaser may obtain future writing-down allowances, in a manner similar to that which applies for industrial buildings.

Where an hotel is located in an enterprise zone, it is advisable to claim the alternative allowances discussed below.

ENTERPRISE ZONES

Substantially increased capital allowances are available for expenditure incurred on assets located in enterprise zones. The cost of constructing an industrial building, a qualifying hotel or a commercial building or structure qualifies for an initial allowance, which unlike other allowances, was not generally withdrawn in 1986. It is a requirement that the expenditure must be incurred, or a contract entered into, within a period of ten years following the date on which the area first became designated as an enterprise zone.

An initial allowance of 100 per cent can be obtained to absorb the entire expenditure. Alternatively, the initial allowance may be reduced to some smaller amount, with annual writing-down allowances not exceeding 25 per cent of original

-------- 66 --------
ENTERPRISE ZONES

Tom has carried on business for many years, preparing accounts to 31 December annually. During the year ended 31 December 1998 he incurred expenditure of £200,000 when constructing an industrial building for use in his business. The building was located in an enterprise zone and in the year of construction Tom decided to claim an initial allowance of only 40 per cent.

Assuming the business continues with accounts being prepared to 31 December annually and all claims are made, the allowances to be deducted from profits will be:

		£
Cost		200,000
Initial allowance – year to 31 December 1998		
40 per cent × £200,000 . . .		80,000
		120,000
Writing-down allowance – year to 31 December 1999		
25 per cent × £200,000 . . .		50,000
		70,000
Writing-down allowance – year to 31 December 2000		
25 per cent × £200,000 . . .		50,000
		20,000
Writing-down allowance – year to 31 December 2001		
25 per cent × £200,000 – but restricted to balance remaining		£20,000

cost until the expenditure has been fully used. Where a building located in an enterprise zone is sold, balancing adjustments must be calculated on a basis similar to that applied on the sale of an industrial building.

AGRICULTURAL BUILDINGS

Expenditure incurred by the owner or tenant of agricultural land on the construction of farm buildings, fences, cottages and other works, such as ditches and drains, will usually qualify for capital allowances. The cost of constructing a farmhouse may also be included but must be restricted to one-third of the capital cost, or a smaller fraction where the amenities of the farmhouse are considered excessive in relation to the agricultural holding.

The calculation of allowances and the effect on those allowances where property is subsequently demolished or sold differs substantially for expenditure incurred before 1 April 1986 and that incurred subsequently.

Expenditure incurred on or before 31 March 1986

For expenditure incurred before 1 April 1986, an initial allowance of 20 per cent could be claimed and usually granted in the year of assessment following that in which the outlay was made. At the taxpayer's option, the initial allowance could be reduced to some smaller amount. An annual writing-down allowance of one-tenth of the expenditure was also granted for the year of assessment following that in which expenditure was incurred and each of the succeeding years until the cost had been fully relieved. Where the maximum initial allowance of 20 per cent was claimed, aggregate allowances of 30 per cent were available in one year and allowances of 10 per cent in each of the seven following years.

Once qualifying expenditure had been incurred allowances remained available and could not subsequently be withdrawn. Nor could any balancing charge or balancing allowance arise on the sale of an interest in agricultural property. Where an interest in such property changed hands before all allowances had been obtained, the benefit of future allowances accrued to the purchaser.

Not later than 5 April 1996 all allowances will have been exhausted for expenditure incurred under this heading.

———67———
AGRICULTURAL BUILDINGS

On 12 April 1991, A incurred capital expenditure of £50,000 on the construction of a farm building. He sold the farm to B on 6 October 1997 with £47,000 being allocated to the building.

If *no election is made* annual allowances will be granted at the rate of £2,000 (4 per cent × £50,000) for 1991–92 and each of the next twenty-four years. These will be allocated as follows:

A

1991–92 to 1996–97 inclusive	£2,000 annually
1997–98 (to 5 October) . .	Half × £2,000

B

1997–98 (from 6 October)	Half × £2,000
1998–99 and the following eighteen years . . .	£2,000 annually

If *an election is made* the effect on A will be:

	£
Cost	50,000
Less writing-down allowances:	
1991–92 to 1996–97 inclusive (6 × £2,000)	12,000
	38,000
Sale price	47,000
1997–98 balancing charge . . .	£9,000

B may obtain annual writing-down allowances calculated on the 'residue of expenditure' of £47,000 (£38,000 + £9,000), which represents that part of A's original cost not covered by allowances, with the addition of the balancing charge. These allowances will be available to B throughout the remaining part of the twenty-five year period, namely eighteen and a half years, at the annual rate of £2,541.

Expenditure incurred after 31 March 1986

For several years no initial allowance was forthcoming to absorb expenditure incurred after 31 March 1986. However, an initial allowance of 20 per cent became available for expenditure incurred between 1 November 1992 and 31 October 1993. No such allowance can be obtained for expenditure incurred subsequently and the first year allowance available for certain expenditure incurred after 1 July 1997 does not apply to agricultural buildings.

Writing-down allowances based on the outlay are given at the rate of 4 per cent annually for the year of assessment in which expenditure is incurred and succeeding years. These allowances are given in addition to the initial allowance, if any, although the aggregate allowances obtained cannot exceed the cost incurred.

Subject to the election mentioned below, no balancing charge or allowance will arise if the property is sold or assets cease to exist. Any purchaser of property will become entitled to the annual writing-down allowance at the rate of 4 per cent annually throughout the remaining part of the 25-year period or, where an initial allowance has been obtained, throughout a shorter period. This writing-down allowance is based on the vendor's original cost and not on the purchase price paid by the purchaser.

However, an election may be submitted where a building, fence or other work on which expenditure has been incurred is demolished, destroyed or otherwise ceases to exist. This election will establish a balancing allowance arising at the time of the event and representing the balance of unused expenditure, as the disposal proceeds will be nil. No future annual writing-down allowances will then be available.

An election may also be made, jointly by the vendor and purchaser, where property on which qualifying expenditure has been incurred is sold. Where such an election is made the disposal proceeds must be compared with the written-down tax value. Should the proceeds exceed this value, a balancing charge will be made on the vendor to recoup previous writing-down allowances and any initial allowance. If the proceeds fall below the written-down tax value the vendor will receive a balancing allowance. The effect on the purchaser is that he will then receive future annual writing-down allowances throughout the remaining twenty-five-year, or shorter, period, based on the 'residue of expenditure', namely the written-down tax value plus any balancing charge or less any balancing allowance.

Broadly stated, the effect of submitting an election is similar to that which applies to industrial buildings and structures. It does, however, remain a matter for decision by the parties whether or not to take advantage of the election procedure.

FORESTRY LAND AND BUILDINGS

Capital expenditure incurred by the owner or tenant of commercial forestry land on the construction of forestry buildings, fences and other structures previously produced an entitlement to capital allowances. These allowances were calculated on a basis similar to those for expenditure on agricultural buildings. It was necessary to demonstrate that an election had been made for the occupation of woodlands to be assessed under Case I of Schedule D. Liability to assessment in this manner generally terminated in 1988, although it continued until 5 April 1993 where an election had been made. No capital allowances care available after the date on which commercial woodlands ceased to be within the charge under Case I of Schedule D. It inevitably follows that all entitlement to capital allowances ceased once the special transitional period ended on 5 April 1993.

OTHER CAPITAL EXPENDITURE

Other expenditure for which allowances are available includes the cost of acquiring patents, 'know-how', expenditure on scientific research, ships, and the capital outlay incurred in working mines and sources of mineral deposits.

PARTNERSHIPS

The allowances mentioned earlier are also available to individuals carrying on business in partnership.

COMPANIES

Capital expenditure incurred by companies will enable the various capital allowances to be claimed, but different rules apply for determining the basis periods into which those allowances fall.

NON-TRADERS

Many of the capital allowances discussed on the previous pages are also available to individuals who incur expenditure on investment assets leased or used by others. This includes expenditure on industrial buildings, hotels, agricultural property and property located in enterprise zones. Allowances must be primarily offset against income arising from the investment, but it is usually possible to absorb surplus allowances against other income as outlined on page 103. A non-trader who incurs capital expenditure on plant and machinery leased to others may obtain the appropriate capital allowances, but these

68
ENTERPRISE ZONES

During the year ended on 5 April 1999, Roy incurred expenditure of £100,000 on the construction of a commercial building for letting in an enterprise zone. He decided to claim an initial allowance of £50,000 in 1998–99 which resulted in annual writing-down allowances of £25,000 for each of the two following years.

In 1998–99 Roy received rent of £10,000 from letting the building to a tenant. This rent must be set against the initial allowance of £50,000, leaving a balance of £40,000.

The other income of Roy for 1998–99 was £85,000. Assuming he was a married man aged 47 entitled to the full married couple's allowance, and made a claim to set the unused initial allowance against other income, the tax payable for 1998–99 becomes:

		£
Total income		85,000
Less	£	
Personal allowance . .	4,195	
Surplus initial allowance .	40,000	44,195
		£40,805

Tax payable:	
Lower rate:	
On first £4,300 at 20 per cent . .	860.00
Basic rate:	
On next £22,800 at 23 per cent . .	5,244.00
Higher rate:	
On balance of £13,705 at 40 per cent	5,482.00
	11,586.00
Less Married couple's allowance – £1,900	
at 15 per cent	285.00
	£11,301.00

are generally only available to be offset against income arising from leasing and cannot be used against other forms of income.

12

Land and property

INTRODUCTION

One of the many changes made to the tax structure in advance of self-assessment affected the taxation of income arising from land and buildings located in the United Kingdom. The change to the new system applied from 6 April 1995 and concerned both the calculation of income and the nature of expenditure which could be subtracted when determining the amount of taxable income.

It was a feature of the former rules that tax became chargeable under Schedule A on the amount of rents or other receipts to which the landlord was entitled during the year of assessment. It was largely immaterial whether sums were actually received, although relief could be obtained for some 'lost rents'.

Expenditure capable of entering into the calculation of income chargeable under Schedule A was both specified and somewhat restricted. In those situations where eligible expenditure incurred by the landlord in respect of a single property exceeded rental income, the excess could usually be set against rental income accruing to the landlord from other properties in the same year. However, the right of set-off was precluded where properties had been let under abnormal conditions. Expenditure which could not be relieved was carried forward to succeeding years and set against income subsequently arising from property. Owners of agricultural property could elect to set excessive expenditure against income generally, but other landlords were unable to relieve expenditure in this manner.

Profits from letting property furnished did not arise from a trade. The actual profits of a year of assessment could be assessed at the taxpayer's option under Schedule A or Case VI of Schedule D. The selection of the proper charging provision could be important where some deficiency was capable of being relieved against amounts chargeable under one heading only. Assessment remained subject to the special treatment of income arising under the 'rent-a-room' scheme and from the provision of furnished holiday accommodation.

Interest paid on a loan applied to acquire property for letting could only enter into the calculation of profits chargeable under Schedule A or Case VI of Schedule D if a number of requirements were satisfied. Any surplus interest which could not be relieved in this manner was carried forward to future years.

LIABILITY NOW

The former basis used for calculating liability under Schedule A often produced difficulties, particularly where an individual retained two or more properties some of which were unlet and others let, perhaps on differing terms. Many of these difficulties were removed by revised provisions which came into operation on 6 April 1995. These provisions did not necessarily apply to a source of income which existed in 1994–95, but which was discontinued in the following year. Nor did those provisions have any application to companies, which continued to use the old approach. In addition, some features of the earlier system emerged largely unscathed, including the taxation of premiums, the 'rent-a-room' scheme, and the treatment of furnished holiday accommodation.

The effect of the revised provisions is to treat income from land and buildings as arising from a 'Schedule A business'. Such income will include profits or gains arising from the exploitation of any estate, interest or right in or over land in the United Kingdom. This will incorporate receipts in the form of rent but may also extend to other items from the exploitation of land. However, there must be excluded from liability under Schedule A:

a The receipt of yearly interest;
b Profits or gains arising from the occupation of woodlands managed on a commercial basis and with a view to the realisation of profits;
c Profits from farming and market gardening;
d Profits from the operation of mines, quarries and other concerns; and
e Rents arising from mines, quarries and similar undertakings.

Calculation of liability

All receipts accruing to an individual from the exploitation of property and forming part of a Schedule A business are gathered together in a single 'pool'. It is not necessary to isolate the different transactions which may produce profits, gains or income.

Unlike the previous approach, the type of expenditure which can be entered in the pool is not closely defined. The pool is attributable to the conduct of a 'Schedule A business' and both the expenditure which can be included and the receipts which must be gathered together will be determined on a basis similar to that used to calculate profits from a trade or profession assessable under Case I and Case II of Schedule D. Therefore many of the comments made on pages 85 and 86 are of application when calculating the profits of a Schedule A business.

The former calculation was based on rents to which a person became 'entitled' in a year of assessment, with relief for 'lost' rents. Although the right to receive rent will be an important matter when completing the Schedule A calculation, neither entitlement nor the special relief for 'lost' rents is a necessary ingredient.

Where income arises from letting property furnished this will be incorporated in the profits of the Schedule A business. That part of the receipts attributable to the use of furniture will be included also unless the provision of furniture comprises an activity of a trade. Where the use of furniture is included a wear and tear allowance can be obtained.

This is given at the rate of 10 per cent of the net rent. No further relief will then be given for the cost of renewing furnishings, linen, crockery and other items. It is not possible to invoke an option to assess income from furnished lettings under either Case VI of Schedule D or Schedule A.

Payments of interest

Payments of interest made after 5 April 1995 on a loan applied to acquire or improve property may usually enter into the calculation of profits arising from a Schedule A business. It remains necessary to demonstrate that the underlying property is used, or is to be used, for the purposes of such a business.

In those cases where interest is paid under the MIRAS scheme in relation to let property, the payer may exercise an option to exclude MIRAS and bring the interest payment into the calculation of profits or losses from the Schedule A business. Adjustments may also be required where part of a single property is used for residential purposes and the remaining part is let (see page 33).

Relief for losses

The entries made in a Schedule A business 'pool' may disclose a deficiency at the end of the year of assessment. This deficiency, treated as a Schedule A loss, can be carried forward and offset against Schedule A business profits for the following year, or years, until the deficiency or loss has been fully absorbed. It is not usually possible to offset a Schedule A loss against the taxpayer's other income.

However, where, or to the extent that, the loss has been created by the inclusion of capital allowances in the 'pool', a claim may be made to set that loss against the taxpayer's income for either the year of assessment in which the loss arose, or the following year. This claim must be made not later than 31 January falling some twenty-two months after the end of the year of assessment to which the claim relates.

A similar claim is available where a loss has arisen from an agricultural estate to the extent that that loss reflects agricultural expenses.

Assessment

The assessment of profits from a Schedule A business will represent the full amount of the profits or gains arising in the year of assessment and calculated after subtracting any Schedule A loss relief. The payment of tax is governed by the self-assessment regime.

Non-resident landlords

Where a non-resident person retains property interests in the United Kingdom any rent or other income arising will incur liability to United Kingdom income tax. To facilitate the collection of tax after 5 April 1996, where rent is paid to a United Kingdom letting, or other, agent that person must account to the Inland Revenue for income tax on a quarterly basis. Tax must be paid at the basic rate of 23 per cent for 1998–99 on the amount of rents less expenses, if any. Where there is no letting agent the tenant may be required to account for income tax in this manner. However, tenants who pay rent not exceeding £100 per week will not have to account for tax unless they are required to do so by the Inland Revenue. The amount of tax accounted for by the agent or tenant will, of course, be deducted by that person when paying rent to the non-resident landlord.

The accountability for tax in this manner can be avoided if the non-resident landlord successfully applies to the Inland Revenue for approval to receive rents and other sums gross. The non-resident will then be directly charged to income tax by applying normal self-assessment rules.

69
SCHEDULE A BUSINESS

During the year ended 5 April 1999 Kevin received the following income:

	£
Rent from letting commercial property on a tenant's repairing lease	19,500
Rent from letting unfurnished flats	6,200
Rent from letting furnished accommodation to students	4,800
Rent from letting agricultural property on a full repairing lease	10,000
	£40,500

Expenses incurred 'wholly and exclusively' for the purposes of the business amounted to £11,600. In addition, Kevin paid interest of £9,000 on a loan applied to acquire the agricultural property.

Based on these short facts, the Schedule A profits chargeable to tax for 1998–99 will be calculated as follows:

	£	£
Rents received		40,500
Expenses	11,600	
Interest	9,000	20,600
Schedule A profits		£19,900

Transitional matters

The change from the old basis to the new, when calculating income chargeable under Schedule A and which generally occurred on 6 April 1995, required the application of transitional rules. These were designed to ensure that the same item of receipt or expenditure was not taxed under both the old and the newly introduced rules. It was also necessary to ensure that such items did not escape inclusion from both headings. As numerous practises had been used in the past, the Inland Revenue merely issued guidance notes which provided taxpayers with a number of options designed to achieve a fair result.

Two additional matters arising from the transition require special comment. Firstly, any unused Schedule A expenditure being brought forward on 6 April 1995 and arising under the 'old' calculations could be carried forward and utilised against subsequent Schedule A business profits, unless the source of income for which that expenditure had been incurred ceased before 6 April 1996.

Secondly, any qualifying payments of interest attributable to let property and which had not been relieved before 6 April 1995 due to the absence of sufficient rental income, could be included as an outlay in the Schedule A computation for 1995–96.

PREMIUMS

Premiums received on the grant of a lease for a term not exceeding fifty years in duration are liable to taxation. The amount of the premium received must be reduced by 2 per cent for every complete twelve months of the lease, excluding the first twelve months, and only the balance remaining will produce

---

70
PREMIUMS ON LEASES

On 25 June 1998 Jacob granted a 21-year lease of property in return for a premium of £40,000. That part of the premium which must be treated as income for 1998–99 and included in the profit arising from a Schedule A business will be calculated as follows:

Number of complete years of the lease	21
Less first year	1
	20

	£
Premium received	40,000
Less	
20 years at 2 per cent = 40 per cent	16,000
Schedule A receipt 1998–99	£24,000

—71—
RENT A ROOM SCHEME
EXEMPTION

David owns 'Fairways' and resides in the property with his wife and family as their only residence. He lets part of the property furnished to a lodger, and information for 1998–99 was as follows:

	£
Gross rents	3,700
Expenses	600

Apart from David, no other person receives any income for letting 'Fairways'. As the gross rents do not exceed £4,250 there will be no taxable profit, nor can relief be obtained for the expenses of £600.

---

liability to income tax and be included in the Schedule A computation of profit.

Any part of a premium excluded from assessment under Schedule A may enter into other calculations of income or gains requiring assessment to income tax or capital gains tax.

The calculation is not affected by the changes which took place on 6 April 1995.

FURNISHED LETTINGS – RENT A ROOM SCHEME

An exemption from tax is available to individuals who receive rent from letting rooms in their own homes. This exemption, known as the 'rent-a-room scheme', extends to owners and tenants who let rooms furnished in their only or main residence. It is a necessary requirement that income from this activity is attributable to the letting of furnished accommodation and assessable under Schedule A. The scheme is confined to the letting of rooms and accommodation in an individual's only or main residence and has no application to similar activities undertaken in some other property. Nor does it apply if the activity is part of a guest house or bed and breakfast business.

Gross rents up to a maximum of £4,250 received in 1998–99 may qualify for complete exemption, but this figure is halved to £2,125 if two or more individuals each receive income from lettings in the same property. The limitation could arise, for example, where an owner lets part of his or her home to a tenant who sub-lets to a sub-tenant. Both the owner and the tenant may each obtain a maximum exemption of £2,125, if of course each individual can treat the property as his or her only

—72—
RENT A ROOM SCHEME
PARTIAL EXEMPTION

Using the basic facts in Example 71, let it be assumed that the figures for 1998–99 were:

	£
Gross rents	8,000
Expenses	3,400

David is now provided with a choice, namely:

a He may file an election and pay tax on the following profit without obtaining any relief for expenses:

Gross rents	8,000
Less basic exemption . .	4,250
Taxable profit	£3,750

b He may decline to file an election and pay tax on the actual profit as follows:

Gross rents	8,000
Actual expenses	3,400
Taxable profit	£4,600

It would be advisable to file an election.

---

or main residence. The same figures applied for 1997–98.

Complete exemption

Where gross rents do not exceed £4,250 (or £2,125 where appropriate) in 1998–99, both receipts and expenses will be disregarded and the rent received incurs no liability to taxation. It remains possible to file an election to avoid taking advantage of this exemption. An election may be beneficial where the expenses incurred exceed rental income, as it will then be possible to carry forward surplus outgoings to a subsequent year or years.

Partial exemption

Gross rents arising in a tax year may exceed the ceiling of £4,250 (or £2,125). The taxpayer is then provided with a choice, namely:

a The individual may elect to suffer tax on that proportion of the gross rents which exceed the ceiling of £4,250 (or £2,125). No relief will then be available for outgoings

b In the absence of an election the individual will incur liability to tax on the difference between gross rents received and expenses paid with no relief under the 'rent-a-room scheme'.

The election must be made not later than 31 January falling some 22 months after the end of the year of assessment to which it applies.

FURNISHED HOLIDAY ACCOMMODATION

A relaxed approach is available for individuals receiving income from the commercial letting of furnished holiday accommodation. Several requirements must be satisfied before these relaxations can apply, including the following:

a The property must be located in the United Kingdom;

b There must be a letting on a commercial basis and with a view to the realisation of profit;

c The tenant or occupier must be entitled to the use of furniture;

d Accommodation must be available for commercial letting as holiday accommodation to the public generally for periods which aggregate at least 140 days;

e The property must actually be so let for at least 70 days; and

f In a period of seven months the property must not normally be in the same occupation for a continuous period exceeding 31 days.

Special rules must be applied to determine whether these requirements are satisfied in a year of assessment. It also remains possible to submit a claim for averaging where some properties in the same ownership would, and others would not, satisfy the several requirements.

Once the existence of qualifying lettings has been established, there are several taxation advantages. Income remains chargeable under Schedule A after 5 April 1995, but for all practical purposes that income is deemed to be derived from a trade. Income is treated as 'earned', losses may be relieved against other income and income can be used to provide cover for personal pension or retirement annuity premiums.

An additional benefit from establishing qualifying furnished holiday lettings is that the disposal of property used for this purpose may enable roll-over relief and retirement relief to be obtained when calculating capital gains tax liability.

The relaxed treatment of furnished lettings is confined to property in the United Kingdom and has no application to property situated overseas, perhaps in Spain, Portugal or France.

COMPLETING THE TAX RETURN

Taxpayers having income from property should complete the supplementary page headed 'Land and Property' and attach it to the tax return form. Part of the supplementary form requires the calculation of profit arising from a Schedule A business in a form not unlike that used to summarise the results of a trade or profession. A further part of the supplementary pages records details of furnished holiday lettings, again in a rather similar form.

AGRICULTURAL LAND

Owners of agricultural land let to tenants are entitled to special relief for expenses. In the ordinary case where property outgoings exceed income in a year of assessment, the excess must be carried forward and set against income accruing in future years, unless the excess is attributable to capital allowances. However, if the expenditure was incurred on land, houses or other buildings comprised in an agricultural estate, the excess may be set against any income of the landlord for the same year.

FARMERS

Farmers who carry out farming on a commercial basis and with a reasonable expectation of profit, and persons who occupy land managed on a commercial basis and with a view to profit, are chargeable in the same manner as other persons who carry on a trade (see page 76). A claim may be made to average profits from farming between two consecutive years. Relief for farming losses may be obtained by setting those losses against other sources of income derived by the farmer, but there can be some limitation in the relief available where losses have been sustained for five consecutive years.

The allowances in respect of plant and machinery referred to on page 94 are available to farmers, and other allowances will frequently be obtained for capital expenditure on agricultural buildings and works (see page 99).

FORESTRY AND WOODLANDS

In earlier times the occupation of woodlands did not give rise to a tax liability unless the woodlands were managed on a commercial basis and with a view to the realisation of profit. If woodlands were managed in this manner the occupier was provided with a choice. He could either choose to be assessed under Schedule B on an assumed annual value or elect to be assessed under Case I of Schedule D as a person carrying on a trade. Persons having the use of woodlands for the purpose of felling and removing timber in connection with an actual trade could not be assessed under Schedule B.

This basis for dealing with commercial woodlands has long been withdrawn by measures spread over a number of years. The effect of these measures is that from 6 April 1993 the occupation of commercial woodlands has been entirely removed from income tax liabilities, reliefs and commitments, unless those woodlands are occupied for the purpose of felling and removing timber in connection with a bona fida trade.

Short rotation coppice

Some farmers produce fuel from the use of short rotation coppice. This involves planting willow or poplar cuttings on farm land. After a year or so the plantings are cut back to ground level which causes the production of shoots. These shoots are harvested every three years or so and made into chips which are then used as fuel. Arguably, the activity could involve commercial woodlands and support exemption from tax on profits arising. However, from 29 November 1994 the activity cannot comprise a use of commercial woodlands but income and expenditure will be included in the calculation of farming profits or losses.

SAND AND GRAVEL QUARRIES

Rents and royalties paid for the use and exploitation of quarries of sand and gravel, sand-pits and brick-fields were previously discharged after deduction of income tax at the basic rate. However, this ceased to apply on 1 May 1995 and all payments are now made gross. The sums received are chargeable to tax under Schedule D.

It is often possible for the recipient of mineral royalties to divide the amounts received into two equal parts. One part will be regarded as a chargeable gain assessable to capital gains tax and the other remains assessable to income tax.

WAYLEAVES

Wayleaves are often payable in the form of a rent attributable to electric, telegraphic or telephone wires or cabling. This rent was previously discharged after deducting income tax at the basic rate but payments made after 5 April 1997 must be discharged gross without any tax deduction. The rent is usually chargeable to income tax under Schedule D, but where wayleaves arise from land producing rents taxable under Schedule A, the wayleaves also may be taxed under this Schedule.

13

Investment income

THE PRESENT AND THE FUTURE

INDIVIDUALS retaining surplus funds, or maintaining an investment portfolio, will be concerned to obtain the maximum income or capital yield from the investment of capital. There are many investment opportunities and the eventual choice will also be influenced by tax considerations.

For the year of assessment 1998–99, which ends on 5 April 1999, income arising from certain investments, notably National Savings Certificates and Children's Bonus Bonds, is exempt from liability to income tax. Exemption also extends to dividends and other revenue arising from Personal Equity Plans and Venture Capital Trusts, together with interest from TESSA arrangements. However, most other forms of income are liable to tax where the investor's income is sufficiently substantial.

In the case of husband and wife 'living together' it is necessary to allocate income between the couple, particularly where income-producing assets are jointly owned. This allocation is required as husband and wife are each independently assessed. Caution must be exercised to ensure that any attempt to transfer future income from one spouse to the other cannot be set aside by the Inland Revenue on the grounds that the transaction represents a 'settlement'.

The treatment of some forms of investment income will be substantially amended on 6 April 1999. This date marks the introduction of Individual Savings Accounts which secure tax advantages to those adopting this form of saving. At the same time the tax credit attaching to United Kingdom company dividends will be reduced and it will no

longer be possible to obtain a repayment of the credit. The tax-free status of income arising from Personal Equity Plans and TESSA's will be preserved but no new Plans or TESSA arrangements can then be entered into.

It must be emphasised that these substantial changes affecting investment income will not be introduced until 6 April 1999. However, many investors will recognise the importance of the arrangements when undertaking their own tax planning.

The present chapter discusses the tax treatment of investment income for the year of assessment 1998–99. A separate chapter, commencing on page 171 outlines the changes which are expected to be introduced on and after 6 April 1999. It should not, of course, be overlooked that further changes may be forthcoming in the future.

RECEIPT OF INVESTMENT INCOME – 1998–99

Income arising on many investments in 1998–99 will be received 'net' after deduction of income tax. Examples include interest received from company debentures, loan interest payable by a company and interest on a reducing number of many Government stocks. Depositors with building societies and banks also receive interest after deduction of income tax although those not liable to tax can arrange to receive income gross. Where the recipient is liable to income tax at a rate which corresponds to the rate of tax deducted, no further tax may be due. Recipients who are not liable, or not wholly liable, may obtain a partial or complete repayment. The gross income, calculated before deduction of income tax, must be included in the figure of total income where the recipient is liable to income tax at the higher rate of 40 per cent but tax will only be charged at the rate in excess of that suffered by deduction.

Dividends paid by United Kingdom companies are not subject to deduction of income tax. However, most dividends have an attached 'tax credit'. The amount of this tax credit effectively represents income tax suffered by deduction from a gross sum representing the aggregate of the dividend paid and the tax credit. Here also a shareholder not liable or fully liable to income tax may obtain a repayment of the tax credit, with those incurring liability to the higher rate of 40 per cent required to discharge further sums.

From 6 April 1998 interest arising on many holdings of government stocks is received gross without deduction of income tax. Gross payments also arise from a limited range of other investments, including interest on Income Bonds issued by the National Savings movement. Any tax on interest of this nature must be satisfied by self-assessment or by adjustment on the notice of coding used for PAYE deduction purposes.

There are complex rules for dealing with certain forms of indirect income. For example, where an investment in an offshore 'roll-up' fund is realised surplus proceeds may be treated as income. Accrued income may also arise on the realisation of deep discounted stock, namely stock issued at a large discount. The special rules which affect interest on National Savings capital bonds are reviewed later.

INVESTMENT INCOME – 1998–99
The taxation of investment income for 1998–99 (and 1997–98 also) draws a distinction between:

a Income from savings; and
b Other income.

The expression 'income from savings' will include:

a Dividends from United Kingdom companies
b Bank interest
c Building society interest
d Interest on Government securities
e All other forms of interest
f The income element of purchased life annuities.

Investment income which does not arise from 'savings' for this purpose will include:

a Income from letting property
b Some annuities
c Pensions.

When paying interest or annuities comprising income from savings the payer will deduct income tax at the lower rate of 20 per cent for 1998–99. Most dividend income retains a tax credit representing one-quarter of the dividend received. In those cases where investment income is not attributable to savings, any tax which must be suffered by deduction will be imposed at the basic rate of 23 per cent which applies for 1998–99.

Income from savings is chargeable to tax at the rate of 20 per cent in the hands of the recipient. This liability will, of course, be matched by the amount of tax suffered by deduction or by the tax credit on dividends. Such income will incur no liability to income tax at the basic rate of 23 per cent. However, where income from savings increases taxable income above the basic rate band of £27,100 for 1998–99, the excess will incur liability at the higher rate of 40 per cent.

This will support the following conclusions in relation to income from savings:

a An individual who is not liable to income tax due to an insufficiency of income may obtain a repayment of income tax deducted, or the tax credit, in full
b An individual who only becomes liable following the receipt of income from savings may recover part of the tax deducted or part of the tax credit
c An individual liable to tax at the lower rate of 20 per cent only will neither pay additional tax nor recover any part of the tax deducted or tax credit
d An individual liable at the basic rate only will neither pay nor recover tax deducted or the tax credit, unless income from savings increases income beyond the basic rate band of £27,100
e An individual liable to tax at the higher rate of 40 per cent will be assessed on the gross amount of income from savings but will receive a reduction in the tax otherwise payable equal to the amount of the tax deducted and the tax credit. As the deduction or credit is given at the reduced rate of 20 per cent this will involve a higher rate liability of 20 per cent (40 per cent less 20 per cent) calculated on the gross sum.

Any investment income which is not derived from savings becomes chargeable in the normal manner, with liability being calculated at the lower rate of 20 per cent, the basic rate of 23 per cent or the higher rate of 40 per cent as appropriate. Where income tax must be deducted from income of this nature deductions will be made at the basic rate of 23 per cent and not at the lower rate of 20 per cent which applies to income from savings.

The following notes may be of assistance in obtaining a fuller understanding of this rather complex area.

DIVIDENDS

Subject to the exceptions mentioned below, each dividend paid by a United Kingdom company in 1998–99 carries a tax credit of one-quarter. This credit effectively represents income tax deducted at the rate of 20 per cent on the aggregate of the dividend and the tax credit. The tax credit is available for repayment where it exceeds the shareholder's liability. In those cases where higher rate income tax must be suffered, further tax will become due.

In certain situations a dividend paid by a United Kingdom company will not carry a tax credit. The first concerns a company receiving income from overseas which has created an entitlement to double taxation relief. It may be in the interests of such a company to elect for dividends paid to its own shareholders to be treated as 'foreign income dividends'. Like other distributions, these are deemed to have suffered income tax at the lower rate of 20 per cent, are not liable to income tax at the basic rate, but remain liable to tax at the higher rate on the grossed-up equivalent. The difference is that foreign income dividends carry no tax credit and a shareholder not liable, or not fully liable, to income tax cannot recover the notional tax of 20 per cent.

A second situation concerns companies purchasing their own shares after 7 October 1996 where the purchase price is effectively treated as a dividend. These distributions are dealt with on a basis identical to foreign income dividends and there is no tax credit capable of being repaid.

Pension funds and other funds administering exempt pension arrangements could previously recover tax credits attaching to dividends received. However, the ability to recover tax credits in this manner was withdrawn for dividends received on and after 2 July 1997. In addition, as discussed on page 171, individuals and trustees will be unable to recover tax credits on and after 6 April 1999 unless their holdings satisfy certain conditions. The rate of credit will be reduced from the same date.

BUILDING SOCIETY INTEREST

When making payments of interest, or crediting interest to a depositor's account, in 1998–99, a building society will deduct income tax at the lower rate of 20 per cent, leaving only the net sum payable or to be credited. Depositors not liable, or not fully liable, to income tax at this rate may recover part, or all, of the tax deducted. Those incurring liability at the higher rate will be assessed to further tax on the gross sum.

It is apparent that substantial administrative problems would arise if small savers received interest after deduction of income tax at the lower rate of 20 per cent and in the absence of tax liability had to reclaim the tax suffered from the Inland Revenue. This problem has been recognised and investors who do not expect to pay income tax may complete a simple registration form. Once this form has been completed and forwarded to the building society concerned, interest will subsequently be paid or credited gross without any deduction of income tax. Should the circumstances of the investor change, the building society must be notified immediately to ensure that in future income tax is deducted from interest. It is possible that some investors may fraudulently complete the registration form or fail to notify the building society of changed circumstances. This is a serious matter as following detection a penalty of up to £3,000 may be incurred.

Many minor children have building society accounts into which pocket money, gifts or earnings are deposited. If sums deposited in a minor child's account by that child's parents, but not by grandparents or others, produce interest in excess of £100 the interest may well be treated as that of the parents for tax purposes. In this situation no registration should be made in an attempt to receive interest gross.

A considerable number of individuals entitled to receive interest gross have failed to register. There will be others having anticipated income close to, or a little in excess of, the threshold at which income tax liability commences who subsequently find there is no liability. These individuals may apply for repayment of excess income tax deducted from payments made.

No tax is deducted from interest on building society TESSA's.

BANK DEPOSIT AND OTHER INTEREST

With limited exceptions, which include National Savings Ordinary Accounts, Investment Accounts and Income Bonds, items of interest paid or credited on bank deposits in 1998–99, are discharged net after deduction of income tax at the lower rate of 20 per cent. Those investors unlikely to incur income tax liability may complete a simple registration form

73
INCOME FROM SAVINGS

Andrew is a single man aged 54. During 1998–99 he received dividends of £1,600 (tax credit £400).

Using these basic facts, it will be assumed that other income, none of which arose from savings, chargeable to income tax was £4,500, £10,000, £30,000 and £40,000 respectively.

Other income £4,500

	£
Other income	4,500
Less Personal allowance . . .	4,195
	305
Add Dividends – gross	2,000
	£2,305

Tax payable:

On £2,305 at 20 per cent . . .	461.00
Less tax credits	400.00
	£ 61.00

Other income £10,000

	£
Other income	10,000
Less Personal allowance . .	4,195
	5,805
Add Dividends – gross	2,000
	£7,805

Tax payable:

On first £4,300 at 20 per cent .	860.00
On next £1,505 at 23 per cent .	346.15
On dividends of £2,000 at 20 per cent .	400.00
	1,606.15
Less tax credits	400.00
	£1,206.15

The dividends have been taxed in full and no further tax is due on those dividends.

Other income £29,000

	£
Other income	30,000
Less Personal allowance . .	4,195
	25,805
Add Dividends – gross . . .	2,000
	£27,805

Tax payable:

On first £4,300 at 20 per cent . .	860.00
On next £21,505 at 23 per cent . .	4,946.15
On dividends:	
On first £1,295 at 20 per cent .	259.00
On balance of £705 at 40 per cent .	282.00
	6,347.15
Less tax credits	400.00
	£5,947.15

This calculation ensures that only to the extent that total income exceeds the basic rate band of £27,100 by £705 will the excess gross dividend of £705 give rise to liability at 40 per cent.

Other income £40,000

	£
Other income	40,000
Less Personal allowance . . .	4,195
	35,805
Add Dividends – gross	2,000
	£37,805

Tax payable:

On first £4,300 at 20 per cent . .	860.00
On next £22,800 at 23 per cent . .	5,244.00
On balance of £10,705 at 40 per cent	4,282.00
	10,386.00
Less tax credits	400.00
	£9,986.00

It is clear that the entire gross dividend of £2,000 is fully taxable at the higher rate of 40 per cent.

NB. These illustrations are of identical application for 1998–99 if dividends were replaced by interest and tax credits by tax suffered by deduction at 20 per cent.

which will enable the bank or other person to discharge interest gross. The formalities of registration, the penalties for false declarations and procedures for the recovery of excessive lower rate income tax deductions are identical to those which affect building society deposits (see above). Banks also may take deposits within the TESSA arrangements and interest credited under these arrangements is not subject to income tax.

Individuals over the age of 64 may obtain an increased personal allowance and married couple's allowance. The amount of any increase will require restriction, or perhaps elimination, where total income exceeds £16,200 for 1998–99. When calculating income for this purpose it should not be overlooked that the gross amount of bank, building society or other interest must be included and not just the net sum received or credited.

————74————
BUILDING SOCIETY INTEREST – LOWER RATE

Jean, a married woman aged 42, earns a salary of £11,000 for 1998–99. She receives interest of £320 on an ordinary building society deposit account and has not registered to receive interest gross. An election has been made to transfer one-half of the married couple's allowance to the wife.

Total income:	£	£
Salary		11,000
Building society interest received	320	
Add Tax deducted at 20 per cent	80	
		400
		11,400
Less Personal allowance . . .		4,195
		£7,205

Tax payable:		
On first £4,300 at 20 per cent . .		860.00
On next £2,505 at 23 per cent . .		576.15
On interest of £400 at 20 per cent .		80.00
		1,516.15
Less Married couple's allowance (one-half) – £950 at 15 per cent . .		142.50
		1,373.65
Less Tax deducted on building society interest		80.00
		£1,293.65

The total tax due is £1,373.65 of which £80 has been suffered by deduction from interest received, leaving the balance to be collected from the salary under the PAYE deduction scheme.

NATIONAL SAVINGS BANK INTEREST

Interest received on deposits with the National Savings Bank is chargeable to income tax. When establishing the total income of an individual for 1998–99, the first £70 of interest received in the year from deposits, other than investment deposits, with the National Savings Bank, is disregarded. If husband and wife each receive interest, both may obtain the £70 exemption. This applies also where husband and wife have a joint holding. Should interest received by one spouse fall below £70 the unabsorbed balance cannot be used to increase the other's exemption limit above £70.

No tax is deducted on payment of interest but tax due will be limited to the lower rate of 20 per cent, unless there is liability to the higher rate of 40 per cent also.

————75————
BUILDING SOCIETY INTEREST – HIGHER RATE

Marcus is a single man and receives building society interest of £1,200 on a non-TESSA account in 1998–99. His other income for the year amounts to £33,000.

Total income:	£	£
Other income		33,000
Building society interest received . . .	1,200	
Add Tax deducted at 20 per cent . . .	300	
		1,500
		34,500
Less Personal allowance . . .		4,195
		£30,305

Tax payable:		
Lower rate:		
On first £4,300 at 20 per cent . .		860.00
Basic rate:		
On next £22,800 at 23 per cent . .		5,244.00
Higher rate:		
On balance of £3,205 at 40 per cent		1,282.00
		7,386.00
Less Tax deducted on building society interest		300.00
		£7,086.00

NATIONAL SAVINGS CAPITAL BONDS

National Savings capital bonds offer a guaranteed return of interest throughout a five-year period. Interest is not paid out but added, without deducting income tax, to the value of the bond. However, the amount of interest added is liable to income tax as if it was actually received by the bond holder.

GOVERNMENT AND OTHER SECURITIES

A special scheme applies for dealing with interest arising on large holdings of securities. The scheme has no application to shares but extends to Government securities, together with most securities issued by companies and local authorities, among others.

Normally, the price paid to acquire securities, together with proceeds arising from the disposal of those assets, will be calculated by inserting an adjustment for accrued interest. This adjustment has no effect for income tax purposes as the holder actually receiving interest is liable to bear tax on the entire amount of that interest at his or her appropriate rate.

76
BANK INTEREST RECEIVED OLDER PERSONS

Cyril, a married man aged 78, receives pensions amounting to £17,700 in 1998–99. He also receives net building society interest of £1,800 in the same year. No TESSA account was involved and Cyril is entitled to the full married couple's allowance.

Total income is calculated as follows:	£	£
Pensions		17,700
Building society interest received	1,800	
Add Tax deducted at 20 per cent	450	2,250
Total income		£19,950

As total income exceeds £16,200, the increased personal allowance of £5,600 must be reduced as follows:

Increased allowance		5,600
Less one-half of excess over £16,200 (£19,950 less £16,200)	1,875	
		£3,725

The personal allowance cannot be reduced below the basic allowance of £4,195. Therefore of £1,875 only £1,405 is needed to produce this result.

The increased married couple's allowance will be:

Increased allowance		3,345
Less one-half of excess as above	1,875	
Deduct sum subtracted from personal allowance	1,405	470
Reduced allowance		2,875

The calculations may now be completed:

Total income		19,950
Less Personal allowance		4,195
		£15,755

Tax payable:

On first £4,300 at 20 per cent		860.00
On next £9,205 at 23 per cent		2,117.15
On interest of £2,250 at 20 per cent		450.00
		3,427.15
Less Married couple's allowance – £2,875 at 15 per cent		431.25
		2,995.90
Less Tax deducted on building society interest		450.00
		£2,545.90

The gross building society interest of £2,250 has been included to calculate total income thereby increasing that income further beyond £16,200. As a result the one-half restriction has reduced allowances by £1,125 (one-half of £2,250), in addition to the restriction arising from the receipt of other income.

77
SAVINGS BANK INTEREST

Charles is a married man and receives a salary of £19,250 for 1998–99. His wife, Sandra, has business profits of £7,400 assessable in the same year. Both have ordinary deposits with the National Savings Bank and the amounts of interest from these deposits otherwise assessable for 1998–99 are as follows:

	£
Husband	90
Wife	37

Assuming neither spouse has reached the age of 65 and the husband is entitled to the full married couple's allowance, the tax payable by Charles will be:

Total income:	£	£
Salary		19,250
Interest	90	
Less exemption	70	
		20
		19,270
Less Personal allowance		4,195
		£15,075

Tax payable:		
On first £4,300 at 20 per cent		860.00
On next £10,755 at 23 per cent		2,473.65
On interest of £20 at 20 per cent		4.00
		3,337.65
Less Married couple's allowance – £1,900 at 15 per cent		285.00
		£3,052.65

The liability of Sandra will become:

Total income:	£	£
Profits		7,400
Interest	37	
Less exemption	37	
		—
		7,400
Less Personal allowance		4,195
Tax chargeable on		£3,205

Tax payable:		
On £3,205 at 20 per cent		£641.00

However, the position is otherwise for securities brought within the scheme as interest is treated as accruing on a day to day basis and this will determine the individual's liability to tax where securities are purchased and sold. For example, where securities are purchased between interest payment dates the purchaser will only bear tax on that part of the interest which accrues for the period from the

78
GOVERNMENT SECURITIES

On 1 May 1998 Jack acquired a holding of securities. Interest at the rate of £6,000 was payable half-yearly on 1 July and 1 January. Gross interest of £6,000 was received by Jack on 1 July 1998. He sold his holding, with settlement on 15 December 1998. If Jack was not within the special scheme his income for 1998–99 would comprise £6,000, representing the gross equivalent of interest actually received.

However, if, as seems clear, the special scheme applies, Jack's income will be calculated as follows:

	£
Interest period to 1 July 1998 – 181 days:	
Period of ownership – 61 days	
Taxable 61/181 × £6,000 . . .	2,022
Interest period to 1 January 1999 – 184 days:	
Period of ownership – 167 days	
Taxable 167/184 × £6,000 . . .	5,446
Taxable income	£7,468

purchase date to the end of the interest period. Similarly, where securities are sold the vendor will bear tax on interest accruing from the commencement of the interest period to the date of settlement.

The scheme will only apply if the nominal value of all securities held by an individual in the year of assessment during which the interest period ends, or in the previous year, exceeds £5,000. The threshold of £5,000 applies separately to a husband and to his wife. Personal representatives are brought within the scheme if the nominal value of securities held in the deceased person's estate exceeds £5,000.

Individuals and personal representatives who do not retain holdings of this magnitude remain unaffected by the special scheme and continue to suffer income tax on the actual amount of interest received.

GILT-EDGED SECURITIES

Throughout a period of many years interest paid to individuals on holdings of Government securities (gilts) has usually been discharged after deduction of income tax. This deduction was limited to tax at the lower rate of 20 per cent for interest paid in 1997–98. There were a number of exceptions, including interest on holdings of $3\frac{1}{2}$ per cent War Loan and gilts purchased through the National Savings Stock Register. Payments of interest on such holdings were discharged gross, a system which also applied where the holder of gilts ordinarily resided outside the United Kingdom.

As a general rule, all payments of interest made on gilts on and after 6 April 1998 will be discharged gross without deduction of income tax. This remains subject to two possible exceptions.

The first exception extends to a holder of gilts who applies for income tax to be deducted at the lower rate of 20 per cent. The second exception is of application to individuals holding gilts on 5 April 1998, as income tax will continue to be deducted on subsequent payments of interest unless the holder applies for payments to be made gross.

PURCHASED LIFE ANNUITIES

Life annuities can be purchased from insurance companies and other financial institutions. Each annuity, which may be paid on an annual or some other periodic basis, contains two elements, namely a capital element and an income element. The amount of each element will be determined by the insurance company or institution responsible for the arrangement.

79
PURCHASED LIFE ANNUITY

Mabel is a widow aged 67. She receives a social security retirement pension and a pension from her late husband's former employers. The gross amount of these pensions was £12,300. In addition she receives £1,500 (gross) annually from a purchased life annuity. The annuity contains a capital element of £850 and an income element of £650.

The actual sum received from the annuity in 1998–99 will be:

	£	£
Capital element		850.00
Income element . . .	650.00	
Less Tax at 20 per cent . .	130.00	520.00
Cash received		£1,370.00

The tax payable becomes:

	£
Total income:	
Pensions	12,300
Annuity (income element only) . .	650
	12,950
Less Personal allowance . .	5,410
	£7,540

Tax payable:	
On first £4,300 at 20 per cent . .	860.00
On next £2,590 at 23 per cent . .	595.70
On annuity of £650 at 20 per cent .	130.00
	1,585.70
Less Tax deducted on annuity . .	130.00
	£1,455.70

The capital element is effectively a return of the purchase price and will not be liable to income tax. However, the income element is taxable and payments will be received after deduction of income tax at the lower rate of 20 per cent for 1998–99. Only the income element will enter into the calculation of the annuitant's total income. As the annuity represents income from savings there will be no liability at the basic rate.

These purchased life annuities must be distinguished from those acquired as part of a pension scheme arrangement. The latter annuities are wholly taxable.

STOCK DIVIDEND OPTIONS
Companies residing in the United Kingdom sometimes offer shareholders the option of receiving a cash dividend or an issue of shares. Where the shareholder decides to accept shares the market value of the holding will sometimes exceed the corresponding cash dividend. However, these arrangements, called stock dividend options, may involve the shareholder in liability to income tax. The value of the shares issued is deemed to represent a sum remaining after deducting income tax at the lower rate of 20 per cent for 1998–99. There can be no assessment to tax at either the lower rate or the basic rate. However, where income is sufficiently substantial the gross sum will incur liability to higher rate income tax, less a notional credit of 20 per cent. Shareholders not liable, or not

fully liable, to income tax cannot obtain any repayment of the notional tax deducted. This arrangement effectively ensures that a shareholder opting to obtain shares will suffer income tax in a manner similar to that which is applied to dividends, but without the ability to recover any tax credit.

Where stock dividend options arise after 5 April 1999, the notional tax is reduced from 20 per cent to the Schedule F ordinary rate of 10 per cent (see page 172).

LIFE POLICIES AND INCOME BONDS
There are a range of products, including life policies, life annuities and capital redemption policies, which may produce liability to income tax on maturity, surrender or assignment. These will not usually comprise normal policies of life assurance but broadly reflect other arrangements, often involving single premiums paid to obtain guaranteed income bonds. Liability may arise on the occurrence of a chargeable event which affects the underlying policy. The amount of any gain arising by reason of this event will be calculated and notified by the insurance company or other financial institution marketing the product. The gain does not incur liability to income tax at the lower rate or the basic rate. Liability is confined to higher rate income tax. A policyholder not liable to tax at the higher rate is unable to recover any of the notional income tax deemed to have been suffered.

SAVE AS YOU EARN
Save As You Earn contracts enable monthly investments to be made throughout a period of five years. At the end of this period, or at the investor's option two years later, the investment may be withdrawn together with a terminal bonus. The bonus is not liable to income tax. Most Save As You Earn contracts are share option related and enable employees to purchase shares in their employing company with the proceeds arising on maturity.

No new 'non' share option related schemes are now available.

PERSONAL EQUITY PLANS
Originally introduced as an incentive to encourage wider share ownership, personal equity plans have been available for several years. However, following the introduction of Individual Savings Accounts on 6 April 1999 no new plans can be obtained on or after that date.

80
STOCK DIVIDEND OPTIONS

Henry has substantial income which attracts considerable liability to higher rate income tax for 1998–99. He retains shares in a United Kingdom company and during the year was provided with an option to take either

a a cash dividend of £4,800; or
b shares issued by the company.

Henry opted to take shares, which had a market value of £5,000 at the time of issue.

For assessment purposes the shares are treated as representing a gross sum of £6,250 from which income tax at the lower rate of 20 per cent has been deducted to produce £5,000. As Henry is already liable to tax at the higher rate of 40 per cent he will incur the following additional liability:

	£
Tax on £6,250 at 40 per cent . . .	2,500.00
Less deemed tax suffered – £6,250 at 20 per cent	1,250.00
Additional liability	£1,250.00

Personal Equity Plans (PEPs) are managed by plan managers, usually financial institutions, which must be approved by the Inland Revenue. Investment is confined to individuals aged eighteen years and above who must be either resident and ordinarily resident in the United Kingdom, or performing duties on behalf of the Crown in some territory overseas.

There are basically two kinds of available PEP, namely a general PEP and a single company PEP. For 1998–99 the maximum permitted cash investment capable of being made by an individual in a general PEP is £6,000. The entire sum may be invested in investment or unit trusts. It remains a condition that at least one-half of the investments made by the investment or unit trusts are in United Kingdom ordinary shares or comparable shares in companies incorporated within a Member State of the European Community, in certain United Kingdom corporate bonds, or preference shares in United Kingdom and European Community companies. Where this 50 per cent level is not achieved the maximum amount of investment capable of being made in unit or investment trusts is limited to £1,500. It is a further condition that this limited investment will only be recognised if the underlying unit or investment trust holds at least one-half of its investments in shares, which need not necessarily be issued by a United Kingdom company or one in the EC. In addition the sum contributed may be directly invested in United Kingdom or European company shares.

It is also possible for an individual to invest up to £3,000 in a single company PEP during 1998–99. This is in addition to an investment in a general PEP. However, an individual cannot invest in more than one general PEP during the year of assessment.

The attraction of a PEP is the exemption from taxation offered to investors. Any dividends paid on investments made by plan managers will have the usual tax credit attached. Managers may obtain repayment of the tax credit from the Inland Revenue on behalf of investors. This ensures that dividend income received by the plan will effectively be realised 'gross' without suffering the inroads of income tax. Some relief may also be available for interest on investments made within the plan. Should gains arise from the disposal of assets held by the plan no liability to capital gains tax will arise.

Plan managers charge a fee for their services and the investor cannot obtain any tax relief for this outlay.

Withdrawal of plans

Since their introduction in 1986 PEPs have grown enormously in popularity and many different forms of plan are available. However, no new PEPs will be issued after 5 April 1999, although holdings existing on that date may be retained and continue to produce tax advantages (see page 173 for further details).

TAX EXEMPT SPECIAL SAVINGS ACCOUNT

A further facility conferring taxation benefits which will shortly be withdrawn is the Tax Exempt Special Savings Account (TESSA), operated by authorised banks and building societies. Among the conditions which must be discharged before the account will be recognised for taxation purposes are the following:

a The account holder must be an individual aged at least eighteen years;
b The account must be identified as a TESSA;
c The holder of the account must not have any other TESSA;
d The account must not be held on a joint basis;
e The account must not be held for the benefit of any person except the holder;
f The account must not be connected with any other account.

A maximum is placed on the amount which can be deposited in a TESSA throughout a five-year period. Deposits must not exceed £3,000 in the first year or £1,800 in each of years two, three, four and five. In addition, the total deposited must be limited to £9,000.

Where these conditions are satisfied, any interest or bonus added to the account will not become liable to income tax if the account is maintained throughout a full five-year period, or until the death of the account holder, whichever event occurs first. Once the five-year period has come to an end any future interest will become chargeable to income tax but the account holder may close the account and open another TESSA attracting similar tax advantages.

It is possible to contemplate the withdrawal of some interest during the five-year period. The amount withdrawn in 1998–99 is not to exceed the interest credited less income tax at the lower rate of 20 per cent. However, should interest in excess of the amount calculated on this basis be withdrawn, or any extraction of capital take place, the tax advantages will be lost. All interest will then be treated as the depositor's income, with that interest deemed to arise at the date exemption was abandoned.

Reinvestment

TESSA's were first made available in January 1991. As a result, many account holders reached the five-year anniversary in January 1996 with others achieving this objective at later dates. As an induce-ment for those with maturing TESSAs to reinvest the proceeds, a relaxation is made in the maximum investment into a new TESSA during the first year. Up to a maximum of £9,000 can be invested in the new TESSA using proceeds arising from the maturity of the old deposit. Only the capital part of the earlier deposit can be used for this purpose and not any accrued interest. The restrictions on the amount which can be deposited in the new account for years two, three, four and five remain. Those who receive the maximum capital repayment of £9,000 on the maturity of the old TESSA and reinvest the entire sum in a new deposit account cannot invest any further amounts in that account during the remaining five-year period. It is a require-ment that the proceeds must be reinvested within a period of six months following the maturity of the original TESSA.

It is unnecessary for the new TESSA to be invested with the same institution in which the old TESSA was held. Where the reinvestment is to take place with a different financial institution and the deposit in the first year is to exceed £3,000 a certificate must be obtained from the old institution. Unless this certificate is forthcoming the new insti-tution will be unable to accept a sum in excess of £3,000. No certificate is required if the new TESSA is to be re-invested in the same institution.

Withdrawal of relief

No new TESSAs will be available after 5 April 1999. TESSAs acquired on or before that date will continue to run and confer tax exemption on interest throughout the remainder of the five-year period. Further details will be found on page 173.

VENTURE CAPITAL TRUSTS

Yet a further facility conferring substantial tax benefits, the venture capital trust, became available for investment during 1995. The general nature of these new trusts has been outlined on page 43. Subject to a maximum investment of £100,000, when subscribing for shares in any year of assessment the investor may obtain income tax relief at the rate of 20 per cent. In addition, any dividends or other distributions received from the investment will be immune from income tax, where of course the underlying requirements are satisfied. It is possible that the investments made by an individual in a year of assessment exceed £100,000. In such a situation it is only dividends and other distributions attributable to the initial £100,000 qualifying for relief which are exempt from liability to income tax. Dividends and distributions on any excess will be chargeable to tax in the normal manner.

An additional attraction of venture capital trusts is freedom from capital gains tax liability where a qualifying holding is retained throughout a five-year period.

SICKNESS AND UNEMPLOYMENT INSURANCE RECEIPTS

For several years many benefits received throughout an initial twelve-month period on some permanent health and similar policies were not charged to income tax. From 6 April 1996 this exemption was extended to all insurance benefits where the person entitled to receive those benefits is sick, disabled or unemployed. This includes benefits which are payable during convalescence or rehabilitation or to top up earned income when it is required following sickness, disability or unemployment. The most common policies falling under this heading com-prise:

a Mortgage payment protection insurance
b Permanent health insurance
c Creditor insurance
d Certain kinds of long-term care insurance.

The exemption does not extend to insurance benefits which are taken into account in computing trading or other business profits. Nor will the exemp-tion apply where the policy premiums have received tax relief or have themselves been deducted in arriving at profits liable to income tax.

Some employers may take out group policies to meet the cost of sick pay for employees. Pay which is funded in this manner remains taxable, except where the employees have themselves contributed to the premium. The proportion of benefits attribu-table to those employee contributions will be excluded from taxation.

DECEASED PERSON'S ESTATE

Personal representatives administering the estate of a deceased person incur liability to income tax for income arising after the time of death. Tax is suffered at the basic rate of 23 per cent, or the lower rate of 20 per cent which applies to income from 'savings' in 1998–99. During, or at the end of, the administration of the estate, income will be distributed to legatees. This income will be treated as having borne tax at the rate suffered by personal representatives. Distributions are now regarded as income for the tax year in which the distribution takes place.

INCOME FROM ABROAD

A taxpayer may receive income from abroad which must suffer United Kingdom taxation. As this income has probably been taxed in a foreign country also, it is effectively taxed twice. To avoid the problems of double taxation, agreements have been entered into between the United Kingdom and many foreign countries. These agreements contain a variety of features. Some exempt income from tax in either the foreign country or the United Kingdom and others provide that the foreign tax suffered will be deducted from the United Kingdom tax due on the same income.

Even where no double tax agreement has been concluded a taxpayer who would otherwise pay tax on the same slice of income both here and abroad is entitled to similar relief.

No relief from double taxation will be granted unless it is claimed by the taxpayer, who must be resident in the United Kingdom. A person not liable to United Kingdom taxation, where, for example, personal allowances exceed income, cannot claim any repayment of foreign tax from the United Kingdom authorities.

Dividends received from overseas companies are not within the United Kingdom 'tax credit' system discussed on page 110. However, the income tax charged on those overseas dividends is generally limited to 20 per cent for 1998–99. Increased liability will arise for individuals liable at the higher rate of 40 per cent.

In addition to dividends, other overseas income which would be similar to 'savings' if arising in the United Kingdom is charged at the reduced rate of income tax, as shown on page 109.

The treatment of some income arising overseas after 5 April 1999 is briefly outlined on page 171.

81
JOINT ASSETS

Bob and Betty are married and the joint owners of commercial property with the husband retaining a beneficial interest of two-thirds and his wife the remaining one-third. Net rental income taxable under Schedule A amounted to £12,000 for 1998–99.

In the absence of a declaration the income will be allocated as follows:

	£
Bob – one-half	6,000
Betty – one-half	6,000
	£12,000

If a declaration is made before the commencement of the year of assessment on 6 April 1998, the allocation becomes:

	£
Bob – Beneficial ownership two-thirds .	8,000
Betty – Beneficial ownership one-third .	4,000
	£12,000

A finding that the declaration was only made on, say, 6 October 1998 and income accrued evenly throughout the year would support the following allocation:

	Bob £	Betty £
Income to 6 October 1998 – £6,000		
Bob – one-half	3,000	
Betty – one-half		3,000
Income from 6 October 1998 – £6,000		
Bob – two-thirds . . .	4,000	
Betty – one-third . . .		2,000
	£7,000	£5,000

HUSBAND AND WIFE – JOINT PROPERTY

A husband and wife 'living together' may jointly retain the ownership of income-producing assets. It is then necessary to allocate any income arising between each party. The general rule is that the income from jointly held assets must be apportioned equally between the couple. This does not apply to earned income, income from a partnership or to some special types of income where the legislation requires a specific allocation.

Where equal apportionment is appropriate it remains possible for this to be varied by making a joint declaration. The declaration does not enable the parties to impose their own allocation but requires income to be apportioned on the basis of each individual's beneficial interest in the asset.

A declaration may be made at any time, but will only apply to income arising subsequently. The declaration cannot be related back to some earlier period.

A separate declaration is required for each jointly owned asset. For example, a husband and his wife may jointly own perhaps five assets. The declaration may apply to any number between one and four, extend to all assets, or the parties may choose not to make any declaration whatsoever. A declaration is only valid if it reaches HM Inspector of Taxes within a period of sixty days from when it was made.

A declaration once made cannot subsequently be withdrawn and will only cease to apply where the couple separate, one spouse dies or there is a change in the beneficial interests.

HUSBAND AND WIFE – TRANSFER OF ASSETS

A deceptively simple method of transferring future income from one spouse to the other is to transfer the ownership of the asset producing that income. Where the transfer is made by way of outright gift, and without any strings attached, the transfer should achieve the required objective. The position will, however, be otherwise if the transferee does not obtain an interest in all income arising, is bound to apply that income for the benefit or advantage of the transferor, or the transferor can benefit from either income or capital in any circumstances whatsoever. Some caution must therefore be exercised when contemplating the transfer of income-producing assets between a husband and his wife.

14

Deeds of covenant

THROUGHOUT A PERIOD of many years, payments made under a properly drawn deed of covenant formed a popular method of transferring income from one person to another. In some cases payments had been made in return for valuable and sufficient consideration but the great majority were devoid of any consideration whatsoever. The continuing use of deeds of covenant as a tax efficient arrangement was severely restricted by the withdrawal of relief for many covenants made after 14 March 1988. This withdrawal had no effect on covenants in favour of recognised charities, nor did it immediately apply to the rapidly diminishing list of non-charitable covenants entered into before that date.

To achieve a proper understanding of the effect which payments made under deed of covenant may now have on taxation liabilities, a distinction must be drawn between:

a Charitable covenants; and
b Other covenants.

None of these matters are affected by the introduction of self-assessment.

CHARITABLE COVENANTS
To qualify for recognition, charitable covenants must require payments to be made to a named charity throughout a period capable of exceeding three years. Many deeds drawn in simple form will be suitable but professional advice should be obtained before entering into deeds containing unusual provisions.

If a covenant is capable of being terminated within the initial three-year period it will not be recognised for tax purposes. To avoid this some covenants are drawn in a form which enables termination to occur at any time after the end of three years. Previously such covenants ceased to qualify immediately the power arose, but this no longer applies and such covenants may now continue without the need for a fresh deed.

When making payments under a deed of covenant drawn in favour of a charity the payer should deduct income tax at the basic rate. This will involve a deduction at the rate of 23 per cent for payments made in 1998–99. The rate at which tax must be deducted is not influenced by the 20 per cent lower rate band. If the payer has taxable income equal to, or in excess of, the gross sum payable, and chargeable at the basic rate, he or she may retain the income tax deducted. This effectively provides relief from income tax at the basic rate if, but only if, the payer exercises the right to deduct tax.

Where the payer's taxable income is not sufficiently substantial to incur liability at the basic rate on an amount equal to payments made under deed of covenant, income tax similar to the amount of tax deducted must be accounted for to the Inland Revenue. This situation may arise where income is exceeded by allowances and reliefs, or occasionally where liability arises at only the lower rate of 20 per cent. The possibility of such a development should not be overlooked by those of modest means when being invited to sign a covenant form.

Some married couples enter into joint covenants. The Inland Revenue will treat payments made under

———— 82 ————
CHARITABLE COVENANTS

Richard is a married man aged 54 earning an annual salary of £25,000 and entitled to the full married couple's allowance. During 1998–99 he made a payment of £500, less tax, to a charity as required by a properly drawn deed of covenant.

The actual payment made will be:

	£
Gross sum	500
Less Income tax at 23 per cent . .	115
Actual payment	£385

The income tax payable by Richard in 1998–99 will be:

	£
Total income	25,000
Less Personal allowance . .	4,195
	£20,805

Tax payable:

On first £4,300 at 20 per cent . .	860.00
On balance of £16,505 at 23 per cent .	3,796.15
	4,656.15
Less Married couple's allowance – £1,900	
at 15 per cent	285.00
	£4,371.15

As Richard suffers tax at the basic rate on an amount of income in excess of the gross covenanted payment, he may retain the tax deducted of £115.

———— 83 ————
RESTRICTION OF RELIEF

Margaret, a married woman aged 40 living with her husband, has earnings of £4,000 for 1998–99. During the year she makes an annual payment of £300, less tax, under a charitable covenant. The actual payment made will be:

	£
Gross sum	300
Less Income tax at 23 per cent . .	69
Actual payment	£231

The income tax payable will be:

	£
Total income	4,000
Less Personal allowance . .	4,195
	NIL

Tax payable:

On £300 at 23 per cent . . .	£69.00

Although income is fully covered by the personal allowance of £4195, income tax must be charged at the basic rate of 23 per cent on £300. This ensures that tax of £69 deducted from the annual payment is fully accounted for.

———— 84 ————
COVENANTS – HIGHER RATE RELIEF

Peter is a married man and has business profits of £75,000 assessable for 1998–99. During the year he made payments under deed of covenant aggregating £20,000 (gross) to several recognised charities.

The actual aggregate payments made to charity in 1998–99 will be:

	£
Gross sums.	20,000
Less Income tax at 23 per cent . .	4,600
Actual payments	£15,400

The income tax payable, assuming Peter is entitled to the full married couple's allowance, will be calculated as follows:

	£
Total income	75,000
Less Personal allowance . . .	4,195
	70,805
Less Gross covenant	20,000
	£50,805

Tax payable:

Lower rate:	
On first £4,300 at 20 per cent . .	860.00
Basic rate:	
On next £22,800 at 23 per cent .	5,244.00
Higher rate:	
On balance of £23,705 at 40 per cent	9,482.00
	15,586.00
Less Married couple's allowance of	
£1,900 at 15 per cent . . .	285.00
	15,301.00
Add tax recovered on covenant .	4,600.00
	£19,901.00

Note: Relief at the basic rate of 23 per cent has been obtained by deducting that amount on payment of the covenant. Relief at the higher rate must therefore be restricted to 17 per cent (40 per cent less 23 per cent). This is achieved in the example by:

a deducting £20,000 when calculating taxable income liable at 40 per cent and

b adding back tax deducted at 23 per cent, namely £4,600.

such covenants as discharged in equal proportions by each spouse, unless there is evidence supporting a different conclusion.

In those cases where the payer's income is sufficiently substantial to incur income tax liability at the higher rate of 40 per cent, covenanted payments may be offset against income otherwise chargeable at that rate.

Thus an individual having suffered sufficient tax on income at the top rate of 40 per cent and making payments of, say, £10,000 (less tax) to a charity obtains the following tax reliefs for 1998–99:

a £2,300 (£10,000 at 23 per cent) by deduction; and

b £1,700 (£10,000 at 40 per cent less 23 per cent) against higher rate liability.

The net cost of the payments becomes £6,000 (£10,000 less (£2,300 plus £1,700)).

The charity receiving payments under a properly drawn deed of covenant may expect to recover income tax suffered by deduction at the basic rate.

Further matters relating to payments made under charitable deeds of covenant are discussed on page 123. In addition, single donations made under the Gift Aid scheme are effectively treated as discharged in a manner similar to payments under deed of covenant (see pages 124 and 126).

OTHER COVENANTS

Payments made under a non-charitable deed of covenant entered into before 15 March 1988 continued to be recognised for taxation purposes. It remained a condition that the deed of covenant had been examined by HM Inspector of Taxes not later than 30 June 1988. In the absence of such an examination the deed could not be accepted and payments made after 5 April 1988 were entirely disregarded for taxation purposes.

Where a non-charitable covenant had been accepted by the Inspector the payer would deduct and retain or account for income tax at the appropriate basic rate in a manner identical to that which applied to a charitable deed of covenant. However, relief was restricted to the deduction of income tax at the basic rate on payment. It was not possible to obtain relief at the higher rate of 40 per cent.

Recognition of these pre 15 March 1988 non-charitable covenants ceased to apply for payments made after 5 April 1995. The payer cannot deduct income tax at the basic rate and must satisfy payments 'gross'. The recipient will not treat the amount received as taxable income, nor can any attempt be made to recover income tax allegedly deducted. Shortly stated, payments under a non-charitable deed of covenant, whether entered into before 15 March 1988 or on or after that date now have no effect for income tax purposes.

Where payments continue to be made under these non-qualifying deeds of covenant they are unlikely to have any effect on capital gains tax commitments. The position would only be otherwise if the disposal of an asset was matched with an undertaking to pay covenanted sums when the value of these sums to the recipient would identify proceeds from the disposal of the asset.

A payment under a non-charitable deed of covenant does reflect the transfer of value for inheritance tax purposes. Unless such a payment can be treated as made out of normal expenditure or fall under one of the exemption headings, it could comprise a potentially exempt transfer entering into the calculation of inheritance tax liability for transactions taking place within a period of seven years before the date of death.

15

Charitable bodies

GENERAL EXEMPTION

Recognised charities are provided with a general exemption from tax where income is applied for charitable purposes. This exemption extends to rents and receipts from land, together with dividends and interest, among other items. Therefore a charity may invest surplus funds and obtain a return which is not eroded by taxation liabilities. Where income is received after deduction, or deemed deduction, of tax, for example on some interest, the charity may obtain a repayment of tax suffered from the Inland Revenue. It is also possible to obtain tax repayments representing the tax credits on dividends, where income arises not later than 5 April 1999.

Trading profits earned by a charity are, however, exempt only where either:

a The trade is exercised in the course of the actual carrying out of a primary purpose of the charity; or

b The work in connection with the trade is mainly carried out by beneficiaries of the charity.

Failure to satisfy one of these conditions will result in the trading profits remaining liable to tax, notwithstanding that the proprietor of the business is a charity. An arrangement often used by charities to avoid this liability is mentioned later.

INDUCEMENTS FOR CHARITABLE FUNDING

In addition to exemptions from tax for income arising on investments made, or profits earned, by a charity, several inducements are available to encourage charitable giving. These inducements, which have been increased by the special Millennium Gift Aid, are discussed below.

Deeds of covenant

On making payments under deed of covenant to a charity an individual may deduct and usually retain income tax at the basic rate of 23 per cent for 1998–99. Additionally, the charity may obtain repayment of the tax deducted from the Inland Revenue. Where the payer is liable to tax at the higher rate of 40 per cent he or she may obtain further relief as shown on page 121. Thus the cost to the covenantor is reduced and the charity obtains the full benefit of the gross payment. If the donor merely made a cash gift equal to the gross sum, no deduction of income tax could be made and the cost to the donor would be correspondingly increased. The position may be otherwise if sufficiently large gifts are made to qualify for relief under the Gift Aid arrangements outlined on the following pages.

The advantages of making payments under deed of covenant are not confined to individuals, as similar payments may be made by companies. On making any payment a company will deduct income tax at the basic rate and account for the tax deducted to the Inland Revenue. The corporate payer obtains relief for corporation tax purposes by setting the gross payment made against profits. The recipient charity retains the normal entitlement of recovering tax suffered by deduction.

Deeds of covenant often provide for the payment

85
DEED OF COVENANT

Bill had entered into a qualifying charitable deed of covenant requiring payments on 15 May annually of such a sum as will, after deduction of income tax at the basic rate for the time being in force, leave the sum of £100.

On these bare facts Bill will have made an actual cash payment of £100 on 15 May 1996. The basic rate of income tax in force at that time was 24 per cent.

Therefore the gross sum required to support a net payment of £100 becomes £131.58. This result can be verified by calculating tax at 24 per cent on £131.58 to produce £31.58.

Later, on both 15 May 1997 and 15 May 1998, Bill will make a further actual cash payment of £100. However, the basic rate of income tax is now 23 per cent. Therefore the gross sum becomes £129.87 on each occasion.

of a fixed annual sum which must be grossed up at the basic rate prevailing at the time of payment. The advantage of this arrangement is that the covenantor may continue to make the same cash payment annually, notwithstanding any change in the basic rate of income tax.

As a general rule, payments made under deed of covenant will only be recognised for tax purposes if they produce no benefit for the payer and place no obligation on the payee to provide some advantage. Small benefits or advantages may be disregarded but those of any substance may not. This prevents many subscriptions being paid in the form of covenanted payments and qualifying for tax relief. However, a relaxation affects payments made to a limited range of charities whose sole or main purpose is the preservation of property or the conservation of wildlife for the public benefit. This also includes museums and supporters' organisations having charitable status. For payments made to these charities, any right of entry to view property or perhaps a collection will not be treated as a benefit which may otherwise disqualify a deed, if the right is limited to the covenantor, or members of the covenantor's family.

Payroll deduction scheme

Limited income tax relief will be available where charitable donations are made by an employee under an approved payroll deduction scheme. These schemes must be operated by an employer through an approved charity agency. Membership is voluntary but those employees who join may contribute up to

£1,200 in 1998–99. Contributions are subtracted from each employee's earnings and the aggregate sums collected paid to an approved agency which is responsible for distributing those funds to the selected charities. The qualifying contributions are also deducted from the employee's earnings when calculating the net sum chargeable to income tax. This effectively provides contributing employees with tax relief for payments made under the payroll deduction scheme.

Costs incurred by an employer when operating the scheme may be subtracted in calculating the employer's profit liable to taxation. In addition, relief can be obtained where the employer contributes towards the costs incurred by the charitable agency when administering the employer's scheme.

Gift Aid scheme

As a further inducement to charitable giving, a Gift Aid scheme is available. Details of the basic scheme are outlined below but the terms of a special Millennium Gift Aid arrangement are discussed later. The basic scheme encourages individuals to make lump sum donations to charity and obtain income tax relief. If the donations are to qualify the following conditions, among others, must be discharged:

a There must be a payment in money.
b The payment must not be subject to any condition leading to repayment.
c The payment must not comprise a covenanted payment to charity.
d The payment must not fall within the payroll deduction scheme.
e No benefit of any substance must be receivable by the donor in return for the donation.
f The sum paid must not be less than £250.

Where the above conditions are satisfied the donor is provided with a choice. He or she may decline to make any attempt to obtain tax relief, in which eventuality the transaction is entirely disregarded for taxation purposes. Alternatively, the individual may provide a certificate confirming that the above conditions have been satisfied and that any tax liability will be discharged. This certificate will identify the donation made as a net sum after deduction of income tax at the basic rate of 23 per cent for 1998–99. The donor must treat the payment on a basis identical to payments made under deed of covenant. The tax deemed to have been deducted can usually be retained and relief will be available at the higher rate of income tax on the gross equivalent.

86
GIFT AID SCHEME

Simon, a married man aged 42, has business profits of £75,000 assessable for 1998–99. During the year he made a single donation of £15,400 to a recognised charity. The payment satisfied the requirements of the Gift Aid scheme and a certificate was provided.

The actual payment of £15,400 must be treated as a net sum calculated as follows:

	£
Gross sum	20,000
Less Income tax at 23 per cent . .	4,600
Actual payment	£15,400

The income tax payable by Simon, assuming the full married couple's allowance can be obtained, will be calculated as follows:

	£
Total income	75,000
Less Personal allowance . . .	4,195
	£70,805
Less Gross Gift Aid	20,000
	50,805

Tax payable:
Lower rate:

On first £4,300 at 20 per cent . .	860.00
Basic rate:	
On next £22,800 at 23 per cent . .	5,244.00
Higher rate:	
On balance of £23,705 at 40 per cent .	9,482.00
	15,586.00
Less Married couple's allowance of £1,900 at 15 per cent	285.00
	15,301.00
Add tax recouped on Gift Aid . . .	4,600.00
	19,901.00

Note: Relief at the basic rate of 23 per cent is deemed to have been obtained by deduction on payment of Gift Aid. Relief at the higher rate must therefore be restricted to 17 per cent (40 per cent less 23 per cent). This is achieved by deducting £20,000 when calculating taxable income liable at 40 per cent and adding back £4,600 representing tax at 23 per cent.

Should the donor have insufficient income to absorb the gross payment he or she will be required to account to the Inland Revenue for the income tax deemed to have been deducted.

No upper limit is placed on the maximum lump sum which individuals may contribute under Gift Aid, providing the minimum of £250 is exceeded.

Company donations

Single lump sum donations made by companies are also capable of being brought within the Gift Aid scheme. It is a condition that on making such a payment a company deducts income tax at the basic rate and accounts for that tax to the Inland Revenue. The net payment actually made must not be less than £250 but there is no upper limit. A recipient charity will recover the amount of income tax deducted.

Some additional requirements must be satisfied where the company retains close company status.

As in the case of single donations made by individuals, companies are not required to apply these arrangements when making lump sum donations to a charity.

Gifts of business equipment

A novel form of relief is made available for business gifts to educational establishments. The relief can be obtained by individuals, partnerships and companies carrying on a trade. Only the transfer of 'equipment' is brought within this relief, with 'equipment' comprising plant and machinery.

Where the equipment is either manufactured or sold by the business the gift of that equipment will not require any adjustment in the calculation of trading profits. However, as the cost of the equipment, or the raw materials and other costs involved in manufacture, will be included in the computation of profits, relief for expenditure is effectively obtained. In those cases where the equipment has qualified for capital allowances, its transfer will be treated as taking place for no consideration.

The transfer must be made to a recognised educational establishment, which can include a university, polytechnic, college and school.

A variation of this relief is available under the Millennium Gift Aid scheme – see above.

Trading profits

Many trades in which charities may wish to become involved will be unable to satisfy the strict requirements outlined on page 123. As a result, trading profits will not secure immunity from taxation and indeed the existence of commercial trading operations may of itself destroy charitable status.

This problem is frequently resolved by forming one or more companies under the ownership of a particular charity. The company will trade with trading profits becoming chargeable to corporation tax in the usual manner. However, each company will enter into a deed of covenant with the charity, requiring payments equal to the amount of profits. The result is that in theory the amount of a qualifying covenanted payment will offset trading profits and no corporation tax will be due. The difficulty with this arrangement, at earlier times, was that if a charitable payment was to be included in calculations for a company's accounting period it had to be paid in that period. In many situations it was not possible to assess the amount of profits realised by a company in an accounting period until a date falling after the end of that period. This often required initial payments to be made based on guesswork, with any further payments being discharged in the following accounting period.

Although the basic requirement remains that payments should be made during an accounting period if they are to be offset against profits for that period, a substantial relaxation was introduced for qualifying payments made by a company in an accounting period commencing on or after 1 April 1997. This relaxation is available where:

a A covenanted donation is made to a charity by a company which is wholly owned by that charity;
b The payment is made after deducting income tax at the basic rate;
c The covenant under which the donation is made required payment to be undertaken in an accounting period ending before the time of payment; and
d The payment is made within nine months following the end of the earlier period.

Where these requirements are discharged the payment may be treated as made in the earlier accounting period. The broad effect of this relaxation is that it is now possible for a payment to be made within a period of nine months following the end of an accounting period and treated as discharged in that earlier period. This enables the profit figure on which the payment may be based to be accurately determined.

Company dividends
Most United Kingdom company dividends received by a charity during 1998–99 will have tax credits attached of one-quarter. Therefore, a charity receiving a cash dividend of £80 may expect to recover the tax credit of £20, which effectively increases the amount of the distribution to £100.

The ability to recover tax credits in this manner will no longer apply on and after 6 April 1999. It is

therefore apparent that charities receiving a substantial part of their income in the form of dividends from United Kingdom companies will suffer a considerable fall in financial returns.

In recognition of this fall, special payments can be made to charities based on the amount of actual dividend income received in a five-year period. Payments will be based on the amounts received, as follows:

Year of assessment	Per cent
Year to 5 April 2000	21
Year to 5 April 2001	17
Year to 5 April 2002	13
Year to 5 April 2003	8
Year to 5 April 2004	4

The phasing out process will therefore terminate on 5 April 2004. No further payments will be made subsequently.

The special payments fall outside the tax system and have no effect whatsoever on companies paying the dividends involved.

Some dividends paid by United Kingdom companies are treated as foreign income dividends. Distributions of this nature do not retain any tax credit, or indeed tax deduction capable of being reclaimed by a charity.

MILLENNIUM GIFT AID
A special group of arrangements under the general heading of 'Millennium Gift Aid' is being introduced to support education and anti-poverty projects in more than sixty of the world's poorest countries. The arrangements will extend from late in the calendar year 1998 to 31 December 2000. Some existing United Kingdom charities will administer the arrangements and further details must await publication on a later date. However, it is intended that two existing reliefs will be modified.

Gift Aid
Individuals may adopt arrangements similar to those made available under the basic Gift Aid scheme but with the minimum donation reduced to amounts in excess of £100 (and not £250 which otherwise applies). It is also proposed that where smaller gifts are made by instalment these will be brought within the scheme once the aggregate instalments exceed £100.

Gifts of business equipment
Gifts of business equipment made to a recognised educational establishment attract the relief outlined

on page 125. Under the millennium arrangements the scheme will be extended to gifts made for the purpose of assisting educational projects within the list of poorer countries.

Other reliefs

Wide-ranging reliefs from capital gains tax and inheritance tax are also available where assets are transferred to charitable bodies.

16

Husband and wife

Marriage

FOR THE YEAR of assessment in which a couple marry, each will receive the normal personal allowance, suitably increased for those over the age of 64.

A married couple's allowance of £1,900 will be available for 1998–99 if the ceremony takes place before 6 May 1998. The married couple's allowance may be increased to some higher figure for those over the age of 64 or 74 years.

However, the amount of the married couple's allowance will be reduced by one-twelfth for each complete month after 5 April until the date of marriage where the event occurs on or after 6 May 1998.

87
RESTRICTED MARRIED COUPLE'S ALLOWANCE

Janet and Michael, both aged 24, were married on 14 November 1998. The married couple's allowance for 1998–99 is £792, calculated as follows:

	£
Full married couple's allowance	1,900
Deduct period before marriage 7/12ths of £1,900	1,108
Married couple's allowance available.	£792

In addition, each individual will obtain a full year's personal allowance of £4,195.

88
YEAR OF MARRIAGE

Mark and Sarah were married on 19 October 1997. Mark earns a salary of £19,500 per annum and Sarah £10,300 per annum. Mark is to obtain the full married couple's allowance. The tax payable for 1998–99 is calculated as follows:

Mark		£
Total income	. . .	19,500
Less Personal allowance	. . .	4,195
		£15,305
Tax payable:		
On first £4,300 at 20 per cent	. .	860.00
On balance of £11,005 at 23 per cent		2,531.15
		3,391.15

Less Married couple's allowance:			
Maximum . . .	1,900		
Deduct period before marriage (one-half of £1,900). . .	950		
Leaving £950 at 15 per cent	. .		142.50
			£3,248.65

Sarah		£
Total income	. . .	10,300
Less Personal allowance	. . .	4,195
		£6,105
Tax payable:		
On first £4,300 at 20 per cent	.	860.00
On balance of £1,805 at 23 per cent		415.15
		£1,275.15

In those cases where the amount of the increased married couple's allowance for older persons must be restricted by reason of the husband's income exceeding £16,200, the restriction must firstly be applied. The one-twelfth limitation will then be made to the reduced married couple's allowance only.

It is possible that the husband will be entitled to the additional personal allowance for a child or children in the year of marriage. He must then choose whether to retain that allowance or abandon the allowance and obtain the married couple's allowance. This choice applies for the year of marriage only. Whilst the additional personal allowance will usually be greater, when making the choice it should not be overlooked that any part of this allowance which cannot be used by the husband is incapable of being transferred to the wife. In contrast, any unused part of the married couple's allowance can be transferred.

The wife may retain the additional personal allowance for the year of marriage if the qualifying child was resident with her before the ceremony took place. Any unused blind person's allowance can be transferred between the couple in that year.

It is possible that a married man already entitled to the married couple's allowance for a year of assessment re-marries in the same year, perhaps following the death of his first wife. In such a situation there will be no restriction to the married couple's allowance, which may be obtained in full. However, only one married couple's allowance can be obtained and not a separate allowance for each wife.

Although a husband may have more than one wife as permitted by his religious or other beliefs, only a single married couple's allowance will be available for each year.

The wife may elect to obtain one-half of the basic married couple's allowance. In addition, husband and wife may jointly elect that the entire basic allowance should be transferred to the wife (see page 17). Either election must be made during the year of marriage, if it is to apply for that year.

Death of spouse

WHERE A HUSBAND and wife are 'living together' and the husband dies, no apportionment of allowances is made. A full year's personal allowance will be granted when calculating the liability of the deceased husband. In addition, a full year's married couple's allowance will be available. It is possible for the personal representatives administering the estate of the deceased husband to transfer any unused married couple's allowance for 1998–99 to the surviving widow.

In the year of her husband's death the widow will obtain the normal personal allowance. In addition, she will qualify for a widow's bereavement allowance. This allowance will be available for the following year also, unless she re-marries in the year of her late husband's death. If the widow has a qualifying child she should be entitled to receive the additional personal allowance.

On the death of his wife the surviving widower is entitled to a full year's married couple's allowance for the year in which death occurs, unless an election has been made to transfer any part of that allowance to the wife. The allowance will not be available for later years unless the widower re-marries. While a widow may obtain a widow's bereavement allowance, usually for two consecutive years, no similar allowance is available to a widower.

Although tax return forms are usually issued during the month of April, the Inland Revenue will, on receiving a request from personal representatives administering the estate of a deceased person, issue forms at an earlier date. This avoids the delay which may otherwise arise when dealing with the deceased's estate. An additional facility available to personal representatives is that the Inland Revenue are prepared to confirm, where appropriate, at an early date that no enquiries are being made into a tax return relating to the deceased's estate. This avoids the delay, which can extend throughout a full twelve months, where the Revenue may select the return for an enquiry.

PENSIONERS AND ELDERLY PERSONS
Pensioners and elderly persons are liable to tax in exactly the same manner as other individuals but the increased personal allowance and increased married couple's allowance mentioned on pages 14 and 15 may be available to those who are in receipt of income falling below, or not substantially exceeding, £16,200 for 1998–99.

Retirement pensions payable under the state scheme and those received from a former employer are subject to tax. A state retirement pension received by a married woman is treated as her income, whether or not it arises from contributions made by the wife or by her husband. Where only small sums of tax are involved on retirement pensions and other income the Inland Revenue may refrain from collecting the amount of tax due (see page 53).

89
DEATH OF HUSBAND

Mr and Mrs G had been married for many years but the husband died on 3 September 1998. Income assessable in 1998–99 was as follows:

Before death

Mr G

	£
Earnings	12,200

Mrs G

Earnings	5,500
Income from letting property . .	450

After death

Mrs G

	£
Pension and taxable social security benefits	5,800
Earnings	6,700
Income from letting property . .	800

Neither individual was over the age of 64 and no election had been made to transfer the married couple's allowance.

Tax payable will be calculated as follows:

Deceased husband (to date of death)

Total income:	£
Own earnings . . .	12,200
Less Personal allowance . . .	4,195
	£8,005

Tax payable:

On first £4,300 at 20 per cent . .	860.00
On balance of £3,705 at 23 per cent	852.15
	1,712.15
Less Married couple's allowance –	
£1,900 at 15 per cent . . .	285.00
	£1,427.15

Mrs G

Total income:	£
Pension and social security benefits	5,800
Own earnings (£5,500 + £6,700) .	12,200
Own property income (£450 + £800)	1,250
	19,250
Less Personal allowance . . .	4,195
	£15,055

Tax payable:

On first £4,300 at 20 per cent . .	860.00
On balance of £10,755 at 23 per cent	2,473.65
	3,333.65
Less Widow's bereavement allowance –	
£1,900 at 15 per cent . . .	285.00
	£3,048.65

CHILDREN'S INCOME

Income accruing to a child will not usually be treated as that of the child's parents. Special rules apply, however, where a parent creates a settlement for, or makes gifts to, such a child. Income arising from the settlement or gift may then be treated as that of the parent until the child reaches the age of 18 or marries, whichever event first occurs. This only arises if the income exceeds £100 in 1998–99.

A minor child can obtain the benefit of a personal allowance of £4,195 for 1998–99 if income received is properly chargeable to income tax as the child's income.

Divorce and separation

MARRIAGE BREAKDOWN

Where a husband and wife are separated by deed of separation, under an order of a court of competent jurisdiction, or are in fact separated in such circumstances that the separation is likely to be permanent, the couple will be treated as not 'living together' for income tax purposes. The loss of the 'living together' status may affect the future availability of allowances. It may also have some application for capital gains tax purposes on the treatment of assets transferred between the parties.

Year of separation

For the year of assessment in which separation occurs a full year's married couple's allowance is available. There will be no reduction in the amount of the allowance, providing the couple were 'living together' at some time during the year. It will remain possible for the husband to transfer any unused part of the married couple's allowance to his separated wife for the year of separation.

The wife will receive the normal personal allowance for 1998–99, perhaps increased to some higher amount if she is over the age of 64. In addition, where a wife has a qualifying child living with her after the date of separation, she may obtain the additional personal allowance of £1,900.

Exceptionally, a husband who was separated from his wife on 5 April 1990 may obtain the married couple's allowance if he is wholly maintaining her but obtains no tax relief for his outlay (see page 22).

90
YEAR OF SEPARATION

Mr and Mrs H, both in their thirties, were living together until July 1998 when they permanently separated. There were two children, aged 10 and 7 years, who continued to reside with their mother after the separation. Both parents were employed, with Mr H receiving earnings of £25,000 and his wife earnings of £11,600 in 1998–99. No maintenance payments were made and the husband was entitled to the full married couple's allowance.

The tax payable by Mr H for 1998–99 will be:

	£
Total income	25,000
Less Personal allowance . . .	4,195
	£20,805
Tax payable:	
On first £4,300 at 20 per cent . .	860.00
On balance of £16,505 at 23 per cent .	3,796.15
	4,656.15
Less Married couple's allowance of £1,900 at 15 per cent . . .	285.00
	£4,371.15

The tax payable by Mrs H becomes:

	£
Total income	11,600
Less Personal allowance . . .	4,195
	£7,405
Tax payable:	
On first £4,300 at 20 per cent . .	860.00
On balance of £3,105 at 23 per cent .	714.15
	1,574.15
Less Additional personal allowance of £1,900 at 15 per cent . . .	285.00
	£1,289.15

As the husband was living with his wife during part of the year, a full year's married couple's allowance is available. The wife can obtain the additional personal allowance as she has at least one qualifying child.

MAINTENANCE PAYMENTS

Payments will frequently be made by a husband to his separated wife, or by a former husband to his divorced former wife, under a binding legal agreement recorded in a separation deed or similar docu-ment or under the terms of a United Kingdom court order. Occasionally such payments may be made by a separated or divorced former wife to her husband or former husband. The nature and treatment of these and other payments for taxation purposes will be governed by the date on which the order or agreement was concluded. It is therefore necessary to examine separately:

a Payments made under 'old' orders and agree-ments, and

b Payments made under 'new' orders and agree-ments.

OLD ORDERS AND AGREEMENTS

The first group incorporates payments under:

a Court orders made before 15 March 1988;

b Court orders applied for before 16 March 1988 and made not later than 30 June in the same year;

c Maintenance agreements made before 15 March 1988; and

d Court orders or maintenance agreements made on or after 15 March 1988 which vary or replace earlier orders or agreements.

The maintenance agreements referred to in **c** and **d** must be binding documents concluded between the parties. Not only is it necessary for these agree-ments to have existed before 15 March 1988 but they must also have been examined by HM Inspector of Taxes not later than 30 June in the same year if they are to be recognised for taxation purposes. Failure to have achieved recognition destroys relief for subsequent payments.

To obtain relief for payments in 1998–99 under 'old' orders or agreements it must be shown that the payments were made:

a To one of the parties of a marriage, including a marriage which has been dissolved or annulled, to or for the benefit of the other party to the marriage and for the maintenance of the other party; or

b To any person under 21 years of age for his own benefit, maintenance or education; or

c To any person for the benefit, maintenance or education of a person under 21 years of age.

All payments falling in the 'old' group will be made gross without deducting income tax.

The payer will obtain income tax relief for pay-ments made in each year of assessment up to an amount not exceeding the payments qualifying for

———91———
PAYMENTS UNDER 'OLD' ORDERS

A husband and wife were divorced in 1983. Under the terms of a pre-1988 court order the former husband was required to discharge maintenance at the rate of £7,000 per annum, payable monthly. He remains unmarried and his income for 1998–99 was £32,000. The former wife had no other income.

The aggregate maintenance payments of £7,000 must be broken down into two parts, namely:

a the first £1,900, and

b the excess of £5,100.

The tax liability of the former husband may now be calculated as follows:

	£	£
Total income . . .		32,000
Less Personal allowance .	4,195	
Excess maintenance payments . . .	5,100	9,295
		£22,705

Tax payable:

On first £4,300 at 20 per cent . .		860.00
On balance of £18,405 at 23 per cent		4,233.15
		5,093.15
Less Maintenance payments – first £1,900 at 15 per cent		285.00
		£4,808.15

The tax liability of the former wife becomes:

	£
Total income	7,000
Less Exempt	1,900
	5,100
Less Personal allowance . . .	4,195
	£905

Tax payable:

On £905 at 20 per cent . . .	£181.00

relief in 1988–89 (twelve months ending on 5 April 1989). These limits will take account of any amending court order or agreement made before 6 April 1989, but subject to this any future increase will not obtain relief.

Relief for the first £1,900 of any maintenance payments made in 1998–99 is restricted to the reduced rate of 15 per cent. The product of the 15 per cent calculation is subtracted from the amount of income tax otherwise payable. If, or to the extent that, payments exceed £1,900 the excess is subtracted from total income and attracts relief at the taxpayer's highest rate of tax suffered.

The reason for the restriction based on £1,900 is to align relief for maintenance payments with that obtained by the married couple's allowance.

The first £1,900 of maintenance payments received in 1998–99 is exempt from liability to income tax. Only the excess, if any, will be treated as income on which the recipient is required to suffer income tax in the normal manner.

Where payments are being made under these 'old' arrangements an election may be submitted to adopt the 'new' rules outlined below. This election could be beneficial where the level of payments made in 1988–89 is less than the married couple's allowance for a future year.

For payments made after 5 April 1999 relief at the reduced rate of 15 per cent becomes a mere 10 per cent. This follows a similar reduction in relief for the married couple's allowance which takes effect at the same time.

NEW ORDERS AND AGREEMENTS

The second group incorporates payments made under 'new' court orders and maintenance agreements concluded after 14 March 1988 other than:

a Court orders applied for before 16 March 1988 and made not later than 30 June in the same year; and

b Court orders or maintenance agreements varying orders or agreements made before 15 March 1988 or falling within **a**.

It is a requirement that payments are made by a spouse or former spouse:

a to or for the benefit of the separated spouse or divorced former spouse for the maintenance of the recipient; or

b to the separated spouse or divorced former spouse for the maintenance by the recipient of any child of the family.

All payments made under orders and agreements of this nature will be discharged gross in 1998–99 without deducting income tax.

The payer will obtain income tax relief on the smaller of:

a the actual payments made in 1998–99; and

b £1,900, which is equal to the basic married couple's allowance for the year.

This relief continues to apply, subject to an adjustment for any changes in the basic married couple's allowance, until the recipient re-marries, if at all. In the somewhat unusual case where an

—92— VARIATION OF 'OLD' ORDER

Using the basic facts in Example 91, let it be assumed that in September 1988 the former wife obtained an order increasing the periodic payments to £9,600 per annum, with the first revised payment falling due in October of that year.

The payments actually made by the former husband in 1988–89 became:

				£
To the date of change .	.	.	.	3,600
From the date of change	.	.	.	4,800
				£8,400

The aggregate amount payable in 1988–89, namely £8,400, will establish the maximum amount which can be recognised for future years. For 1998–99 relief for the first £1,900 will be restricted to 15 per cent, with the balance of £6,500 obtaining relief at the top rate suffered. The revised calculation of tax payable then becomes:

Former husband

	£	£
Total income		32,000
Less Personal allowance . .	4,195	
Excess maintenance payments . .	6,500	10,695
		£21,305

Tax payable:

On first £4,300 at 20 per cent	.	.	860.00
On balance of £17,005 at 23 per cent	.		3,911.15
			4,771.15
Less Maintenance payments – first £1,900 at 15 per cent . . .	.		285.00
			£4,486.15

Former wife

Total income:	£
Maintenance payments – restricted .	8,400
Less Exempt	1,900
	6,500
Less Personal allowance . .	4,195
	£2,305

Tax payable:

On £2,305 at 20 per cent . . .	£461.00

Although the actual maintenance payments made in 1998–99 were greater than £8,400 the amount in excess of payments due in 1988–89 must be disregarded.

—93— PAYMENTS UNDER 'NEW' ORDERS

Norman separated from his wife in 1990. Under a court order made on 12 August 1990, Norman was required to make monthly payments of £500 to his separated wife; the first payment falling due on 15 August 1990. Norman received a salary of £29,000 for 1998–99 but his separated wife received no other income.

Payments made under the court order in 1998–99 will aggregate £6,000 (12 × £500). Norman will obtain relief on only £1,900, which is less than the payments made. His liability for 1998–99 then becomes

				£
Total income				29,000
Less Personal allowance . .				4,195
				£24,805

Tax payable:

On first £4,300 at 20 per cent	.	.	860.00
On balance of £20,505 at 23 per cent	.		4,716.15
			5,576.15
Less Maintenance payments – £1,900 at 15 per cent . .	.		285.00
			£5,291.15

The separated wife has no taxable income as the payments received from her husband are ignored. There is no liability to tax, nor can the wife obtain any tax repayment as no tax has been suffered by deduction.

individual is making payments to more than one divorced former spouse or separated spouse all payments must be aggregated when establishing the £1,900 limitation.

Apart from limited relief where payments are made to a divorced former spouse or a separated spouse, no other tax relief whatsoever will be available to the payer. It follows that relief cannot be obtained for payments made to a child or those falling due under an affiliation order.

Relief on £1,900, or some lower figure, is given at the reduced rate of 15 per cent for 1998–99. It is not subtracted when calculating income but deducted from income tax otherwise payable. For payments after 5 April 1999 the rate of 15 per cent is reduced to a mere 10 per cent.

In the case of all payments falling within the second group and made under a court order or maintenance agreement, the recipient is immune from any taxation liability.

CHILD SUPPORT AGENCY

The Child Support Agency is responsible for a great deal of work associated with child maintenance.

Included in this work is the collection of certain maintenance payments which are then forwarded to the person entitled. This function will not affect the treatment of maintenance payments for tax purposes, notwithstanding the involvement of an 'intermediary'.

RECONCILIATION

It is possible that a separated couple achieve a reconciliation. For the year of assessment in which this occurs a full year's married couple's allowance will be available.

17

Tax Returns and Administration

There are many matters related to compliance and administration which must be resolved before the tax affairs of an individual can be fairly dealt with. The chapter commencing on page 1 outlined the requirement to complete a tax return form following the introduction of self-assessment and also reviewed the dates on which both income tax and capital gains tax must be paid. There are a number of other matters which loosely fall under the heading of 'administration' and for convenience these have been gathered together in the present chapter.

THE TAX RETURN
A completed tax return form is central to the recently introduced system of self-assessment. Information recorded on the return will be inserted by the taxpayer and must reflect a proper view of his or her affairs for the year of assessment to which the return relates. It is this information which will be received by the Inland Revenue and used to calculate the amount of income tax and capital gains tax due when the return is submitted not later than 30 September. Subsequent returns, which should be submitted not later than the following 31 January, will have attached the taxpayer's calculations of any income tax and capital gains tax due. Information disclosed by a fully completed tax return will initially be accepted by the Inland Revenue. A detailed examination will then be undertaken and this may result in the commencement of an enquiry into the taxpayer's affairs.

Returns which have not been fully completed will usually be sent back to the taxpayer for any oversight or failure to be remedied. It is therefore in the taxpayer's interest to ensure that before any tax return is submitted to the Inland Revenue, steps are taken to establish the accuracy of all information which may be recorded.

The tax return guide
A tax return guide should be received together with the tax return form. Most documents of this nature are issued by the Inland Revenue during the month of April following the end of the previous year of assessment on 5 April. Before attempting to complete the return reference should be made to the guide which contains a great deal of helpful information.

Supplementary pages
The basic tax return forwarded to individuals is a document of some eight pages. In addition, there are a number of supplementary pages which may require completion. The purpose of these supplementary pages is to ensure that the basic tax return is not overburdened by the inclusion of material which will not be relevant to many taxpayers.

Page 2 of the basic tax return lists the several supplementary pages. 'Yes' and 'No' boxes are shown against each supplementary page and it is for the taxpayer to tick the appropriate box. Should the 'Yes' box be ticked in one or more places the supplementary page, or pages, should be obtained and completed before proceeding to the rest of the basic return. Where the appropriate supplementary page has not been received, a telephone call to the relevant Inland Revenue office will rapidly remedy the position.

Brief details of the supplementary pages and the information which should be inserted are given below.

Employment
Details of an employment should be inserted, together with a note of income received, taxable benefits and expenses. In addition, details of any lump sum payments will be shown. A separate supplementary 'Employment' page will require completion where there are two or more employments.

Share schemes
Details of any share schemes, including the issue of shares and the exercise of option rights, need to be inserted.

Self-employment
Individuals who are self-employed must complete a detailed statement of income and outgoings where turnover exceeds £15,000. Any capital allowances will be shown, together with claims for loss relief. Businesses having a balance sheet will complete details of assets and liabilities. Where the annual turnover falls below £15,000 a simple entry will suffice.

Partnership
Individuals carrying on business in partnership will insert details of their partnership shares. This includes profits, chargeable gains and any other matter which may be relevant. It will not be overlooked that, in addition, a separate partnership return will have to be completed by a representative of the partnership.

Land and property
A detailed profit statement of rents and other receipts, together with outgoings, is required. Where furnished holiday lettings are involved a separate statement is necessary.

Foreign
Interest, dividends, pensions and other income from overseas will be inserted. Deductions for foreign tax suffered, which affects both income tax and capital gains tax, will also need to be shown.

Trusts
Those individuals receiving income from trusts and settlements will insert the appropriate details. This supplementary page is also used for recording income received from the estate of a deceased person.

Capital gains
Details of capital gains and any capital losses will need to be recorded.

Residence
This supplementary page is used where an individual claims that he or she is not resident, not ordinarily resident or not domiciled in the United Kingdom. Further details relating to the residential status may also be required.

The basic return
Once any supplementary pages have been fully completed it is time to turn to the remaining part of the basic tax return. This part is broken down into a number of sections, each commencing with a question requiring a tick against 'Yes' or 'No'. Where the response is 'yes' details must be shown. These details relate to such matters as interest and dividends received, pensions and social security receipts, together with other information. Further sections involve claims for a range of reliefs and also details needed to obtain allowances.

Those taxpayers requiring to calculate their own income tax or capital gains tax will insert the appropriate details and complete a calculation form. A claim may also be submitted for a repayment of tax, where excessive tax has been suffered.

Dealing with pence
Income, together with tax deducted from interest and tax credits attaching to dividends, will rarely arise in exact pounds. This could create uncertainty when completing a tax return as taxpayers are encouraged to ignore pence and insert only complete pounds. However, the Inland Revenue will accept that income or gains should be rounded down by ignoring odd pence. In contrast, tax deducted and tax credits should be rounded up to the next complete pound. Where there are two or more similar items, for example, two or more dividend receipts or two or more receipts of interest, it is the aggregate

94
ROUNDING FIGURES

Karen received a dividend of £34.60 with a tax credit of £8.65. This was the only dividend received during 1997–98. The amounts entered on the tax return will be:

Dividend	Tax credit	Dividend plus tax credit
£34	£9	£43

If Karen had received several dividends aggregating £237.40, with tax credits totalling £59.35, the entry would be:

Dividend	Tax credit	Dividend plus tax credit
£237	£60	£297

Rounding must be applied to the aggregate sum and not to each dividend separately.

---

figure which should be subjected to the rounding process and not each item.

The completed return

Once the return has been fully completed and the appropriate supplementary page, or pages, attached, it only remains to sign and date the declaration before submitting the document to the Inland Revenue.

Partnerships, trustees and persons administering the estate of a deceased person are also required to submit tax returns. Here also, returns may be submitted not later than 30 September where the Inland Revenue are required to calculate tax due, or by the following 31 January should the calculation be completed by the taxpayer.

At first glance the tax return form may appear to represent a somewhat daunting document. In some situations taxpayers with complex tax affairs will require the services of professionals to assist with the completion work. Others who are content to undertake completion themselves should carefully read both the tax return guide and the tax return before proceeding.

Common errors

It is found that a not insignificant number of returns contain fundamental errors and have to be sent back to the taxpayer by the Inland Revenue. Among the more common errors are the following:

a Failure to sign and date a return.
b Failure to complete page 2, dealing with supplementary pages.
c Failure to enclose supplementary pages.
d Failure to fully complete supplementary pages, particularly those dealing with self-assessment and land and property.
e Failure to tick the 'Yes' or 'No' box at the commencement of each section in the basic return.
f Failure to distinguish between 'gross' and 'net' interest and dividends. For example, reading from left to right, the interest section requires:

Amount of tax deducted	Tax deducted	Gross amount before tax

In the case of dividends, the sequence, again from left to right, reads:

Dividend	Tax credit	Dividend plus credit

Should the wrong sequence be followed confusion is inevitable.

Recognition that errors of this nature do arise may help others to avoid the same pitfalls.

Date of delivery

Completed tax returns must be 'delivered' to the Inland Revenue by a specified date, usually 30 September or 31 January following the end of the year of assessment to which they relate. This implies the date a return is received and not that on which it may be posted. In those situations where the appropriate Inland Revenue office is closed on the specified date, usually at weekends, a return received immediately the office reopens should be treated as delivered on the day of closure.

DATE OF PAYMENT

Should the payment of tax be made after the due date a liability to interest, and perhaps surcharges, may well arise. It is therefore necessary to identify the effective date of payment.

Where payment is made by cheque, cash or postal order handed in at an Inland Revenue office, or received by post, the day of receipt by the Inland Revenue will identify the date of payment. However, where a payment of this nature is received by post following the day on which an Inland Revenue office has been closed, the date of payment will be that on which the office was first closed or, for payments received on a Monday, the effective date will be the previous Saturday.

Payments made by electronic transfer will be treated as made one working day immediately before the date that the value is received.

Finally, payments by Bank Giro or Girobank are treated as received three working days prior to the date of processing by the Inland Revenue.

REPAYMENT OF TAX SUFFERED

Some items of investment income are received after deduction of income tax at the lower rate of 20 per cent for 1998–99. These may include interest on building society and bank deposits, although many depositors not liable to income tax may arrange to receive interest gross. Other examples of income received after deduction of income tax include interest on some Government securities and also certain annuities. Income tax is not strictly deducted from dividends paid by United Kingdom companies but for 1998–99 each dividend has a tax credit equal to one-quarter of the sum received, which effectively represents income tax at the rate of 20 per cent on the aggregate amount.

Where tax has been suffered by deduction, or a tax credit is available, it may be possible to obtain a complete or partial repayment. This may arise where the recipient has insufficient income and does not receive the full benefit of personal and other allowances, or is not fully liable to tax on the amount deducted or that treated as deducted. Repayment situations are not confined to income tax suffered on investment income but may arise where excessive deductions have been made under the PAYE scheme, where there are claims for loss relief or claims are submitted for some other relief.

Stringent time limits apply for submitting claims and elections and there is a wide range of different limits which must be observed. However, claims for the repayment of income tax suffered may be forwarded within a period of six years following the end of the year of assessment to which the claim relates or by 31 January falling some five years and ten months after the end of the year in the case of

---

— 95 —
REPAYMENT CLAIM

The total income of Robin, a widower aged 72, for 1998–99, was as follows:

	£	£
State retirement pension . .		3,364
Dividends received . . .	960	
Add Tax credits at 1/4th . .	240	
		1,200
Total income		£4,564

The taxpayer is entitled to a personal allowance of £5,410 and as total income does not exceed this amount no tax is due. The tax credits of £240 on dividends received may be reclaimed from the Inland Revenue.

— 96 —
REPAYMENT CLAIM

Gwen is a single woman aged 58. She receives an annuity (not being a purchased life annuity) of £9,000 (tax deducted £2,070), building society interest of £600 (tax deducted £120) and cash dividends of £1,200 for 1998–99.

Total income:		£	£
Annuity (gross)			9,000
Building society interest (gross) . .			600
Dividends received . . .		1,200	
Add Tax credits at 1/4th . .		300	1,500
			11,100
Less Personal allowance			4,195
			£6,905

Tax payable:		£
On first £4,300 at 20 per cent . .		860.00
On next £505 at 23 per cent . . .		116.15
On dividends and interest of £2,100 at 20 per cent		420.00
		1,396.15
Less		
Tax on annuity . . .	2,070.00	
Tax credits . . .	300.00	
Tax on interest . . .	120.00	
		2,490.00
Repayment due		£1,093.85

1996–97 and later years. Before contemplating future repayment claims the claimant should consider whether it is possible to arrange for interest to be received 'gross', or indeed that a claim for repayment is justified.

Repayment claims relating to 1996–97 and later years may be included in a tax return form. In theory, this form need not be completed and delivered until 31 January following the end of the year of assessment. However, individuals entitled to repayment may well be able to submit fully completed returns on a much earlier date. This should enable the repayment procedure to commence without undue delay.

If a taxpayer who is entitled to a repayment does not receive a tax return form for completion he or she should contact the local Inland Revenue office without delay.

The effect of claims for the repayment of tax suffered by deduction in 1998–99 is shown by examples on the following page.

Dividends received after 5 April 1999 will no longer have any tax credit attached and available for

— 97 —
REPAYMENT CLAIM

Ralph, a married man entitled to the full married couple's allowance, receives interest on investments of £2,400 gross (tax deducted £480) in 1998–99. He has National Savings Bank interest of £90 on an ordinary deposit account, National Savings Income Bonds interest (paid gross) of £275 and business profits of £4,380 chargeable in the same year.

	£	£
Total income:		
Business profits		4,380
Investment income (gross) . . .		2,400
National Savings Bank interest	90	
Less Exempted . . .	70	
		20
Income Bond interest		275
		7,075
Less Personal allowance . . .		4,195
		£2,880
Tax payable:		
On £2,880 at 20 per cent . . .		576.00
Less Married couple's allowance -£1,900		
at 15 per cent		285.00
		291.00
Less Tax suffered by deduction . .		480.00
Repayment due		£189.00

repayment unless they arise from an Individual Savings Account or Personal Equity Plan. This will inevitably reduce the number of repayment claims.

REPAYMENT SUPPLEMENT
Where a repayment of income tax or capital gains tax has been claimed there may also be an entitlement to a repayment supplement. At earlier times, this entitlement did not arise unless the repayment occurred more than twelve months following the end of the year of assessment in which the original payment was made. However, the position is otherwise for repayments of income tax and capital gains tax attributable to payments made after the inception of self-assessment on 6 April 1996. As a result, the repayment supplement will be calculated from the date on which the original tax was paid, notwithstanding that that payment may have been made in advance, in arrears or on the normal due date. This relaxation does not extend to tax deducted at source, namely under the PAYE scheme or to tax credits on dividends.

The rate at which the repayment supplement falls due has been amended from time to time. The table below records the rates used in the last six years. The formula which applies to determine these rates was amended on 5 February 1997. One effect of this amendment was to reduce the rate at which the repayment supplement has been payable subsequently.

REPAYMENT SUPPLEMENT		
From	**To**	**Per cent**
6 October 1991	5 November 1992	9.25
6 November 1992	5 December 1992	7.75
6 December 1992	5 March 1993	7
6 March 1993	5 January 1994	6.25
6 January 1994	5 October 1994	5.5
6 October 1994	5 March 1995	6.25
6 March 1995	5 February 1996	7
6 February 1996	5 February 1997	6.25
6 February 1997	5 August 1997	4
6 August 1997		4.75

SCHEDULES AND CASES
To facilitate the collection of income tax each source of income is allocated to a Schedule. The scope of each Schedule is given below but it must be borne in mind that there is only one income tax and the use of the various Schedules in no way affects this principle.

Schedule	Source of income includes
A	Income from land and property in the United Kingdom.
B	Previously woodlands managed on a commercial basis and with a view to the realisation of profit but this Schedule has now been abolished.
C	Previously interest and dividends on Government or public authority funds and certain payments made out of the Public Revenues of overseas countries but this schedule also has been abolished.
D	This Schedule is divided into the following Cases: Case I – trades; Case II – professions and vocations; Case III – interest, annuities, annual payments and discounts; Case IV – securities located outside the United Kingdom; Case V – possessions located outside

the United Kingdom;

Case VI – annual profits or gains not chargeable under any other Case or Schedule.

E This Schedule includes three Cases and extends to emoluments from offices and employments of profit and also to pensions arising in the United Kingdom.

F Company distributions.

Case IV of Schedule D now has no application to companies.

INCOME LIABLE TO ASSESSMENT

In general, liability to United Kingdom income tax extends to all income arising in England, Scotland, Wales and Northern Ireland. Additionally, individuals who are regarded as resident in the United Kingdom are usually liable to income tax on income arising overseas. However, in the case of individuals resident in the United Kingdom but either domiciled abroad, or, being British subjects, ordinarily resident abroad, only overseas income actually remitted to, or received in, the United Kingdom will suffer income tax.

RESIDENCE

Liability to United Kingdom income tax may arise on overseas income if an individual becomes resident here and this is of particular importance to visitors and other persons whose stay is only intended to be temporary. In the absence of residence no part of the visitor's income arising overseas will be subject to United Kingdom taxation, whether remitted here or retained abroad.

A visitor is regarded as resident for any income tax year (commencing on 6 April) if he or she is present in the United Kingdom for periods amounting to six months or more during that year. There are no exceptions to this rule.

Difficult cases arise where an individual is in the United Kingdom for a period falling short of six months, but if visits are made year after year, and are for substantial periods, residence will be acquired. For this purpose visits are usually regarded as substantial if they average three months or more per annum over a four-year period. When establishing the duration of visits for this purpose, days spent in the United Kingdom which were beyond the individual's control may be ignored. This may arise in the case of illness and also in the case of individuals affected by the outbreak of hostilities overseas. Where an individual comes to the United Kingdom to commence permanent residence or with the intention of remaining

for at least three years, he or she will be treated as becoming resident from the date of arrival.

An individual's status of residence strictly applies throughout a full year of assessment. It is not possible to be resident for part only of a tax year. In practice, however, where an individual comes to the United Kingdom to take up permanent residence, or to stay for at least two years, the year may be split with residence commencing on the date of arrival. A similar approach is adopted where an individual leaves the United Kingdom and ceases to be both resident and ordinarily resident in this territory.

The residence status of a wife must be determined separately from that of her husband. However, where the husband leaves the United Kingdom to take up employment overseas and is accompanied by his wife at or about the time of departure, the residential status of the husband may be adopted by the wife also.

The significance of 'splitting' a year of assessment is that certain items of income arising in the 'non-resident period' may be exempt from United Kingdom taxation.

REMISSION OF TAX

By concession, the collection of arrears of income tax or capital gains tax may be waived where those arrears have arisen through the failure of the Inland Revenue to make proper and timely use of information supplied by:

a The taxpayer about his or her own income, gains or personal circumstances;

b An employer, where the information affects the taxpayer's coding; or

c The Department of Social Security, where the information affects a taxpayer's entitlement to the State retirement, disability or widow's pension.

However, the concession will normally be given only where the taxpayer:

a Could reasonably have believed that his or her tax affairs were in order; and

b Was notified of the arrears more than twelve months after the end of the tax year in which the Inland Revenue received the information indicating that more tax was due; or

c Was notified of an over-repayment after the end of the tax year following the year in which the repayment was made.

In exceptional circumstances arrears of tax notified twelve months or less after the end of the relevant tax year may be waived if the Inland Revenue:

a Failed more than once to make proper use of the

facts they had been given about one source of income; or

b Allowed the arrears to build up over two whole tax years in succession by failing to make proper and timely use of information they had been given.

Previously, the amount of tax waived was governed by the gross income of the taxpayer. However, this approach ceased to apply on 11 March 1996 and it follows that all taxpayers, whatever their level of income, are now treated on an identical basis where the collection of outstanding tax is attributable to a failure to make use of information. Taxpayers seeking remission of tax should not disregard the requirement that they 'reasonably believed' their affairs to be in order.

INTEREST AND PENALTIES

Failure to discharge, or to disclose, tax liabilities promptly may have serious repercussions resulting in an obligation to satisfy interest and penalties. The law on this subject is extremely complex and the comments made below provide little more than broad guidelines. In particular some different, or additional, liabilities may be incurred following the introduction of self assessment. Individuals should never disregard the possibility of additional obligations arising where there is a failure to comply with statutory requirements.

INTEREST ON OVERDUE TAX

When tax for 1995–96 and earlier years falls due for payment, it must be satisfied not later than the due and payable date. Overdue tax for these years incurs a liability to interest, calculated from the 'reckonable date' to the date of payment. The reckonable date is broadly that on which tax falls due, but may be affected by such matters as an appeal against an assessment and the increase of an estimated assessment which is adjusted to the proper amount later.

However, in those cases where tax, either income tax or capital gains tax, for 1995–96 (or 1996–97 for some partnerships) or any earlier year is assessed on or after 6 April 1998, that tax will be treated as becoming payable on 31 January following the end of the year of assessment to which it relates.

Following the introduction of self-assessment, different rules apply for 1996–97 and later years when calculating liability to interest. The nature of this liability and the calculations involved are outlined on page 7. Failure to discharge tax on the prescribed date, frequently 31 January following the end of the year of assessment, will involve an automatic liability to interest.

Any interest paid cannot be subtracted when calculating the payer's income chargeable to tax.

The rates at which interest has been imposed have changed on numerous occasions, and rates for the last six years are shown by the preceding table. A revised basis for calculating interest was introduced on 5 February 1997 which resulted in an increase in the rate of interest chargeable.

INTEREST		
From	**To**	**Per cent**
6 October 1991	5 November 1992	9.25
6 November 1992	5 December 1992	7.75
6 December 1992	5 March 1993	7
6 March 1993	5 January 1994	6.25
6 January 1994	5 October 1994	5.5
6 October 1994	5 March 1995	6.25
6 March 1995	5 February 1996	7
6 February 1996	5 February 1997	6.25
6 February 1997	5 August 1997	8.5
6 August 1997		9.5

INTEREST ATTRIBUTABLE TO OFFENCES

If an assessment is raised not later than 5 April 1998 for 1995–96 (1996–97 for some partnerships) or earlier years to make good a 'loss of tax' due to failure on the part of a taxpayer to provide notice, complete a tax return, or to supply proper accounts or other information, a liability to satisfy interest may also arise. In the past, this situation often developed where a taxpayer had failed to disclose details of taxable income in sufficient time for assessments to be raised before the normal due and payable date. Interest runs from the date on which tax ought to have been satisfied, and not from the date when an assessment was issued, to the date of payment. It was by no means uncommon for interest calculated on this basis to extend over many years and actually exceed the tax payable which had to be satisfied in addition.

The Inland Revenue have powers to mitigate the interest charged under this heading. Such interest displaces interest otherwise chargeable where overdue tax is satisfied late. Here also, any interest paid cannot be subtracted when calculating income chargeable to tax. Rates of interest charged for recent years are identical to those appearing in the table on this page.

This special basis of charging interest for earlier years has no application where assessments are raised on and after 6 April 1998. Nor can it apply to assessments attributable to 1996–97 and future years, unless those assessments relate to a limited range of partnerships for that year only.

PENALTIES

The Taxes Acts provide a wide range of penalties for failure to notify the Inland Revenue of tax liabilities and other matters. This broadly involves the commission of fraud or neglect, with additional offences introduced by self-assessment.

Among the offences is failure to complete properly a tax return, or to provide notification of liability where no return form has been received. There may also be a failure to provide many other returns required by the legislation. A much more serious offence giving rise to penalties is the deliberate understatement or omission of profits, gains or income.

The maximum amount of penalties chargeable may vary considerably between relatively nominal sums to 100 per cent of the under-assessed tax. In very serious situations a criminal prosecution may result.

Where penalties fall due, these must be satisfied in addition to tax and interest, but the Inland Revenue retain wide powers to mitigate amounts otherwise payable. Like interest, penalties incurred cannot be deducted when calculating the payer's income chargeable to income tax.

APPEALS

Appeals against income tax assessments must be made in writing to HM Inspector of Taxes within thirty days of the date appearing on the notice of assessment. The required notice of appeal must state the grounds on which the appeal is made, for example, 'on the grounds that the assessment is excessive'.

Most appeals can be settled by agreement with the local Inspector, but it is as well to be represented professionally if the appeal is to be heard personally by the General (Local) or Special Commissioners.

If no appeal is made against an assessment, or if an assessment is confirmed on appeal, it cannot afterwards be reopened unless, exceptionally, it was made on the basis of an error or mistake in the taxpayer's return.

No award of costs is made at the conclusion of appeal hearings before the General Commissioners, nor are details of the hearings made available for examination by the public. However, the Special Commissioners do retain powers to award costs where either party has acted 'unreasonably' in pursuing the appeal. In addition, the Special Commissioners retain powers to publish details of important decisions.

Following the introduction of self-assessment, few formal assessments will be raised for 1996–97 and future years. This indicates that the number of future appeals will substantially diminish. However, some assessments will be forthcoming as the result of offences or underdeclarations of income or gains. Other assessments will be raised late for earlier years. These will often involve appeals.

18

Capital gains tax

WHERE A GAIN or loss arises from the disposal of land, securities or other assets, it is necessary to establish whether the transaction forms part of a business. A finding that the financial result is derived from a business of dealing will require that any profit must be assessed to income tax in a manner identical to that which applies to other business profits, with relief being granted for losses on a similar basis.

In those cases where the transaction does not form part of a business undertaking and any surplus proceeds are not otherwise chargeable to income tax the transaction may be affected by capital gains tax.

The application of capital gains tax has changed on numerous occasions since its introduction in 1965. Significantly, a further batch of fundamental changes were introduced in the spring of 1998 and these considerably affect future events.

It should be emphasised that these recent changes did not affect many areas of capital gains taxation but required:

a The withdrawal of the former indexation allowance and its replacement by a taper.
b The phasing out of retirement relief.
c The partial withdrawal of bed and breakfast transactions.
d The withdrawal of reinvestment relief and extension of deferral relief.
e The extension of capital gains tax to some individuals not resident in the United Kingdom.
f Changes in the calculation of tax payable by trustees and personal representatives.

These changes, together with other matters affecting liability to capital gains tax, are reviewed in the succeeding pages of this chapter.

DISPOSAL OF ASSETS

Liability to capital gains tax may be incurred where chargeable gains arise on the disposal of assets. The expression 'disposal' usually involves a change of ownership but certain 'deemed' disposals are treated as having taken place and these also may produce potential liability to capital gains tax. 'Assets' include nearly all forms of 'property'; an expression which extends to stocks, shares, unit trust holdings, land, buildings, jewellery and antiques, among others.

RESIDENCE OVERSEAS

Unless assets are used for the purposes of a business carried on in the United Kingdom an individual who is neither resident nor ordinarily resident in this territory will not become liable to capital gains tax. This has enabled some individuals having substantial assets to leave the United Kingdom for a comparatively short length of time and to realise assets when they no longer reside in the United Kingdom, thereby avoiding liability.

In future however, the period spent overseas will have to be lengthened considerably following the introduction of new rules. These rules apply to individuals who:

a Have been resident in the United Kingdom for any part of at least four out of the seven tax years immediately preceding the year of departure, and

b Become not resident and not ordinarily resident for a period of less than five years, and

c Own assets before they leave the United Kingdom.

Where those assets are realised between the date of departure and the date of return any capital gain arising will be vulnerable to capital gains tax. Should the disposal occur in the year of departure, the chargeable gain, if any, will be assessed in that year. In contrast, where the gain arises from disposals undertaken in subsequent years it will be assessed to United Kingdom capital gains tax in the year of return. The revised rules apply to individuals who leave the United Kingdom on and after 17 March 1998.

BED AND BREAKFAST TRANSACTIONS

Individuals requiring to realise gains or losses will often enter into 'bed and breakfast' transactions. In their simplest form these transactions involve selling shares and reacquiring those shares shortly afterwards. The objective is to realise a chargeable gain to absorb the exempt amount or to offset losses. They may also result in losses being incurred which can be offset against chargeable gains.

The future use of bed and breakfast transactions has been restricted for disposals taking place on and after 17 March 1998. In future, where shares are 'reacquired' within a period of 30 days following the date of disposal the transaction will fail to produce the required gain or loss.

EXEMPTIONS AND RELIEFS

The potential scope of liability to capital gains tax is extremely wide but numerous exemptions are available. For example, gains arising on the disposal of private motor vehicles, National Savings Certificates and Premium Savings Bonds, together with sums received on the maturity or surrender of normal policies of life assurance and sums received from the sale of most chattels which have a predictable life of less than fifty years, are exempt. Gains arising on the disposal of goods and chattels not otherwise exempted, usually those with a life expectation of more than fifty years, will be exempt if the disposal proceeds, but not the gains, do not exceed £6,000. Should the proceeds exceed £6,000 by a small amount, the gains otherwise arising on disposal may be reduced. The disposal of gilt-edged securities, marketable securities issued by public corporations and guaranteed by the government, together with most fixed interest stocks, are also exempt.

No liability to capital gains tax arises on assets retained at the time of an individual's death. However, personal representatives, legatees and others taking assets on death are deemed to acquire those assets for a consideration representing market value at the time of death. This use of market value will establish the notional cost of acquisition should the personal representatives, or other persons, subsequently undertake the disposal of assets in circumstances requiring the calculation of chargeable gains. It will also determine the date on which individual assets are treated as acquired.

The disposal of assets to a recognised charity, or to certain national institutions, will incur no liability to capital gains tax. Further, a claim may be made to exclude from liability gains arising on the disposal of works of art, historic houses, and other assets of national interest, if a number of conditions are satisfied.

These exemptions are given in addition to the annual exemption of £6,800 which applies for 1998–99.

TRANSFERS BETWEEN HUSBAND AND WIFE

Transfers of assets between a husband and wife 'living together' will incur no liability to tax. This is achieved by applying the assumption that assets are transferred for a consideration which produces neither gain nor loss to the transferor.

In those cases where the parties are not 'living together', for example by reason of separation, liability to tax will arise in the normal manner.

PRIVATE RESIDENCES

An exemption which is of considerable interest to many individuals arises on the disposal of a private residence. Where the property has been used as an individual's only or main residence throughout the period of ownership, or from 31 March 1982 if later, no chargeable gain will arise on disposal by that individual. In other situations, involving such use throughout part only of the ownership period, some portion of the gain may be chargeable. However, where a property has been occupied for a qualifying purpose at some time in the ownership period, it will be treated as so occupied in the final three years of ownership, whether so occupied or not.

An individual can have only one qualifying residence at any time. If two or more main residences are held simultaneously, perhaps a town house and a seaside cottage, the individual may select which property should qualify for exemption. In the case of husband and wife 'living together', the couple cannot each have a qualifying residence at the same time. Any selection must be made by written notice within a period of two years from the date an additional property is acquired.

In addition, where an individual realises gains from the disposal of a private residence previously occupied by a dependent relative, rent-free and without other consideration, exemption from capital gains tax may be forthcoming. This exemption cannot be obtained, however, where the dependent relative first commenced to occupy the property after 5 April 1988.

Employees occupying job-related accommodation and self-employed individuals required to occupy accommodation in connection with their business may also establish a qualifying residence which is either used or intended to be used on some future occasion.

RETIREMENT RELIEF

Where an individual undertakes the disposal of business assets the gain arising may be reduced or eliminated by retirement relief. This relief is available for gains realised in recent years on the disposal of:

a The whole or part of a business carried on by a sole trader or by individuals in partnership;

b Assets used for the purposes of a business in **a** which has ceased; and

c Shares or securities issued by a company where the following requirements are satisfied:

  i the company was a trading company;

  ii the individual retained at least 5 per cent of the voting rights; and

  iii the individual was a full-time working director, officer or employee of that company or an associated company.

For disposals made after 29 November 1993 and not later than 5 April 1999, the maximum amount of retirement relief will comprise:

a 100 per cent of gains up to £250,000, plus

b 50 per cent of the gains between £250,000 and £1,000,000.

This formula could produce maximum retirement relief of £625,000 calculated as follows, if gains were £1,000,000 or more:

	£
On first £250,000 at 100 per cent	250,000
On balance of £750,000 at 50 per cent	375,000
	£625,000

98
RETIREMENT RELIEF

On 27 February 1998, John realised gains of £530,000 from the disposal of business assets. At the time of disposal John was 53 years of age and had carried on business for more than ten years.

As the maximum ten-year period is satisfied the appropriate percentage becomes 10/10ths. The chargeable gains assessable to capital gains tax will be calculated as follows:

Aggregate gains	£530,000

Maximum relief 10/10ths × £1,000,000 = £1,000,000

	£
Available relief:	
On first £250,000 at 100 per cent .	250,000
On balance of £280,000 at 50 per cent .	140,000
Total relief	£390,000

	£
Aggregate gains	530,000
Less retirement relief: maximum . .	390,000
Assessable chargeable gains, 1997–98	£140,000

A finding that John had only carried on the business for exactly four years would limit retirement relief to the following:

Appropriate percentage = 4/10ths
Maximum relief 4/10ths × £1,000,000 = £400,000

	£
Available relief:	
On 4/10ths of £250,000 = £100,000 at	
100 per cent	100,000
On £400,000 *less* £100,000 = £300,000	
at 50 per cent	150,000
Total relief	250,000

	£
Aggregate gains	530,000
Less retirement relief	250,000
Assessable chargeable gains, 1997–98	£280,000

In most situations the total gains arising on disposal will fall below, perhaps substantially below, £1,000,000. However, the above approach may be used to establish the amount of available retirement relief.

Maximum relief will only be forthcoming where the business has been carried on, or the shares retained, throughout a minimum ten-year period. If those conditions are satisfied for less than ten years, but more than twelve months, the amount of retirement relief will be reduced. Relief is then governed by the 'appropriate percentage', which represents that part of the ten-year period throughout which the conditions are satisfied, and comprises the aggregate of:

a The appropriate percentage of £250,000, plus
b One-half of the gains exceeding the product of **a** but which do not exceed the appropriate percentage of £1,000,000.

Retirement relief cannot exceed the gains less losses arising on disposal, as it merely serves to reduce or eliminate the net gains. However, apart from premature retirement on the grounds of ill-health, physical retirement is usually unnecessary and 'retirement relief' may be available for two or more separate disposals undertaken by the same individual until maximum relief has been obtained. With few exceptions retirement relief is given as of right and does not require the submission of any claim.

Individuals who have reached the age of 50 years on or before the disposal date may qualify for retirement relief. In the case of disposals made before 28 November 1995 the higher age of 55 years applied. Retirement relief may also be available for disposals made by an individual before reaching the age of 50 (or 55) years if that individual was compelled to retire from business early on the grounds of ill-health.

Withdrawal of retirement relief

With the introduction of taper relief for disposals taking place after 5 April 1998 a decision was taken to phase out retirement relief. However, this relief remains available in full for disposals undertaken on or before 5 April 1999.

The amount of relief for each of the four following years will then be progressively reduced until it ceases to apply for disposals carried out after 5 April 2003, as shown by the following table:

Year of disposal	100 per cent relief	50 per cent relief
	Gains up to	Gains between
	£	£
1998–1999	250,000	250,001–1,000,000
1999–2000	200,000	200,001– 800,000
2000–2001	150,000	150,001– 600,000
2001–2002	100,000	100,001– 400,000
2002–2003	50,000	50,001– 200,000

ROLL-OVER RELIEF – BUSINESS ASSETS

Gains arising from the disposal of many assets used for the purpose of a business may be 'rolled over' and offset against the cost of acquiring a replacement asset. This avoids any liability on the gain, but as

99
RETIREMENT RELIEF PHASING OUT

Using the basic facts in Example 98, let it be assumed that the disposal occurred three years later on 27 February 2001. The net chargeable gains, subject to a further adjustment for taper relief will then be calculated as follows:

Maximum ten-year period satisfied.

Appropriate percentage 10/10ths.

Maximum relief 10/10ths × £600,000 = £600,000

Available relief:

	£
On first £150,000 at 100 per cent	150,000
On balance of £380,000 at 50 per cent	190,000
Total relief	£340,000

	£
Aggregate gains	530,000
Less retirement relief – maximum	340,000
Chargeable gains (subject to taper relief) 2000–2001	£190,000

Only four-year period satisfied.

Appropriate percentage 4/10ths.

Maximum relief 4/10ths × £600,000 = £240,000

Available relief:

	£
On 4/10th × £150,000 = £60,000 at 100 per cent	60,000
On £240,000 less £60,000 = £180,000 at 50 per cent	90,000
Total relief	£150,000

	£
Aggregate gains	530,000
Less retirement relief	150,000
Chargeable gains (subject to taper relief) 2000–2001	£380,000

the cost of the replacement asset is reduced a correspondingly increased gain may arise from the eventual disposal of that asset.

It remains a requirement that both the old and the replacement assets fall within a restricted list. This list includes land and buildings occupied and used for the purposes of the business, goodwill, fixed (but not moveable) plant and machinery, aircraft, hovercraft and ships. It also includes milk quotas, potato quotas and other agricultural quotas, together with qualifying property used to provide furnished holiday accommodation and commercial woodlands.

100

ROLL-OVER RELIEF
BUSINESS ASSETS

On 30 March 1998, Bob sold freehold premises used for the purposes of his business. The chargeable gain arising on disposal was calculated as follows:

	£
Disposal proceeds	150,000
Less cost	60,000
	90,000
Less indexation allowance – say	38,000
Chargeable gain	£52,000

Bob purchased replacement premises at a cost of £200,000 on 18 July 1998, and made a claim for roll-over relief with the following results:

	£
Gain arising on disposal	52,000
Less roll-over relief	52,000
Chargeable gain 1997–98	NIL

	£
Cost of replacement premises	200,000
Less roll-over relief	52,000
Deemed cost of acquisition	£148,000

If a disposal is to be matched with an acquisition, the replacement asset must usually be acquired within a period commencing twelve months before and ending thirty-six months following the disposal of the old asset.

Only limited roll-over relief will be available where the consideration used to acquire the replacement asset falls below the amount of consideration received from the disposal of the old asset.

A similar form of roll-over relief may be available where an interest in land is disposed of to an authority possessing compulsory purchase powers. In circumstances such as these it is frequently possible to roll-over the chargeable gain arising against the cost of acquiring some other interest in land. The only limitation is that the interest acquired must not be, or subsequently become, the acquirer's qualifying only or main residence.

A written claim must be made if roll-over relief is to be obtained for gains arising on the disposal of business assets or interests in land. Such a claim will usually be made when completing the annual tax return form. However, this form must normally be received by the Inland Revenue not later than 31 January following the end of the year of assessment in which the disposal took place. As roll-over relief enables disposals to be matched with acquisitions made in the succeeding three-year period, it is apparent that part of this three-year period will remain when the appropriate date of 31 January is reached. To overcome this problem it is possible to submit a provisional claim for roll-over relief. This claim will prevent capital gains tax becoming payable on the gain, or part of the gain, which it is intended to roll-over. At a later date finality will be achieved by inserting accurate figures which either confirm the accuracy of the provisional claim or indicate that a gain remains chargeable to capital gains tax.

The availability and application of roll-over relief is unaffected by the changes to capital gains tax introduced in the spring of 1998.

REINVESTMENT RELIEF

For several years a form of roll-over relief has been available where gains arising on the disposal of an asset are matched with consideration given to acquire shares in an unlisted trading company or the unlisted holding company of a trading group. To obtain this relief, known as reinvestment relief, it is a requirement that shares must be acquired within a period commencing twelve months before and ending thirty-six months following the disposal date.

However, reinvestment relief has been withdrawn and cannot apply to acquisitions made after 5 April 1998. The following comments extend only to earlier acquisitions.

Not all acquisitions of shares in unlisted companies are available for reinvestment relief as a range of trading activities may disqualify some trading companies. Subject to this, where qualifying shares are acquired and a claim for reinvestment relief is made, the amount of that relief will comprise the smallest of:

a the gain arising on disposal;

b the actual consideration given to acquire new shares, or market value where those shares are acquired otherwise than by way of a transaction at arm's length; and

c the amount which the claimant may specify.

Heading c is a most important matter as this may enable the claimant to restrict the amount of reinvestment relief for the purpose of absorbing the annual exemption, or perhaps losses, on the balance remaining.

The amount for which a reinvestment relief claim is made will be deducted from the gain arising on disposal of the 'old asset' and also subtracted from the cost of acquiring qualifying shares.

———— 101 ————
REINVESTMENT RELIEF

On 22 January 1998, Betty realised a chargeable gain of £75,000 from the sale of a painting. She invested £51,000 when acquiring shares in A Ltd, a qualifying company, on 14 March 1998, and made a claim for reinvestment relief. No entitlement to enterprise investment scheme relief arose.

Reinvestment relief will be available on the smallest of

a the gain of £75,000;
b the consideration given to acquire shares, namely £51,000; and
c any amount which may be specified, falling between £1 and £50,999.

Assuming Betty claims maximum relief under **b**, the effect on capital gains tax liability will be as follows:

				£
Gain on disposal of painting	.	.	.	75,000
Less Reinvestment relief	.	.	.	51,000
Chargeable gain 1997–98	.	.	.	£24,000

				£
Cost of acquiring shares	.	.	.	51,000
Less roll-over relief	.	.	.	51,000
Deemed cost of acquisition	.	.	.	NIL

Note: Reinvestment relief can be obtained as shares in A Ltd were acquired before 6 April 1998.

Any gain which has been rolled over in this manner will become chargeable to capital gains tax if the claimant emigrates from the United Kingdom within a period of three years following the acquisition of shares. Liability will also arise should the share issuing company cease to qualify as an eligible trading company within the three-year period.

Claims for reinvestment relief will usually be made in the tax return, although they are capable of being submitted separately. It is not possible to take advantage of the provisional claim procedure mentioned on page 147, which is limited to potential claims for roll-over relief on the disposal of business assets and certain interests in land. It follows that if gains arising in a year of assessment have not been matched with an investment before the following 31 January, capital gains tax will have to be paid. Any valid claim made subsequently will result in a repayment, or partial repayment, of that tax.

It must again be emphasised that reinvestment relief has been withdrawn and cannot apply to shares acquired after 5 April 1998.

DEFERRAL RELIEF

There are two types of investment which enable the capital gain arising on disposal of some other asset to be deferred. Both investments require a share subscription and may confer income tax relief. The investments and the nature of deferment relief are outlined below.

Enterprise investment scheme shares

Investments up to a maximum of £150,000 (or £100,000 for 1997–98 and earlier years) made during a year of assessment in shares issued by a company to which the enterprise investment scheme applies, qualify for income tax relief at the reduced rate of 20 per cent (see page 41). In addition, where a chargeable gain arises from the disposal of some other asset after 28 November 1994, a claim may be made to match that gain with the cost of acquiring shares eligible for enterprise investment scheme relief. For shares acquired after 5 April 1998 it is not necessary for relief to actually be obtained, if the shares would otherwise qualify for that relief. The sum matched in this manner will comprise the smallest of:

a the gain arising on disposal;
b the cost of acquiring eligible shares; and
c the amount which the claimant may specify.

The amount identified by this calculation is not subtracted from the cost of acquiring eligible shares. The amount involved, representing all or part of the chargeable gain arising on the disposal of the asset, will be deferred until the eventual disposal of the shares takes place or some other event occurs.

Therefore the effect of the relief is in the nature of a deferral of liability and not that of a liability being rolled over against the cost of acquiring shares.

It remains a requirement that eligible shares must be acquired within a period commencing twelve months before and ending thirty-six months following the disposal of the asset if deferral relief is to be obtained.

Venture capital trust shares

A further form of deferral relief is available where the disposal of an asset takes place after 5 April 1995 and the chargeable gain arising is matched with an investment in shares issued by a venture capital trust which satisfies the requirements outlined on page 43. An individual may invest up to a maximum of £100,000 in a year of assessment when acquiring venture capital trust shares. Should an investment take place, it becomes possible to match the disposal of an asset with the cost of acquiring shares and

102
DEFERRAL RELIEF
ENTERPRISE INVESTMENT SCHEME

Barry realised a gain of £80,000 on 17 May 1998 from the disposal of some land. Eight months later, on 16 January 1999, he subscribed £60,000 when acquiring shares in X Ltd. The subscription comprised eligible shares qualifying for enterprise investment scheme relief. This relief reduced Barry's income tax liability by

£60,000 at 20 per cent **£12,000**

In addition, Barry claimed deferral relief on the maximum sum available, namely, the subscription cost of £60,000.

On 31 January 2004 Barry sold his entire holding of shares in X Ltd. The substantial gain arising on disposal was not chargeable to capital gains tax as all requirements had been satisfied throughout a five-year period.

The effect of the claim for deferral relief will be as follows:

	£
Gain on disposal of land	80,000
Less Deferral relief	60,000
Chargeable gain 1998–99 . . .	**£20,000**
Postponed gain becoming chargeable in 2003–2004 on the disposal of shares (£80,000 less £20,000) . . .	**£60,000**

A similar set of calculations would apply if Barry had subscribed £60,000 for shares in a capital venture trust.

---

submit a claim for relief. Any claim will be based on the smallest of:

a the amount of the gain arising on disposal;

b the consideration applied to acquire qualifying shares in a venture capital trust; and

c the amount which the claimant may specify.

Here also, the amount on which relief is claimed will not be subtracted from the cost of acquiring shares in a venture capital trust. The amount involved, representing all or part of the chargeable gain arising on disposal of the asset, will be deferred until a disposal of qualifying venture capital trust shares occurs or some other event takes place. Only at that time will the amount of the deferred gain become chargeable to capital gains tax.

It is a necessary requirement that the subscription for shares in a venture capital trust takes place within a period commencing twelve months before and ending twelve months following the disposal of the other asset.

Making claims

Claims for deferral relief must be made before that relief will be forthcoming. These claims will usually be included in a tax return but are capable of being submitted separately. The provisional claim procedure mentioned on page 147, which applies to roll-over relief for business assets, has no application to claims for deferral relief.

HOLD-OVER RELIEF

Where assets are transferred by way of gift, or for an inadequate consideration, the disposal proceeds actually passing, if any, and the corresponding cost of acquisition to the transferee, will be deleted and replaced by market value. A similar adjustment must be made for all transactions between 'connected persons', an expression which applies to near relatives and many other closely associated individuals and companies.

The insertion of market value may well produce chargeable gains accruing to the transferor which are not actually realised gains. However, where the transferor is an individual and the transferee resides in the United Kingdom a claim for hold-over relief may be available. The effect of this claim is that the chargeable gain will be reduced to nil and the amount of the reduction subtracted from the cost of acquisition (namely market value) to the transferee. As the transferee's cost is reduced, he or she may well incur an increased chargeable gain from the eventual disposal of the asset. A similar claim is available for assets transferred by trustees.

Only limited hold-over relief may be available if the transferee provides some consideration for the asset. Any hold-over relief previously granted may be withdrawn should the transferee emigrate from the United Kingdom within the succeeding six-year period before undertaking a disposal of the asset transferred.

Only a limited range of assets qualify for hold-over relief. These assets comprise:

a Assets used for the purposes of a business carried on by the transferor, or by a company in which the transferor retains a significant interest

b Agricultural property

c Shares or securities in unlisted trading companies

d Shares or securities in listed trading companies, where the transferor retains a substantial interest.

No restriction is placed on the range of assets where the transfer is a lifetime transfer, other than a potentially exempt transfer, which is taken into account for inheritance tax purposes.

103
GIFTS AND HOLD-OVER RELIEF

On 14 October 1997, a father gifted shares in a family trading company to his son. The shares, which retained a market value of £50,000 at the time of the transfer, had been acquired by the father for £6,000 in 1985 and the transaction fully satisfied the requirements for hold-over relief.

If no claim is made, the chargeable gain accruing to the father will be:

			£
Disposal proceeds (market value)	.	.	50,000
Less cost .	.	.	6,000
			44,000
Less indexation allowance – say	.	.	4,000
Chargeable gain 1997–98	.	.	£40,000

However, should a claim for hold-over relief be made there will be no chargeable gain accruing to the father. The son's cost of acquisition must then be adjusted as follows:

			£
Cost of acquisition (market value)	.	.	50,000
Less father's chargeable gain	.	.	40,000
Deemed cost of acquisition	.	.	£10,000

CALCULATION OF GAINS AND LOSSES

Where the disposal of an asset takes place and none of the exemptions from capital gains taxation apply it becomes necessary to calculate the gain or loss arising. This task remains whether the various reliefs mentioned earlier, for example, retirement relief, roll-over relief, reinvestment relief and deferral relief, apply. Substantial changes affecting the calculation have been introduced for disposals taking place on and after 6 April 1998. These directly involve the replacement of the indexation allowance by taper relief and other changes linked with that withdrawal.

It must however, be stressed that none of these changes affects the calculation of the basic gain or loss as it is only adjustment made after that calculation has been completed which have changed.

For disposals taking place before, on, or after 6 April 1998 the calculation of the basic gain or loss will broadly reflect the difference between the acquisition cost of an asset and the disposal proceeds, with an adjustment for incidental costs of both acquisition and disposal, together with costs incurred when carrying out improvements or alterations to the asset.

There is a significant alteration in the computation

104
CALCULATION OF GAIN
VALUE AT 31 MARCH 1982

Norman purchased an asset at a cost of £8,000 on 27 March 1972. The asset realised £100,000 when sold on 9 October 1998. Market value at 31 March 1982 was agreed to be £42,000.

The chargeable gain arising on disposal becomes:

				£
Disposal proceeds .	.	.	.	100,000
Less deemed cost: market value at				
31 March 1982	.	.	.	42,000
				58,000
Less indexation allowance (based on				
market value at 31 March 1982) – say			41,500
Chargeable gain 1997–98	.	.	£16,500

procedure for assets acquired before 31 March 1982. These assets are deemed to have been acquired for a 'cost' representing market value on that date. The position will only be otherwise where this approach produces an excessive gain or loss exceeding the actual gain or loss incurred, or converts a gain into a loss or a loss into a gain. It remains possible to file an election to adopt market value at 31 March 1982 for all assets (but not some only) held on that date. Where such an election is made, any distortions in the gain or loss are ignored. The election must be submitted within a period of two years following the end of the first year of assessment commencing on 6 April 1988 in which the first disposal of an asset held on 31 March 1982 is made.

Once the basic gain or loss has been calculated it is necessary to examine separately the adjustments required for disposals taking place

a on or before 5 April 1998; and

b on or after 6 April 1998.

DISPOSALS BEFORE 6 APRIL 1998
Where the disposal of an asset takes place on or before 5 April 1998 the first step is to calculate the basic gain or loss arising, as explained above. The second step is to calculate the amount of any indexation allowance.

The indexation allowance
The indexation allowance is calculated using monthly figures taken from the retail prices index. There are two components, namely:

——— 105 ———
INDEXATION ALLOWANCE

Cyril purchased shares at a cost of £10,000 on 12 June 1982. He realised £42,000 from selling the shares on 24 January 1998. Figures extracted from the retail prices index (as adjusted) were as follows:

June 1982 (RI)	.	.	.	.	81.85
January 1998 (RD)	.	.	.	.	159.50

The indexation allowance becomes:

$$\frac{159.50 - 81.85}{81.85} = 0.949$$

£10,000 × 0.949	.	.	.	.	**£9,490**

The chargeable gain for 1997–98 will be:

				£
Disposal proceeds .	.	.	.	42,000
Less Cost .	.	.	.	10,000
Gain				32,000
Less indexation allowance	.	.	.	9,490
Chargeable gain 1997–98	.	.	.	**£22,510**

——— 106 ———
INDEXATION ALLOWANCE – LOSSES

Jane purchased property at a cost of £80,000 on 14 September 1988. The property realised £95,000 when sold on 15 February 1998. Retail prices index figures were:

September 1988	108.4
February 1998	160.3

The indexation allowance will be:

$$\frac{160.3 - 108.4}{108.4} = 0.479$$

£80,000 × 0.479	.	.	.	.	**£38,320**

The calculation continues:

				£
Disposal proceeds .	.	.	.	95,000
Less cost .	.	.	.	80,000
				15,000
Less Indexation allowance (restricted)				15,000
Gain or loss 1997–98	.	.	.	**NIL**

Although an indexation allowance of £38,320 is available, this cannot be used to create a loss and can only apply to reduce the gain to nil.

RI – which represents the figure extracted from the index for the month of March 1982, or the month in which expenditure is incurred, whichever is the later, and

RD – which is the index figure for the month in which the disposal takes place.

The allowance will then comprise:

$$\frac{RD - RI}{RI} \times \text{Expenditure}$$

Where two or more items of expenditure have been incurred in relation to an asset in different months, for example, when carrying out improvements to property, separate calculations must be prepared for each item. Retail prices index figures used to establish factors RI and RD are shown by the tables on the following page.

For the disposal of assets acquired before 31 March 1982 the computation of the indexation allowance will proceed by applying the assumption that those assets were acquired for a consideration reflecting market value on that date. In the case of assets acquired or expenditure incurred subsequently, the actual amounts involved will be used as representing cost.

Before an indexation allowance can be calculated, the disposal must be matched with a corresponding acquisition of an asset. This should not give rise to difficulty where there is a single acquisition followed by a single disposal. However, problems do emerge when dealing with a holding of shares or securities. The holding may have been created by acquisitions made on two or more occasions, only part of the aggregate holding may be realised and many listed holdings will be affected by bonus issues, rights issues, exchanges and reorganisations. Complex rules must then be followed to identify the disposal with the matching acquisition before the calculation of gain or loss can proceed and the indexation allowance be identified.

The indexation allowance must be subtracted from the basic gain to identify the chargeable gain assessable to capital gains tax, or which may be subjected to one of the several reliefs, for example, retirement relief or roll-over relief. However, for several years a restriction has been placed on the ability to create or increase the amount of a capital loss by the application of the indexation allowance. In summary form:

a an indexation allowance remains available to reduce a basic gain to a smaller chargeable gain;

b the indexation allowance may be used to reduce a gain to nil but not to convert that gain into a loss; and

RETAIL PRICES INDEX 1982–1987*						
Month	1982	1983	1984	1985	1986	1987
Jan		82.61	86.84	91.20	96.25	100.0
Feb		82.97	87.20	91.94	96.60	100.4
Mar	79.44	83.12	87.48	92.80	96.73	100.6
Apr	81.04	84.28	88.64	94.78	97.67	101.8
May	81.62	84.64	88.97	95.21	97.85	101.9
Jun	81.85	84.84	89.20	95.41	97.79	101.9
Jul	81.88	85.30	89.10	95.23	97.52	101.8
Aug	81.90	85.68	89.94	95.49	97.82	102.1
Sep	81.85	86.06	90.11	95.44	98.30	102.4
Oct	82.26	86.36	90.67	95.59	98.45	102.9
Nov	82.66	86.67	90.95	95.92	99.29	103.4
Dec	82.51	86.89	90.87	96.05	99.62	103.3

*Note: The Retail Prices Index was repositioned at 100 in January 1987. For the purpose of this Table earlier figures have been recalculated by reference to the repositioned standard.

RETAIL PRICES INDEX 1988–1993						
Month	1988	1989	1990	1991	1992	1993
Jan	103.3	111.0	119.5	130.2	135.6	137.9
Feb	103.7	111.8	120.2	130.9	136.3	138.8
Mar	104.1	112.3	121.4	131.4	136.7	139.3
Apr	105.8	114.3	125.1	133.1	138.8	140.6
May	106.2	115.0	126.2	133.5	139.3	141.1
Jun	106.6	115.4	126.7	134.1	139.3	141.0
Jul	106.7	115.5	126.8	133.8	138.8	140.7
Aug	107.9	115.8	128.1	134.1	138.9	141.3
Sep	108.4	116.6	129.3	134.6	139.4	141.9
Oct	109.5	117.5	130.3	135.1	139.9	141.8
Nov	110.0	118.5	130.0	135.6	139.7	141.6
Dec	110.3	118.8	129.9	135.7	139.2	141.9

RETAIL PRICES INDEX 1994–1998					
Month	1994	1995	1996	1997	1998
Jan	141.3	146.0	150.2	154.4	159.5
Feb	142.1	146.9	150.9	155.0	160.3
Mar	142.5	147.5	151.5	155.4	
Apr	144.2	149.0	152.6	156.3	
May	144.7	149.6	152.9	156.9	
Jun	144.7	149.8	153.0	157.5	
Jul	144.0	149.1	152.4	157.5	
Aug	144.7	149.9	153.1	158.5	
Sep	145.0	150.9	153.8	159.3	
Oct	145.2	149.8	153.8	159.5	
Nov	145.3	149.8	153.9	159.6	
Dec	146.0	150.7	154.4	160.0	

c where a loss arises without incorporating the indexation allowance, no such allowance can be used to increase the loss.

Capital losses

Not all disposals will produce gains and inevitably some will give rise to capital losses. Any capital losses arising in a year of assessment must be set against chargeable gains, if any, realised in the same year. If a surplus of losses remains these may be carried forward to future years.

Capital losses brought forward from a previous year of assessment may be subtracted from the net gains arising in the subsequent year. However, the application of earlier losses in this manner is not to reduce the net gains for the subsequent year below the exempt amount for that year. Any surplus losses brought forward from earlier years which cannot be relieved against net gains of a subsequent year may be carried forward and utilised in future years.

income chargeable to income tax in the same year or the previous year. Certain losses from hobby farming and non-commercial activities cannot be relieved in this manner.

If income is not sufficient to absorb the available losses a claim may be made to set the surplus against chargeable gains. Any remaining business losses which cannot be set against income or gains can only be carried forward and set against future profits from the same business.

Where a claim is made to set business losses against net capital gains those losses must be used in priority to any capital losses brought forward from an earlier year.

If relief cannot be given, or fully given, for the post-cessation expenses (mentioned on page 88) against income for the year of assessment in which payment takes place, a claim can be made to treat the unrelieved expenditure as an allowable loss in the same year. This will enable that part of the outlay which is not relieved for income tax purposes to be set against chargeable gains.

107
USING CAPITAL LOSSES

At the end of 1996–97 Alan had unused capital losses of £11,800 carried forward to 1997–98.

He realised chargeable gains of £16,000 and capital losses of £7,300 from disposals taking place in 1997–98.

The losses must be dealt with as follows for 1997–98:

	£
Chargeable gains	16,000
Less Capital losses	7,300
	8,700
Less Losses brought forward (part) . .	2,200
	6,500
Less Exempt amount	6,500
Tax chargeable on	NIL

The capital losses of £7,300 arising in 1997–98 must be set against chargeable gains for the same year. It then remains to reduce the net gains remaining by £2,200 to the exemption threshold of £6,500.

The balance of capital losses brought forward from 1996–97, namely £9,600 (£11,800 less £2,200), will be carried forward to 1998–99.

Business losses

Where business losses arise from carrying on a trade, profession or vocation during a year of assessment a claim can be made to set those losses against

---

108
USING BUSINESSES LOSSES

Susan had unused capital losses of £15,000 being carried forward at the end of 1996–97. In 1997–98 she realised chargeable gains of £21,000 and capital losses of £4,500. During the same year Susan suffered a loss of £18,400 when carrying on a trade. A claim was made to offset part of this loss against income but £7,260 remained unrelieved. Susan then made a separate claim to set this unrelieved balance against her net capital gains for 1997–98.

The result of this claim for capital gains tax purposes is as follows:

	£
Chargeable gains	21,000
Less Capital losses	4,500
Net gains	16,500
Less Business losses	7,260
	9,240
Less Capital losses brought forward (part)	2,740
	6,500
Less Exempt amount	6,500
Tax chargeable on	NIL

The business loss of £18,400 has been fully relieved, partly against income and partly against chargeable gains. The balance of capital losses carried forward to 1998–99 will be £12,260 (£15,000 less £2,740).

Annual exemption

The balance of net gains remaining, if any, will then be reduced by subtracting the exempt amount for the year of assessment concerned. For 1997–98 this was £6,500, with the figure for earlier years being shown on page 155.

DISPOSALS ON OR AFTER 6 APRIL 1998

Where the disposal of an asset takes place on or after 6 April 1998 it remains to calculate the basic gain or loss in the normal manner. A number of deductions may then be made from the aggregate gains arising in a year of assessment.

Indexation allowance

There can be no indexation allowance for assets acquired on or after 1 April 1998. However, where there is a disposal made on or after that date of an asset acquired previously some indexation allowance may be available. This restricted allowance will be calculated on the assumption that the disposal occurred during the month of April 1998. Therefore, the indexation allowance will represent the increase, if any, in the retail prices index between the month of acquisition and April 1998. It is not significant whether the disposal takes place in April 1998 or at any future date. In all situations the indexation allowance will be calculated to the month of April 1998, if of course the asset was acquired before 1 April in the same year.

Capital losses and business losses

The next step is to subtract from the gain remaining after the deduction of the restricted indexation allowance any capital losses which may have arisen during the year of assessment in which the disposal occurred. Capital losses brought forward from earlier years may also be deducted but not to reduce the net gains remaining below £6,800 for 1998–99.

Should a claim be made to relieve unused trading losses, these also will be subtracted.

Calculation of net gains

As a result of these adjustments the net sum remaining will represent the basic gain less the restricted indexation allowance, capital losses for the same year of assessment, capital losses brought forward from earlier years and any trading losses for which a claim has been made.

Taper relief

The net gains calculated on this basis may now be reduced further by the application of tapering relief.

This relief is governed by two factors, namely:

a the number of complete years of ownership falling after 5 April 1998; and
b the nature of each asset.

Only complete years of ownership falling after 5 April 1998 will count. However, where an asset acquired before 17 March 1998 is involved the number of complete years of ownership will be increased by one. For example, an asset may have been acquired on, say, 12 December 1997 and disposed of on 15 July 2000. The number of complete years of ownership falling after 5 April 1998 is clearly two but as the acquisition occurred before 6 April 1998 this may be increased to three.

The number of complete years falling, or treated as falling, after 5 April 1998 will be used to determine the percentage of the net gain chargeable to capital gains tax. The percentage is shown by the following table:

Number of complete years after 5.4.98	Gains on Business Assets Percentage chargeable	Gains on Non-Business Assets Percentage chargeable
0	100	100
1	92.5	100
2	85	100
3	77.5	95
4	70	90
5	62.5	85
6	55	80
7	47.5	75
8	40	70
9	32.5	65
10 or more	25	60

Additional tapering relief applies to business assets, in contrast to other assets. For this purpose a business asset will include:

a An asset used for the purposes of a trade carried on by the individual, either alone or in partnership, or by a qualifying company of that individual.
b Assets held for the purposes of a qualifying office or employment to which the individual is required to devote substantially the whole of his or her time.
c Shares in a qualifying company which the individual may hold.

For this purpose a company is treated as a qualifying company if it is a trading company, or the holding company of a trading group, and the individual holds shares which entitle him or her to exercise at least:

a 5 per cent of the voting rights of the company and the individual is a full-time working officer or employee of that company, or

b 25 per cent of the voting rights in that company in other cases.

Suitable adjustments must be made where an asset has been partly used as a business asset throughout the ownership period.

Calculating taper relief

The net gains for a year of assessment may arise from two or more disposals. Some disposals may have involved business assets and others non-business assets. Aggregate gains may have been offset by current or earlier losses. It then remains to identify those transactions which qualify for taper relief. There is no set order but the identification is to be made on whatever basis secures the greater taper relief. For example, where losses are involved it may be advantageous to set these against gains arising on the disposal of non-business assets before absorbing gains on business assets. However, the reverse approach may apply where non-business assets have been held for a substantial period of

---

109
TAPERING RELIEF

Simon acquired shares in a listed company in July 1992 at a cost of £20,000. The shares realised £57,000 when sold on 21 November 2001. The holding does not comprise a business asset.

The indexation allowance, calculated from July 1992 to April 1998 was, it will be assumed, given at the rate of 0.158.

The period of complete years of ownership after 5 April 1998 is 3. This may be increased by one year to 4 as the shares were acquired before 17 March 1998.

Before subtracting any exempt amount which may be available, the chargeable gain assessable to capital gains tax for 2001–2002 is calculated as follows:

	£
Disposal proceeds	57,000
Less cost	20,000
Gain	37,000
Less indexation allowance	
£20,000 × 0.158	3,160
Net gain	£33,840

Tapering relief then reduces the net gain to the following:

Gain chargeable 90% × £33,840	. .	£30,456

110
TAPERING RELIEF
LOSSES

Assume in the previous example that the share transaction was the only profitable disposal carried out by Simon in 2001–2002. If in addition he realised the following capital losses:

a Losses in 2001–2002	£7,400
b Losses brought forward from previous year	£8,900

the position would be as follows:

		£
Disposal proceeds		57,000
Less cost		20,000
Gain		37,000
Less indexation allowance . .		3,160
		£33,840

	£	
Less losses:	£	
Current	7,400	
Brought forward	8,900	16,300
Net gain		£17,540

Tapering relief

Gain chargeable 90 per cent × £17,540	£15,786

---

time but business assets have been retained for a much shorter period.

In those cases where taper relief must be applied to two or more disposals, each calculation will be carried out separately and the aggregate amount of relief subtracted from net gains to establish the remaining chargeable gains assessable to capital gains tax.

Annual exemption

Finally, the annual exempt amount, given at the rate of £6,800 for 1998–99, must be subtracted from the gain remaining after applying tapering relief.

ANNUAL EXEMPTION

The significance of the annual exemption for disposals taking place before, on or after 6 April 1998 has been discussed earlier. For 1998–99 the exempt amount is £6,800. The corresponding figure for the six earlier years is shown by the following table:

	£		£
1992–93	. 5,800	1995–96 .	6,000
1993–94	. 5,800	1996–97 .	6,300
1994–95	. 5,800	1997–98 .	6,500

If the exempt amount is not utilised, or fully utilised, in any year the balance remaining cannot be carried forward to succeeding years. It is therefore advisable to use fully the exempt amount wherever possible.

A husband and wife 'living together' each have the benefit of the exempt amount, without reference to the gains, if any, realised by the other spouse.

111
CALCULATION OF TAX PAYABLE

Martin realised chargeable gains of £12,700, calculated after deducting any tapering relief, during 1998–99. The amount chargeable to capital gains tax becomes:

	£
Chargeable gains	12,700
Less exempt amount . . .	6,800
Tax chargeable on	£5,900

To establish the amount of capital gains tax payable for 1998–99, Martin's marginal rate of income tax must be determined. It was found that he incurred liability at the basic rate on £12,000. As a further £10,800 would produce liability at the basic rate only, capital gains tax will be due as follows:

On £5,900 at 23 per cent . . .	£1,357.00

If the income of Martin for 1998–99 produced, say, £21,200 liable at the basic rate, capital gains tax due would be:

	£
On first £1,600 (£22,800 less £21,200) at 23 per cent	368.00
On balance of £4,300 at 40 per cent . .	1,720.00
Capital gains tax payable 1998–99 . .	£2,088.00

If the income of Martin for 1998–99 was already sufficient to produce income tax liability at the higher rate of 40 per cent, the capital gains tax payable becomes:

£5,900 at 40 per cent	£2,360.00

Finally, a finding that the income of Martin was only sufficient to produce income tax liability at the lower rate of 20 per cent on income of £1,850 would support the following liability:

	£
On first £2,450 (£4,300 less £1,850) at 20 per cent	490.00
On balance of £3,450 at 23 per cent . .	793.50
Capital gains tax payable 1998–99 . .	£1,283.50

CALCULATION OF TAX PAYABLE

Where net gains remaining before 6 April 1998, or tapered gains remaining on or after this date, exceed the exempt amount for a year of assessment the excess is chargeable to capital gains tax. The first step when calculating liability is to establish:

a The amount of net gains arising in the year of assessment which exceeds the exempt amount; and

b The taxable income of the individual which is chargeable to income tax for that year. This will determine the amount of income charged at the lower rate, the basic rate or the higher rate.

Liability to capital gains tax is then calculated by reference to the individual's marginal rate of income tax. This requires that the amount of the excess net gains must be added to income chargeable to income tax, with income tax rates being used to establish liability on the excess. The tax remains a capital gains tax notwithstanding the use of income tax rates.

It will be recognised that where income is sufficiently substantial to incur liability at the higher rate of 40 per cent for 1998–99, net chargeable gains will be assessed at the rate of 40 per cent. If the individual has not fully utilised the basic rate 23 per cent band of £22,800, the net gains may be wholly assessed at 23 per cent or partly assessed at 23 per cent with the balance taxable at 40 per cent. Where the 20 per cent lower rate band has not been fully used, any balance may be applied to calculate the tax due before proceeding to the basic rate and higher rate.

TAX PAYABLE – HUSBAND AND WIFE

A husband and wife 'living together' are separately assessed to capital gains tax. Each receives an annual exemption of £6,800 for 1998–99, and the calculation of tax payable by one spouse entirely disregards the profits, gains and losses of the other.

RETURNS

Details of disposals made during the year ended 5 April 1998, together with the resultant chargeable gains arising on those disposals, should be entered on the tax return form for 1997–98. For this purpose, supplementary pages headed 'Capital Gains' are supplied and should be attached to the completed form.

However, this information need not be supplied where:

a Gains arising from the disposal, if any, of an only or main residence are fully exempt from capital gains tax; and

b Gross proceeds from all other disposals do not exceed £13,000; and

c Total chargeable gains did not exceed the exemption limit of £6,500.

A similar approach is expected to apply when completing the tax return for 1998–99 with the substitution of £13,600 for £13,000 and £6,800 for £6,500.

In the absence of a tax return form, liability to capital gains tax should be notified to the Inland Revenue not later than 5 October following the end of the year of assessment in which the disposal occurred. It is probable that notification will produce a tax return form requiring completion.

TRUSTS

Complex provisions apply to the taxation of chargeable gains accruing to trustees. Where the trustees are resident in the United Kingdom, they will usually suffer capital gains tax at the appropriate rate. Trustees residing overseas are unlikely to be taxed directly but gains accruing to those trustees may be assessed on United Kingdom beneficiaries, or perhaps on the settlor, namely the individual who created the trust.

Following changes in the structure of capital gains tax all gains accruing to trustees after 5 April 1998 are taxed at the rate of 34 per cent. This rate applies also to gains realised by personal representatives administering the estates of deceased persons. Trustees and personal representatives are entitled to an annual exemption and tapering relief will also apply.

19

Companies

PROFITS AND INCOME accruing to individuals are subject to income tax and any chargeable gains arising to such persons are assessable to capital gains tax. In contrast, profits, income and chargeable gains accruing to companies resident in, or carrying on business in, the United Kingdom, are assessed to corporation tax.

Corporation tax is charged on the profits, gains and income of an accounting period and this will usually be the period for which accounts are made up annually. In arriving at assessable profits a deduction may be claimed for capital allowances where expenditure is incurred on the acquisition of plant, machinery, industrial buildings and similar assets.

Individuals suffer income tax on profits and income, with chargeable gains becoming assessable to capital gains tax. In contrast, profits, income and chargeable gains accruing to companies resident or carrying on business in the United Kingdom are assessed to corporation tax.

Corporation tax is charged on the profits, gains and income of an accounting period. This period will usually be that for which accounts are made up annually, but it cannot exceed twelve months in duration. In arriving at assessable profits a deduction may be available for capital allowances where expenditure is incurred on the acquisition of plant, machinery, industrial buildings and similar assets. Profits from letting property are chargeable and from 1 April 1998 the Schedule A computational rules used by individuals are also extended to companies, with some modifications.

Substantial charges will shortly be introduced governing the date on which corporation tax must be paid by larger companies and also the compliance requirements which all companies must satisfy. The nature and application of these changes is outlined on page 161.

RATES OF CORPORATION TAX

The rates at which corporation tax must be paid are fixed by reference to a financial year which commences on 1 April and ends on the following 31 March. In the many cases where the company accounting year does not terminate on 31 March the results of an accounting period must be apportioned on a time basis. This apportionment assumes significance where there is a change in the rate of corporation tax.

The full rate of corporation tax which has been charged in recent years and that which is to apply in the immediate future is as follows:

	Per cent
1 April 1991 to 31 March 1997. .	33
1 April 1997 to 31 March 1999. .	31
1 April 1999 to 31 March 2000. .	30

SMALL COMPANIES' RATE

Where the profits of a United Kingdom resident company do not exceed stated limits, the full rate of corporation tax is reduced to the small companies' rate. The application of the reduced small companies' rate is governed by the amount of profits and not by the size of the company.

The small companies' rate used for recent years and that which is to apply for the future is as follows:

	Per cent
1 April 1991 to 31 March 1996	. 25
1 April 1996 to 31 March 1997	. 24
1 April 1997 to 31 March 1999	. 21
1 April 1999 to 1 April 2000 .	. 20

Full small companies' rate relief is available where profits do not exceed a 'lower limit'. Marginal relief will be forthcoming where profits exceed this limit but do not exceed an 'upper limit'. This marginal relief is calculated by subtracting from the liability determined at the full corporation tax rate a fraction of the difference between profits and the upper limit. Marginal relief ceases to have any application where profits exceed the upper limit as all profits are then chargeable at the full companies' rate.

The effect of marginal relief is to steadily increase the average rate of corporation tax from the small companies' rate to the full rate as the amount of profit escalates. To achieve this result, profits falling in the margin incur a tax rate of 33.5 per cent for the year to 31 March 1999.

The lower and upper limits which have been used in recent years are as follows:

Year Ending 31 March	Lower Limit £	Upper Limit £
1992/1993/1994	250,000	1,250,000
1995/1996/1997, 1998, 1999 and 2000	300,000	1,500,000

The fraction to be used in the calculation becomes:

Year ending 31 March	
1992, 1993, 1994, 1995 and 1996	1/50th
1997	9/400ths
1998, 1999 and 2000	1/40th

Some modification to the calculation is necessary where there are associated companies, namely companies under common control, or the accounting period is less than twelve months. Adjustments must also be made for accounting periods overlapping 31 March where a change in rate or rates arises. The small companies' rate is not available to close investment-holding companies. These are companies which neither carry on a trade nor derive income from most forms of property letting.

112
SMALL COMPANIES' RATE

The trading profits, calculated after subtracting capital allowances, accruing to Y Ltd in the twelve-month period ending on 31 March 1999 were £160,000. These profits fall below the ceiling of £300,000 and the corporation tax payable becomes:

£160,000 at 21 per cent	£33,600

113
SMALL COMPANIES' RATE OVERLAPPING PERIOD

Using the basic facts in Example 112, let it be assumed that the twelve-month period ended on 31 December 1999. Profits of £160,000 must now be allocated as follows:

	£
Period to 31 March 1999 – 90 days:	
90/365 × £160,000	39,452
Period from 1 April 1999 – 275 days:	
275/365 × £160,000	120,548
	£160,000

In each period profits are rateably below the annual lower limit of £300,000 and the small companies' rate relief applies.
Corporation tax payable becomes:

	£
On £39,452 at 21 per cent . .	8,284.92
On £120,548 at 20 per cent . .	24,109.60
	£32,394.52

CHARGEABLE GAINS
The calculation of chargeable gains and capital losses accruing to companies is made on a basis similar to that used for individuals where the disposal takes place on or before 5 April 1998. The indexation allowance can be subtracted from gains but cannot be used to create or increase losses. Where the disposal identifies assets acquired before 1 April 1982 the calculation may usually proceed by treating those assets as acquired at market value on 31 March 1982.

However, the withdrawal of the indexation allowance and the introduction of tapering relief, which applies to individuals for disposals made after 5 April 1998, has no application to companies. The

114

MARGINAL SMALL COMPANIES' RATE RELIEF

X Ltd realised trading profits, calculated after deducting capital allowances, of £520,000 for the twelve-month period ending on 31 March 1999. Marginal small companies' rate relief applies and the corporation tax payable is as follows:

Trading profits	£520,000
Tax on £520,000 at 31 per cent (full rate)	161,200
Less marginal relief:	
£1,500,000 less £520,000 = £980,000	
× 1/40th	24,500
Tax payable	£136,700

The same result can be achieved by the following calculation:

	£
On first £300,000 at 21 per cent . .	63,000
On balance of £220,000 at 33.5 per cent	73,700
Tax payable	£136,700

calculation will continue to apply the rules in application before that date.

Unlike individuals, the annual exemption of £6,800 has no application to companies.

Any chargeable gains, calculated after subtracting allowable losses, become assessable to corporation tax. Those gains, or net gains, are included in profits and may benefit from the application of small companies' rate relief.

115

CHARGEABLE GAINS

A Ltd prepares accounts to 31 March annually. Trading profits, suitably adjusted for tax purposes by subtracting capital allowances, amounted to £180,000 for the year ending 31 March 1999.

On 12 January 1999, the company realised a chargeable gain of £45,000 from the disposal of an asset.

Aggregate profits do not exceed £300,000 and the small companies' rate applies. Corporation tax payable will therefore be calculated as follows:

	£
Trading profits	180,000
Chargeable gain	45,000
Total profits	£225,000
Tax on £225,000 at the small companies'	
rate of 21 per cent . . .	£47,250

As a review is being undertaken of the treatment of capital gains realised by companies, it seems probable that the approach outlined above will be amended on some future occasion.

INTEREST PAYMENTS

When making payments of yearly interest and other annual sums (but not dividends), a company will deduct income tax at the lower rate of 20 per cent. Any tax must usually be paid over to the Inland Revenue and cannot be retained by the paying company. Some relief for the outlay is available, however, as the gross interest, or other payment, may usually be deducted from profits chargeable to corporation tax, unless the payment represents a 'distribution'.

A revised basis for allocating payments of interest to company accounting periods was introduced on 1 April 1996.

CHARITABLE PAYMENTS

Annual payments made to a charity under a properly drawn deed of covenant are satisfied 'net' after deducting income tax at the basic rate of 23 per cent (and not at the lower rate of 20 per cent). This tax must be accounted for to the Inland Revenue but the gross sum may be relieved when calculating the paying company's liability to corporation tax. A similar procedure applies to single donations made under the Gift Aid scheme.

DISTRIBUTIONS

Payments made by a company which are treated as distributions cannot be included in the calculation of profits. The expression 'distribution' has a wide meaning and includes dividends paid on shares, some benefits provided to shareholders and perhaps payments made by a company when purchasing its own shares.

Dividends and other qualifying distributions are paid in full without deduction of income tax. However, when making such a distribution on or before 5 April 1999 the paying company is required to make a payment of advance corporation tax (ACT) to the Inland Revenue. The rate at which ACT is payable changed on earlier occasions but for distributions made between 6 April 1994 and 5 April 1999 has been set at one-quarter. For example, should a company pay a cash dividend of £80 it will be required to account for ACT of £20 (namely, one-quarter of £80).

Any ACT paid may usually be offset by the paying company against its liability to corporation tax for the accounting period in which the distribution was made. Therefore, as the title suggests, ACT is really an advance payment of corporation tax where the company has sufficient profits chargeable to that tax. Should the corporation tax liability be insufficient to absorb payments of ACT the surplus may be carried forward to future periods or perhaps carried back to earlier periods.

ACT will cease to be payable for distributions made on and after 6 April 1999. This is explained by the introduction of new arrangements for the payment of corporation tax, as outlined below.

The treatment of dividends received by shareholders before 6 April 1999 is discussed on page 109. A further discussion, to be found on page 171, deals with dividends received on and after that date.

PAY AND FILE

A revised system for administering the assessment and collection of corporation tax from companies was introduced for accounting periods ending on and after 1 October 1993. The system is known as 'pay and file' and, as the title suggests, requires companies to discharge corporation tax and to submit both accounts and tax returns at a later date.

Pending the introduction of substantial changes which affect larger companies and are reviewed later, corporation tax becomes due and payable nine months following the end of a company's accounting period. Failure to discharge the proper amount of tax on that date will incur a liability to interest, which commences to run from the end of the nine-month period. Supporting accounts and corporation tax returns must be filed within a period of twelve months commencing on the annual accounting date. Should a company fail to satisfy this obligation a liability to penalties will arise. The amount of these penalties increases as the period of failure lengthens.

When applying 'pay and file' it should not be overlooked that the word 'company' has an extended meaning for corporation tax purposes. In addition to the more familiar public and private company it also extends to clubs, associations and similar bodies.

SELF-ASSESSMENT

Individuals, trustees, personal representatives and some others liable to account for income tax became subject to the self-assessment regime on 6 April 1996. However, the regime had no application to companies chargeable to corporation tax. This distinction will shortly be remedied as companies will become liable to self-assessment for accounting periods ending on or after 1 July 1999. As no accounting period of a company can have a duration exceeding twelve months, no company can enter self-assessment until 2 July 1998 at the earliest.

The introduction of self-assessment will not, of itself, affect the date on which a company must file corporation tax returns. However, once self-assessment applies to an accounting period it will remain for the company's representatives to calculate the amount of tax due and insert the calculations on the return.

PAYMENT OF CORPORATION TAX

The obligation imposed on a company to discharge ACT where dividends and other distributions are made will cease to apply on 6 April 1999. In recognition of this change a new system of discharging corporation tax will apply to larger companies. The system will affect company accounting periods ending on and after 1 July 1999.

A 'large' company will have annual profits of at least £1.5 million and under the revised system must discharge corporation tax liability by four instalments. Where two or more companies comprise a group the profit level of £1.5 million will apply to the combined group as a whole and not to members individually.

The revised payment structure will be phased in throughout a number of years to achieve a smooth transition from the present system which requires all corporation tax to be paid nine months after the end of the accounting period.

Companies whose profits do not reach the £1.5 million threshold are unaffected by the new system and will continue to discharge corporation tax on a date falling nine months after the end of the accounting period in which profits arise.

It may be possible to obtain future relief for any unused ACT which remains for dividends or distributions made before 6 April 1999.

20

Value added tax

VALUE ADDED TAX is charged on the value of supplies made by a registered trader and extends both to the supply of goods and also to the supply of services. Special rules must be applied to determine the nature of the supply and also the time at which that supply is made.

For many years value added tax was charged on the value of most goods imported into the United Kingdom, unless the importation was of a temporary nature. With the inception of the European Single Market value added tax is no longer charged on a range of goods imported by a trader from a Member State of the European Community. In substitution for liability at the point of importation, value added tax is imposed on the person who 'acquires' goods. Goods obtained from suppliers outside the Single Market continue to attract tax on importation.

A registered trader will both suffer tax (input tax) when obtaining or acquiring goods or services for the purposes of a business and charge that tax (output tax) when supplying goods or services to customers and others. It is necessary for the trader to calculate both the input tax suffered and the output tax charged, or chargeable, during an accounting period. Should the output tax exceed the input tax qualifying for relief, the difference must be paid over to Customs and Excise. However, if the input tax exceeds the output tax a repayment will usually be due.

Not all input tax can be included in the calculation as some outgoings, for example supplies involving business entertaining and supplies relating to domestic accommodation provided by a company for use by directors and their families, must be disregarded. Nor can tax suffered on the supply of a new motor car be relieved as input tax, unless the vehicle has been imported or supplied to car dealers for resale, is acquired by taxi, self-drive hire firms or driving schools for business use, is acquired solely for business use, perhaps a business of leasing, or falls within a limited range of special vehicles.

Value added tax returns are usually submitted for accounting periods of three months, although some repayment traders may submit returns on a monthly basis. Very large traders will also submit returns on a three-monthly basis, although they must account for tax due at more frequent intervals. An optional scheme is available for traders having an annual taxable turnover falling below £300,000 on joining the scheme. Such traders may, if they so wish, render returns on an annual basis. Nine equal payments of value added tax will then be made on account, with a final, tenth, balancing payment accompanying submission of the return.

REGISTRATION
The collection and repayment of value added tax is confined to registered traders, an expression which includes individuals, partnerships and companies carrying on a trade, profession or vocation and certain other activities. Mandatory registration is confined to those making taxable supplies exceeding certain thresholds. These thresholds are amended periodically and from 1 April 1998 an unregistered trader must register:

a at any time, if there are reasonable grounds for

believing that the value of taxable supplies in the next thirty days will exceed £50,000; or

b at the end of any month if the value of taxable supplies in the last twelve months then ending has exceeded £50,000.

A person liable to be registered under **a** is required to notify liability, and will be registered with effect from the date he or she becomes so liable. If a person is liable to registration under **b**, he or she must notify liability within thirty days of the end of the month concerned and will be registered with effect from the end of the month in which the thirtieth day falls, unless registration from an earlier date is agreed.

These stringent time limits must be fully recognised when commencing a new business, or where the value of taxable supplies increases, as failure to notify Customs and Excise promptly may result in demands for value added tax which ought to have been paid on earlier occasions.

A trader whose taxable supplies do not reach the mandatory registration threshold may apply for voluntary registration. This may sometimes be thought advisable, as only registered traders can obtain relief for input tax suffered. Persons acquiring an existing registered business as a going concern must usually register immediately.

Registered traders may seek cancellation of their registration where the value of taxable supplies does not exceed certain limits. From 1 April 1998, an application for de-registration can be made if the value of taxable supplies is not expected to exceed £48,000 in the year then beginning.

EXEMPT SUPPLIES

Supplies of certain goods and services which comprise 'exempt supplies' are not chargeable to value added tax. These include the provision of finance, insurance and education, together with burial and cremation facilities. The granting of a lease or licence to occupy land will usually represent an exempt supply not chargeable to value added tax, but there are numerous exceptions. In particular, transactions affecting new non-domestic buildings may represent standard rated supplies. It is also possible for the landlord of a non-domestic building to exercise an option to treat rents as standard rated supplies. The purpose of such an election will be to avoid, or to limit, restrictions otherwise affecting the ability to recover input of tax suffered.

In those cases where a trader makes exempt supplies, no value added tax will be added to the prices charged, and in the absence of sufficient taxable supplies it may not be mandatory to register. A trader who is registered but who makes exempt supplies may be unable to fully recover the input tax suffered when obtaining goods or services.

Where a trader makes some taxable supplies and the input tax attributable to exempt supplies does not exceed £7,500 in a twelve-month period, it may be possible to obtain relief for all input tax suffered. However, this relief is severely restricted by a requirement that input tax attributable to exempt supplies must not exceed one-half of all input tax for the period involved.

BAD DEBTS

Tax is charged on the supply of goods or services and not on the amount actually received for the supply, unless the supplier is operating a special scheme. As special schemes only require receipts to be included, those operating these schemes effectively obtain relief for bad debts. The range of special schemes which provide effective relief for bad debts may also extend to registered traders having an annual turnover falling below £350,000. Such traders may, at their option, adopt a system of cash accounting which only recognises payments actually made and received. Since the amount of any bad debt will not be 'received' traders adopting this scheme are not required to account for tax on that debt.

For other traders not within the special schemes relief may be available for the value added tax element of bad debts suffered. This relief is limited to a genuine bad debt more than six months old and which has been written off in the books of the trader. The six-month period will commence to run from the date on which the payment for the supply falls due or, if later, the time of supply.

In those situations where the supplier obtains bad debt relief the person to whom the supply has been made must refund any value added tax for which input tax relief may have been claimed in relation to the supply.

RATES OF TAX

Value added tax is levied at three rates, namely:

a A zero, or nil, rate;

b A standard rate of 17.5 per cent; and

c A reduced rate of 5 per cent on supplies of domestic fuel (reduced from 8 per cent on 1 September 1997). From 1 July 1998 this rate also applies to the installation of energy saving materials under certain government grant schemes.

ZERO RATING

Zero rating extends to many supplies, including the following:

a The supply of food and drink for human consumption. This does not include such items as ice cream, chocolates, sweets, crisps and alcoholic drinks. Nor does it include supplies made in the course of catering, for example, at a wedding reception or dinner, or supplies for consumption in a restaurant or cafe. Take-away supplies of 'cold' foods for consumption off the supplier's premises are zero rated but the supply of 'hot' food and drink, for example, fish and chips or a container of hot tea, are taxable at the standard rate

b Sewerage and water services, unless supplies are made for non-domestic purposes

c Books, booklets, brochures, pamphlets, leaflets, newspapers, journals and periodicals

d Talking books for the blind and handicapped and wireless sets for the blind

e Supplies made in the construction of the following:

   i A dwelling, for example, a house or flat. This may include the construction of a garage if work is undertaken at the same time as the construction of the dwelling.
   ii New buildings used as children's homes, old people's homes and to provide student accommodation, but not hotels or prisons.
   iii New buildings to be used by a charity for non-business purposes, for example, churches.
   iv Substantial alterations to listed buildings used for a purpose within i, ii or iii.

   The construction of other buildings, for example, offices, shops and factories, is not zero rated.

f Transport of passengers in a vehicle, ship or aircraft designed or adapted to carry not less than twelve passengers

g Exports, including those to Member States in the Single Market where the required documentation is forthcoming

h Supply of drugs, medicines, medical and surgical appliances

i Supply of clothing and footwear suitable for young children.

This list is not intended to be exhaustive but it provides some indication of those supplies which may, and those which may not, be zero rated for value added tax purposes. In addition, a number of supplies made to charities obtain the benefit of zero rating and incur no liability to value added tax.

FARMERS

An optional flat-rate scheme may be used by farmers engaged in crop production, stock farming, forestry, fisheries and processing. It cannot be used by individuals whose primary activity is to buy and sell animals, nor can animal trainers qualify. Persons who purchase dairy products from farmers and those operating sawmills are excluded from the scheme.

Where a farmer uses the flat rate scheme he will not be registered for value added tax purposes. In the absence of registration there will be no right to recover input tax. However, the farmer may make a special addition of 4 per cent to sale prices and retain that addition in lieu of relief for input tax. Non-farming activities undertaken by a farmer and which cannot be brought within the flat-rate scheme must be dealt with separately. It will not be possible to add the flat-rate addition to non-farming supplies of this nature. Where the value of taxable supplies attributable to non-farming activities is sufficiently substantial to require registration, or the farmer registers on a voluntary basis, he can no longer use the flat-rate scheme.

Persons to whom supplies are made by a farmer can treat the 4 per cent addition as input tax and obtain relief for that tax in the normal manner.

ADMINISTRATION

Value added tax is administered by HM Customs and Excise and not by the Board of Inland Revenue. The tax performs no role whatsoever in the United Kingdom income tax system.

Registered traders should recognise that the application and administration of value added tax involves the satisfaction of many compliance requirements. Failure to submit value added tax returns, or to account for the proper amount of tax due promptly, may involve liability to penalties and interest.

21

Inheritance tax

INTRODUCED to replace estate duty, capital transfer tax imposed a wide-ranging liability to tax on lifetime gifts and also on the value of an individual's estate immediately before the time of death. Complex rules were included to deal with settled property held in trust. The potential scope of capital transfer tax was substantially redrafted for events taking place after 1 March 1986. Whilst much of the former administrative framework remained, the tax was re-named inheritance tax. The following comments outline the nature and scope of inheritance tax as that tax applies to events occurring on and after 19 March 1986.

When examining these comments it must be emphasised that the introduction of independent taxation, which applies to income tax and capital gains tax, had absolutely no effect on inheritance tax. There was no need for this system to be extended to inheritance tax as husband and wife have been separately taxed since the introduction of capital transfer tax in 1974.

Liability to inheritance tax extends to assets located in the United Kingdom. The tax also applies to assets located overseas if the person concerned was domiciled in the United Kingdom at the time of the transfer or other event. There are two main occasions of charge, one affecting a limited range of lifetime transfers and the other of much wider application to the value of an estate immediately before death.

LIFETIME TRANSFERS
Lifetime gifts and other transfers which deplete the value of an individual's estate may fall into four broad categories, namely transactions to be disregarded, exempt transfers, potentially exempt transfers and chargeable transfers.

Transactions disregarded
Some lifetime gifts and dispositions are entirely disregarded and incur no liability to inheritance tax, notwithstanding the value of the transferor's estate is reduced. These include dispositions not intended to confer any gratuitous benefit, the provision of family maintenance, the waiver of the right to receive remuneration and dividends, and the grant of agricultural tenancies made for full consideration.

Exempt transfers
Transfers of value which can be treated as 'exempt transfers' also avoid liability to inheritance tax. These include the following:

a A transfer by an individual to his or her spouse. This is subject to modification if the transferee is not domiciled in the United Kingdom
b The first £3,000 of transfers made in a year ending on 5 April. If the total value of transfers taking place in any year falls below £3,000 the excess may be carried forward for one year only and utilised in that year
c Transfers of value made by a transferor to any person in a year ending on 5 April if the value transferred does not exceed £250
d A transfer made as part of the transferor's normal expenditure and satisfied out of income

e Outright gifts made in consideration of marriage to the extent that the value transferred by any one transferor in respect of a single marriage does not exceed:

  i £5,000 if the transferor is the parent of either party to the marriage;

  ii £2,500 if the transferor is a party to the marriage or a grandparent or remoter ancestor of either party;

  iii £1,000 if the transferor is any other person.

f Transfers made to a charity where the assets transferred become the property of that charity or are held in trust for charitable purposes only

g The transfer of property to a political party. If this exemption is to apply it must be shown that at the most recent General Election at least two members of the party were elected to the House of Commons. Alternatively, the requirement will be satisfied if a single member is elected with not less than 150,000 votes being cast for members of that party

h Transfers made to an extensive list of institutions, including the National Museum, the National Trust for Places of Historic Interest or Natural Beauty, a local authority, and many others

i Transfers of heritage property and other assets of value to the nation made to an approved body not established or conducted for profit.

Potentially exempt transfers

If a transfer is neither to be disregarded nor treated as an exempt transfer it may comprise a potentially exempt transfer. This represents a transfer made by an individual to:

a A second individual;

b Trustees administering an accumulation and maintenance trust; or

c Trustees administering funds for a disabled or handicapped person.

The range of potentially exempt transfers also includes certain transactions affecting settled property in which an individual or individuals retain a life interest in possession. Most transfers made by an individual to such a trust may be treated as potentially exempt transfers and the termination of an interest in possession during lifetime may usually receive similar treatment.

As the title suggests, potentially exempt transfers are potentially exempt from liability to inheritance tax and no tax will become payable at the time of the transfer. The absence of liability will be confirmed should the transferor survive throughout a period of seven years from the date of the gift or other disposition. However, if the transferor dies within the seven-year inter vivos period tax becomes payable, calculated at the full rate or rates in force at the time of death. The amount of tax calculated on this basis may then be reduced to the following percentages by applying a form of tapering relief, which is governed by the length of the period between the date of the gift and the date of death:

Period of years before death	Percentage
Not more than 3. . . .	100
More than 3 but not more than 4	80
More than 4 but not more than 5	60
More than 5 but not more than 6	40
More than 6 but not more than 7	20

Chargeable transfers

Finally, a limited range of lifetime transfers will incur liability to inheritance tax. These are restricted to transfers involving trusts, other than those falling within the exempt and potentially exempt transfer rules, transfers to non-individuals and transfers affecting close companies. Tax is payable at one-half the full rate or rates but should the transferor die within a period of seven years from the date of the lifetime chargeable transfer additional tax may become payable. This additional tax is calculated by substituting the full rates, less a deduction for any tapering relief.

GIFTS WITH RESERVATION

Troublesome rules apply where a lifetime gift is made but the transferor continues to enjoy some benefit in the subject matter of the gift. This will frequently arise, for example, where parents transfer the ownership of the matrimonial home to children but continue to reside in the property without payment of a commercial rent. Where a gift with reservation is made it becomes necessary to establish the period throughout which the transferor continued to enjoy a benefit. If the benefit ceased to be enjoyed more than seven years before the date of the transferor's death no additional liability to inheritance tax will arise. A finding that the benefit was enjoyed immediately before the time of death will require that the value of the asset must be included when calculating the value of the deceased's estate on which inheritance tax becomes payable. Finally, if the transferor ceased to enjoy the benefit within a period of seven years before death he or she is treated as having made a potentially exempt transfer equal to the value of the asset at the time the benefit ceased.

DEATH

Immediately before the time of death an individual is deemed to make a transfer of value equal to the value of his or her estate, representing the value of assets less liabilities. However, exempt transfers involving transfers to a surviving spouse, charities, political organisations and national bodies will not incur inheritance tax liability, subject to limited exceptions. Inheritance tax payable is calculated by applying the full rate or rates. In addition, death may trigger liability to tax on potentially exempt transfers, and also further liability for chargeable lifetime transfers made within a period of seven years before death.

VALUATION

The value transferred by lifetime transfers will usually reflect the fall in the value of the transferor's estate. Often this fall will be identical to the value of the asset transferred, but there are many exceptions, particularly where an individual transfers part only of his or her shareholding interest in a closely controlled company. Immediately before the time of death a person is treated as having transferred his or her entire estate for a consideration reflecting the value at that date. Therefore, the value transferred will represent the excess, if any, of the value attributable to assets, less liabilities.

BUSINESS ASSETS

In general, the value of property comprised in an individual's estate will reflect the price which that property might reasonably have been expected to fetch on a sale in the open market. However, where the transfer relates to certain assets the value transferred, both by lifetime transfers and on death, may be reduced by a percentage. When calculating this percentage a distinction must be drawn between dispositions, deaths and other events occurring:

a Before 10 March 1992;
b After 9 March 1992 but before 6 April 1996; and
c After 5 April 1996.

Events before 10 March 1992

The percentage deductions available for transfers and other events taking place shortly before 10 March 1992 are shown by the following table:

Asset	Percentage deduction
Business or interest in a business	50
Controlling shareholding interest in any company . . .	50
More than 25 per cent interest in an unlisted company. . .	50
Not more than 25 per cent interest in an unlisted company . .	30
Land, buildings, machinery or plant used by a controlled company or partnership	30

Where a controlling shareholding interest exists it is immaterial whether the underlying company is listed or unlisted on a Stock Exchange when determining the availability of the 50 per cent deduction. However, the percentage deduction for minority shareholding interests cannot apply to shares in a listed company including a company dealt in on the Unlisted Securities Market.

Events after 9 March 1992 but before 6 April 1996

For transfers and events taking place after 9 March 1992 but before 6 April 1996, most percentage deductions were increased considerably to the levels shown by the following table:

Asset	Percentage deduction
Business or interest in a business	100
More than 25 per cent holding in an unlisted company. . .	100
More than 25 per cent holding in a USM company . . .	100
Controlling shareholding interest in a listed company . . .	50
Not more than 25 per cent holding in an unlisted company . .	50
Not more than 25 per cent holding in a USM company . . .	50
Land, buildings, machinery or plant used by a controlled company or partnership	50

As a result of these changes, holdings in companies dealt in on the Unlisted Securities Market became treated in the same manner as unlisted holdings. This treatment applied also to companies dealt in on the Alternative Investment Market, introduced during 1995.

Events after 5 April 1996

Yet further increases in some percentage deductions have been introduced for transfers and events taking place after 5 April 1996. As a result of these changes all holdings of unlisted shares, including those dealt in on the Unlisted Securities Market (which ceased to exist at the end of 1996) and the Alternative Investment Market, now qualify for a deduction at the rate of 100 per cent. Other percentage deductions remain unchanged and the revised list is as follows:

Asset	Percentage deduction
Business or interest in a business	100
All unlisted holdings, including those in USM and AIM companies	100
Controlling shareholding interest in a listed company . . .	50
Land, buildings, machinery or plant used by a controlled company or partnership	50

One significant effect of these increased percentage deductions is that interests in many family businesses, whether carried on by sole traders, partnerships or closely controlled companies, can be transferred without incurring any liability to inheritance tax.

Generally

It remains a general requirement in all cases that assets must have been owned for a minimum period of at least two years before the date of the lifetime disposition or death if the percentage deduction is to be forthcoming.

Only part of the value may qualify for the percentage deduction if not all assets of a business are used for a qualifying purpose.

AGRICULTURAL PROPERTY

The value of agricultural property transferred may also qualify for a percentage deduction. This is limited to the agricultural value and where, for example, property retains an 'excessive' development value no deduction will be available for the excess. Agricultural property includes short rotation coppice farming for events after 5 April 1995.

To obtain this relief the property must either have been owned by the transferor for a period of seven years and used for agricultural purposes or occupied by the transferor for those purposes throughout a

---

116
BUSINESS ASSETS RELIEF

The issued share capital of A Ltd, an unlisted company, comprised 100 ordinary shares of £1 each. Mr B retained 20 shares at the time of his death on 10 May 1998. It was agreed that these shares had a value of £80,000 and fully qualified for business assets relief.

The value to be included in the estate of Mr B for inheritance tax purposes is calculated as follows:

	£
Value of shares – as agreed . . .	80,000
Less 100 per cent business assets relief .	80,000
Value to be included	NIL

period of two years. Land managed under the terms of certain Habitat Schemes is treated as occupied for agricultural purposes.

The percentage deductions for transfers and other events taking place before 10 March 1992 are:

Asset	Percentage deduction
Owner-occupied farmland . .	50
Farm tenancies	50
Land subject to a tenancy not terminating within twelve months	30

For events and transfers taking place after 9 March 1992, the percentage deductions become:

Asset	Percentage deduction
Owner-occupied farmland . .	100
Farm tenancies	100
Land subject to a tenancy not terminating within twelve months	50

The deduction for land subject to a tenancy is increased to 100 per cent from 1 September 1995, but only for leases that commence, or are deemed to have commenced, on or after that date.

CALCULATION OF TAX PAYABLE

The value of each non-exempt lifetime gift or disposition is added to the value of previous dispositions, if any, to establish the rate of tax on the

————117————

CALCULATION OF TAX PAYABLE – GIFTS WITHIN SEVEN YEARS BEFORE DEATH

After making sufficient small gifts to exactly absorb the annual exemption, Mr R gifted freehold property to his son on 24 May 1994. The value of the property at this time was £265,000 and it did not qualify for business assets or agricultural property relief. Mr R died on 7 August 1998 without making any further gifts.

The gift was a potentially exempt transfer incurring no immediate liability to inheritance tax. However, as death occurred within the seven-year period, following the making of the gift this will trigger liability. The tax payable will be calculated as follows:

		Cumulative total
	£	£
Value of gift		265,000
Tax payable		
On first £223,000 . . .	NIL	
On balance of £42,000 at 40 per cent	16,800	
	£16,800	£265,000

As death occurred more than 4 years and less than 5 years from the date of the gift, the tapering relief shown on page 166 is available. The tax payable will therefore be reduced to:

$$£16,800 \times 60 \text{ per cent} = £10,080$$

current transfer. On death the value of the estate, after excluding any exempt transfers, will be added to the cumulative total of lifetime dispositions, if any, and tax calculated on the additional slice. This cumulative procedure affects only dispositions taking place within a period of seven years before the current transfer. Any dispositions made before the commencement of the seven-year period are ignored.

In those limited situations where inheritance tax becomes payable on a lifetime gift or disposition the value transferred must be 'grossed up' by including tax payable, unless the obligation is discharged by the transferee.

RATE OF TAX

Before 15 March 1988 inheritance tax was charged at different rates on each slice of the value transferred added to the cumulative total, if any. As the amount

————118————

CALCULATION OF TAX PAYABLE ON DEATH

Using the facts in Example 117, let it be assumed that the value of Mr R's estate at the time of death on 7 August 1998 was £300,000, after subtracting all reliefs and exemptions.

The total inheritance tax then becoming due will be calculated as follows:

		Cumulative total
		£
Re gift within previous seven years £10,080		265,000
Re value on death		300,000
Tax payable		
On £300,000 at 40 per cent	£120,000	
		£565,000

Therefore the total inheritance tax payable is £130,080 (£10,080 + £120,000).

added to the cumulative total increased, the rate of tax increased also.

This system was virtually abandoned for events occurring after 15 March 1988. Only two 'rates' now apply to calculate liability, namely:

a A nil rate; and

b A positive rate of 40 per cent.

A nil rate band of £215,000 applied to calculate liability for events occurring in the twelve-month period ending on 5 April 1998. This was increased to a threshold of £223,000 for events taking place subsequently, reflecting the increase in the retail prices index for the period ending in September 1997. The positive rate has consistently remained at 40 per cent from 16 March 1988. This positive rate must be reduced by one-half to 20 per cent for chargeable lifetime gifts.

When calculating rates of tax it will not be overlooked that the calculation will be governed by the top slice of the cumulative total.

Tables setting out the rates of inheritance tax which have applied since 17 March 1986 appear on page 192.

SETTLED PROPERTY

Complex rules apply when establishing inheritance tax liability for settled property held by trustees. In general, where a beneficiary retains an interest in possession the settled property to which that interest relates will be effectively treated as being in the ownership of the beneficiary. Property held by discretionary trusts is subject to a ten-year periodic charge, with interim charges where property leaves the trust before the first ten-year anniversary or between anniversaries. An accumulation and maintenance trust for the benefit of individuals below the age of twenty-five years will not be subject to the ten-year periodic charge, nor will liability to inheritance tax usually arise on the removal of property from such a trust.

These brief comments provide no more than a bare outline of the rules to be applied and in all cases consideration must be given to the trust deed or other document governing the administration of settled property.

22

Investment income after 5 April 1999

Some significant changes will apply to the taxation of certain income received by individuals on and after 6 April 1999. The changes affect the treatment of tax credits on dividends and, perhaps more importantly, the identity of income made exempt from liability to income tax. The amendment of exempt income has been made necessary by the introduction of Individual Savings Accounts.

The nature and extent of these changes are outlined below. It will be recognised however, that further changes and amendments may be introduced at a later date.

DIVIDENDS

Dividends received from United Kingdom companies before 6 April 1999 usually have an attached tax credit representing one-quarter of the dividend received. Therefore, of the aggregate sum (dividend plus tax credit) the tax credit represents 20 per cent.

From 6 April 1999 the tax credit will be reduced to one-ninth of the dividend received. Thus of the aggregate sum of the dividend and tax credit, the tax credit itself will represent only 10 per cent.

The method of taxing dividends in 1999–2000 and future years is also changed. There will be two rates, namely:

a A Schedule F ordinary rate of 10 per cent, and
b A Schedule F upper rate of 32.5 per cent.

Either or both rates may be changed from time to time.

The Schedule F ordinary rate will apply where the dividend is not subject to higher rate income tax in the hands of the shareholder. As the ordinary rate of 10 per cent will exactly match the tax credit, also of 10 per cent, no income tax will be due at the lower or the basic rate.

Where, or to the extent that, the dividend incurs tax liability at the higher rate, tax will be imposed on the aggregate of the dividend and the tax credit not at 40 per cent but at the Schedule F upper rate of 32.5 per cent. Tax calculated on this basis will then be reduced by the tax credit of 10 per cent reflecting tax already suffered on the dividend.

The Schedule F ordinary rate of 10 per cent and the Schedule F upper rate of 32.5 per cent have been selected to avoid any additional tax being imposed on dividends, as the example on the next page illustrates.

Repayment of tax credit

A further change affecting dividends is that from 6 April 1999 it will no longer be possible for individuals to obtain a repayment of a tax credit where the shareholder is not liable, or not fully liable, to income tax. Credits may be recovered however, where dividends arise on shares in a Personal Equity Plan or an Individual Savings Account.

Dividends from overseas

Dividends received from companies outside the United Kingdom do not carry any tax credit. However, where a dividend of this nature becomes taxable in the United Kingdom the shareholder is deemed to have suffered notional tax equal to 10 per cent of the aggregate dividend and tax. Therefore the dividend received from overseas is taxed on a

119
DIVIDENDS

Assume throughout that a cash dividend of £80 is received, with other income absorbing all available allowances and reliefs.

1998–99	£
Cash dividend	80.00
Add tax credit – one-quarter	20.00
Gross	£100.00

Individual not liable at higher rate:

	£
Lower rate tax on £100.00 at 20 per cent	20.00
Less tax credit	20.00
Additional income tax	NIL

Individual liable at higher rate:

	£
Higher rate tax on £100.00 at 40 per cent	40.00
Less tax credit	20.00
Additional income tax due	£20.00

1999–2000	£
Cash dividend	80.00
Add tax credit – one-ninth	8.89
Gross	£88.89

Individual not liable at higher rate:

	£
Ordinary rate tax on £88.89 at 10 per cent	8.89
Less tax credit	8.89
Additional income tax	NIL

Individual liable at higher rate:

	£
Upper rate tax on £88.89 at 32.5 per cent	28.89
Less tax credit	8.89
Additional income tax	£20.00

Although different rates of tax have been used, the liability for 1999–2000 is identical to that for the previous year, 1998–99.

Pence have been used to produce an accurate comparison but these would be ignored when completing a self-assessment income tax return form.

---

basis identical to a dividend received from a United Kingdom company.

Foreign income dividends
Foreign income dividends paid by a United Kingdom company carry no tax credit but are deemed to have suffered notional income tax at the rate of 20 per cent. No foreign income dividends are capable of being paid or received after 5 April 1999.

Exemption
In those situations where dividend income arises from investments forming part of a Personal Equity Plan or Individual Savings Account no liability to income tax will arise (see later).

STOCK DIVIDEND OPTIONS
The value of shares issued under stock dividend option arrangements in 1998–99 is deemed to represent a sum remaining after deducting income tax at the lower rate of 20 per cent. Whilst a not dissimilar approach applies for stock dividends received on and after 6 April 1999, the value is deemed to reflect a net sum remaining after subtracting Schedule F ordinary rate tax of 10 per cent.

THE INDIVIDUAL SAVINGS ACCOUNT
A new form of investment, the Individual Savings Account (ISA), will become available on 6 April 1999. Individuals who are resident and ordinarily resident in the United Kingdom may subscribe to the ISA if they are over the age of 18 years.

The three components
An ISA can include three components, namely:

a cash;
b stocks and shares; and
c life insurance.

The cash component may incorporate bank and building society deposit accounts, supermarket savings accounts and National Savings products which are not otherwise tax-free, together with a range of similar items.

Ordinary shares, fixed interest preference shares and fixed interest corporate bonds with at least five years to run to maturity and issued by companies incorporated throughout the world may be included in the stocks and shares component. This will also incorporate units in United Kingdom authorised unit trusts and shares in many approved investment trusts. However, unlisted shares and those traded on the Alternative Investment Market must be excluded.

The life insurance component offered by insurance companies and friendly societies will usually be of the single premium type. No tax will be payable on maturity proceeds and sums invested by the insurer receive favourable treatment.

Subscription limits
In the first year, namely 1999–2000, savers may subscribe up to a maximum of £7,000. Of this sum, no more than £3,000 may be lodged in the cash component and no more than £1,000 in life

insurance. Any balance remaining, or indeed the entire subscription, may be allocated to stocks and shares.

For 2000–2001 and each future year the maximum subscription will be reduced to £5,000, of which no more than £1,000 may go into cash and £1,000 into life insurance.

In all years husbands and wives will each retain their own £7,000 or £5,000 limit.

Marketing

ISAs will be marketed by financial institutions or by independent persons offering other people's products. In each case, however, the ISA will be administered by a manager.

Savers will have a choice when selecting the required manager. One option is to use a single manager who can offer an account which may include all three components but must include the stocks and shares component. Individual savers may choose, for example, to allocate their entire subscriptions to stocks and shares.

The second option is to approach separate managers, one for each of the three components. Where this option is exercised only £3,000 can be allocated to stocks and shares, £1,000 (or £3,000 in 1999–2000) to cash and £1,000 to life insurance.

Other matters

Shares received from an approved profit-sharing or savings-related share option scheme may be transferred into the stocks and shares component at market value. The value will count towards the annual subscription limit but no capital gains tax will be payable on the transfer. It will not be possible to transfer shares acquired under a public offer or received when a building society or insurer demutualises.

Tax advantages

The attraction of ISAs is the tax relief which subscriptions may eventually confer. No liability to income tax or capital gains tax will arise on the underlying investments.

For the five-year period commencing on 6 April 1999 and ending on 5 April 2004, dividends paid by United Kingdom companies on stocks and shares will carry a tax credit of 10 per cent which can be recovered within the account. This credit will also be available for dividends attributable to policies obtained through the life insurance component.

The availability of tax exemptions will not be influenced should withdrawals be made from an ISA. However, once the maximum permitted subscription has been made in any year no further subscriptions will be permitted, notwithstanding the amount of any withdrawal.

PERSONAL EQUITY PLANS

No new personal equity plans (PEPs) will be available after 5 April 1999. However, there is no need for existing PEP holders to transfer their holdings to an Individual Savings Account as the holding will retain exemption from both income tax and capital gains tax.

PEPs retained on 5 April 1999 may continue to be held independently of an ISA and will not affect the future level of subscriptions to the new product.

As a general rule, tax credits attaching to dividends paid by United Kingdom resident companies will cease to be repayable after 5 April 1999. However, throughout a period of five years commencing on 6 April 1999 and ending on 5 April 2004, tax credits at the rate of 10 per cent will be repayable on dividend income received from a PEP investment.

This suggests that where PEP investments have been acquired previously and are retained on 5 April 1999, steps should be taken to ensure that there is no subsequent disposal or other event which may lead to relief being lost.

TESSAs

No new TESSAs will be available after 5 April 1999. Those existing on that date, whether reflecting original investments or reinvestments, will continue to run for the full five-year period. Once a TESSA matures it will be possible to transfer the proceeds, but not the amount of accumulated interest, to an Individual Savings Account.

INCOME FROM SAVINGS

In future, income from savings, as defined on page 109, must be broken down between two headings, namely:

a dividends and other distributions from United Kingdom companies, together with similar receipts from companies overseas, and
b other savings income.

Dividends and other receipts under heading a will be subject to Schedule F ordinary tax at the rate of 10 per cent and Schedule F upper rate tax at the rate of 32.5 per cent, as outlined above. Remaining income from savings will be chargeable to income tax at the lower rate of 20 per cent, or at the higher

120
INCOME FROM SAVINGS

After subtracting available allowances and reliefs, the income of Simon which did not arise from 'savings' for 1999–2000 was £24,000. In addition he received:

Dividends (including tax credits £200)	£2,000
Other income from 'savings' (including tax deducted of £700)	£3,500

Assuming that the basic rate band ended at £27,100, tax payable becomes:

	£
Non 'savings' income	24,000
Add other income from savings (excluding dividends)	3,500
	27,500
Add dividends	2,000
	£29,000

	£
Tax on other income from savings	
Excess over 27,100 = £400	
£400 × 40 per cent	160.00
Tax on dividends	
Excess over £27,100 – all	
£2,000 × 32.5 per cent . . .	650.00
	810.00

	£	
Less		
Tax deducted on other income		
£400 × 20 per cent	80.00	
Tax credits on dividends	200.00	280.00
Income tax due . . .		£530.00

rate of 40 per cent where income is sufficiently substantial.

The expression 'income from savings' includes both dividends and other forms of savings income. It is only to the extent that the combined savings income exceeds the basic rate tax band that liability at the Schedule F upper rate or the higher rate arises. As these two rates differ, one imposed at 32.5 per cent and the other at 40 per cent, it is necessary to establish an order of priority.

Where all income from savings exceeds the basic rate tax band there is no difficulty in applying the respective rates of 32.5 per cent and 40 per cent. However, where part of the combined income from savings falls below the basic rate band and the other part exceeds that band:

a the first addition will reflect income from savings which is not liable at 32.5 per cent, and

b the remaining addition will be limited to dividend income which is liable to the upper rate of 32.5 per cent.

NATIONAL SAVINGS PRODUCTS

National Savings products may be brought within the 'cash component' of an Individual Savings Account. However, those products which are already exempt from liability to tax, for example, National Savings Certificates and Premium Bonds, will continue to retain that exemption and will not be included in ISAs.

Married couples
Some practical considerations

Independent taxation of husband and wife is a well-established feature of the United Kingdom taxation code. However, problem areas do sometimes arise and it may be of interest to readers if a number of matters which occasionally create difficulty are briefly examined. As this section affects only a husband and wife 'living together', the following comments are limited to a married couple retaining such a status.

DEEDS OF COVENANT
When making payments under a properly drawn charitable deed of covenant the payer will deduct income tax at the basic rate of 23 per cent for 1998–99. Where the payments are made out of income chargeable to income tax the amount of tax deducted may be retained. It is also possible to offset the covenanted payments against income generally for the purpose of obtaining relief at the higher rate where income is sufficiently substantial. In those cases where the payer does not have sufficient taxable income to provide cover for the payment the tax deducted must be paid over to the Inland Revenue.

Husbands and wives 'living together' are advised to carefully consider which spouse should be making covenanted payments. If payments are made by a wife who has little or no income she may be required to account to the Inland Revenue for basic rate income tax deducted. In addition, there will be no relief at the higher rate. Where her husband is liable at this rate there will be a substantial advantage if the husband, rather than the wife, makes covenanted payments. In some situations, and with the consent of the charity concerned, it may be thought advisable for a wife to discontinue future payments due under an existing covenant, with these payments being replaced by a new deed of covenant entered into by her husband. If the gross amount of the covenant remains unaltered this will not affect income reaching the charity but will provide the 'household' with increased tax relief.

In the case of joint covenants the Inland Revenue will usually maintain that payments should be treated as made equally by husband and wife, unless there is evidence to support a different conclusion.

ENTERPRISE INVESTMENT SCHEMES
Both a husband and his wife may independently obtain relief at the reduced rate of 20 per cent on investments up to £150,000 made under enterprise investment scheme arrangements. As 20 per cent is equal to the lower rate it may be largely immaterial which spouse invests, although the investor must have a sufficient tax liability to absorb the relief.

However, where one spouse has and the other does not have capital gains capable of being used to provide deferral relief for an investment this may be an important factor when reaching a decision.

VENTURE CAPITAL TRUSTS
The identity of the spouse who should subscribe for shares in a venture capital trust raises considerations

similar to those affecting investment in enterprise investment schemes.

MORTGAGE INTEREST

Only interest on the first £30,000 of a qualifying loan applied to acquire an individual's residence can obtain tax relief, usually under the MIRAS deduction scheme. In the case of husband and wife 'living together' £30,000 is the maximum amount of aggregate loans made to the couple on which relief will be forthcoming.

It remains possible for the couple to submit an 'allocation of interest' election, which enables the interest paid to be apportioned between them in whatever proportions they consider advisable. The election must be submitted within a period of twelve months following the end of the year of assessment to which it relates. It will then continue in force until being revoked by either spouse.

With the restriction of relief to a reduced rate of only 10 per cent the election has lost much of its former importance. However, there may occasionally be an advantage where interest is paid outside the MIRAS scheme or where one spouse is over the age of 64.

MARRIED COUPLE'S ALLOWANCE

Where a couple are 'living together' a married couple's allowance may be obtained. In the absence of any election this allowance must be used by the husband and only where he has insufficient income can any unused balance be transferred to his wife. In the absence of other action the decision whether to transfer is that of the husband only.

However, the wife may elect, as of right, to obtain one-half of the basic married couple's allowance, leaving the husband with the balance of that allowance. Alternatively, the couple may jointly elect that the entire basic allowance should be allocated to the wife only. Notwithstanding any election, if the spouse entitled to any part of the married couple's allowance is unable to utilise that part against taxable income, the unused portion may be transferred to the other spouse.

An election must be submitted before the commencement of the year of assessment to which it is first to apply. An exception arises in the year of marriage where the election may be submitted at any time in that year. Disregarding matters of 'fairness', an election could be beneficial for 1998–99 where the husband has little or no income liable to tax. However, with relief falling to 10 per cent on 6 April 1999 the election is now of somewhat limited importance.

LIFE ASSURANCE RELIEF

Where substantial premiums are paid on life assurance and other policies taken out before 14 March 1984, tax relief may be forthcoming but this could be restricted by reference to the payer's income. The income of husband and wife cannot be merged for this purpose as consideration must be confined to the income of the spouse paying premiums. This may become a factor when deciding which spouse should receive income.

JOINT CHEQUE ACCOUNTS

Many married couples maintain joint bank current or cheque accounts. Where a cheque is drawn on such an account to discharge a liability it may become uncertain whether the payment is being made by the husband or by his wife. Little difficulty emerges where the cheque is drawn to discharge a joint liability and in practice it is unlikely that the Inland Revenue would dispute the identity of the alleged drawer in other cases. However, for the avoidance of doubt, where a cheque is to be drawn to satisfy a payment attracting tax relief, perhaps a donation made under the Gift Aid scheme, it may be considered advisable to open a separate account in the sole name of the drawer. This should place beyond doubt the identity of the person involved.

PARTNERSHIPS

Where the income of one party to a marriage substantially exceeds that of the other there is an obvious advantage from the transfer of future income by that party. One possible method of achieving this where a business is carried on by, say, a husband in his capacity as a sole proprietor is to admit the wife as a partner. This will enable partnership profits to be shared between husband and wife. However, caution must be exercised to ensure that a 'genuine' partnership exists between the parties and not merely a 'paper' or 'sham' arrangement which will fail to withstand detailed scrutiny.

DIRECTORSHIPS

A further method of providing one spouse, usually a wife, with income is for the wife to be appointed a director or employee of a company controlled by her husband. If this results in the earnings of the husband being reduced the Inland Revenue may decline to accept that income really has been derived by the wife. This rejection should be successfully opposed by the ability to demonstrate that real services have been provided in return for the remuneration paid.

JOINT INCOME

Some income-producing assets may be held jointly by a husband and his wife. The general rule is that any income arising from such assets must be apportioned equally between the couple. However, it is possible to submit a joint declaration requiring the income to be apportioned by reference to the beneficial interests held by the husband and by the wife. The declaration must be forwarded to the Inland Revenue within a period of sixty days from the date on which it has been made and will only apply to income arising subsequently.

Where a husband and wife jointly retain income-producing assets the ability to submit an election, or indeed the ability to refrain from making any such election, is important. The election applies separately to each asset, and in some situations it will be advisable to submit an election for a number of assets only and to refrain from making any election for the remainder. Numerous cases will undoubtedly arise where wisdom indicates the inadvisability of submitting any election whatsoever.

TRANSFER OF ASSETS

Where a wife has little, if any, income and her spouse retains a range of income-producing assets, consideration may well be given to the transfer of an asset for the purpose of establishing future income accruing to the wife. If such a transfer is to be effective for income tax purposes it must comprise an 'outright gift'. Should any 'strings' be attached to the gift, or the transferor be entitled to enjoy any benefit whatsoever from the asset transferred, the transaction is likely to be ineffective. All future income from an ineffective transfer will remain that of the transferor for income tax purposes.

LOSSES CARRIED FORWARD

Losses incurred by a husband or wife from the carrying on of a trade, profession or vocation may be carried forward and offset against future profits. Losses incurred by a spouse may only be carried forward and offset against future profits from the same business carried on by this same spouse. It is not possible for those losses to be carried forward and used by the other spouse.

CAPITAL GAINS TAX

For capital gains tax purposes a husband and his wife each have an annual exemption of £6,800 for 1998–99. Any unused part of the annual exemption cannot be carried forward and will be lost. This may suggest the wisdom of transferring assets from one spouse to another before those assets are sold to a third party, thereby enabling the gain to be realised in the most tax efficient manner.

Problems may arise where gains or losses accrue from the disposal of a jointly owned asset. It will be necessary to allocate the gains or losses between the joint owners. No election is possible to determine the basis of allocation, which will probably proceed by an equal apportionment unless there is clear evidence that the beneficial interests support a different allocation. In some cases a husband and his wife may consider it advisable to adjust their interests to obtain the most tax efficient basis of apportionment.

SELF-ASSESSMENT

It is a well recognised feature of independent taxation that a husband and wife are separately assessed. This situation has not altered with the introduction of self-assessment. However, it is now even more important that the tax affairs of husband and wife are properly separated and not confused. Should confusion arise, entries affecting the affairs of one spouse may be inadvertently recorded on the tax return of the other. This could have most serious consequences which eventually create a liability to discharge both interest and penalties.

24

Hints on saving tax

ALL TAXPAYERS are understandably anxious to reduce their tax commitments. This can be achieved by:

a Taking advantage of all available allowances and reliefs.
b Carefully planning the dates on which transactions or events take place;
c Taking steps to increase the reliefs which can be obtained; or
d Refraining from action which will increase the amount of tax payable.

The requirements of one individual will differ from those of another, and there are often personal or business considerations which will outweigh possible tax savings. For example, ready access to savings may be more important than the amount of tax incurred on income arising. But few financial transactions can be safely carried out without considering the effect on tax liabilities. The following notes outline some areas where tax savings can be achieved, or additional obligations avoided. Other matters have been reviewed in the previous chapter dealing with the taxation of married couples.

PERSONAL MATTERS

Allowances
All individuals are entitled to a personal allowance and should make sure that this is being claimed and used. Those approaching the age of 65 or 75 and who do not receive tax return forms must advise the Tax Office if the increased personal allowances are to be forthcoming. Those who do receive tax returns will make the necessary claim when completing the return. Most other allowances will only be given where they are claimed.

Married Couple's Allowance
It is possible for a married woman 'living with' her husband to obtain one-half, or perhaps all, of the married couple's allowance. This requires the submission of a claim before the commencement of a year of assessment and may be advantageous where the husband suffers little or no liability to income tax. With relief restricted to the reduced rate of 10 per cent for 1999–2000 any advantage will be small.

Marriage
In the year of marriage the married couple's allowance reduces by £158.33 (at 1998–99 rates) for each complete month from 5 May to the date of the ceremony. For example, by postponing the wedding from, say, 30 April to 15 May, the allowance will fall by £158, which represents some £23.70 with relief calculated at the reduced rate of 15 per cent or £15.80 when the rate is further reduced to 10 per cent. This amount is small but may justify advancing the ceremony by days, weeks, or even months.

Marriage breakdown
On the breakdown of a marriage leading to separation or divorce, a great many tax considerations will arise. Where maintenance payments are made under a 'new' Court order or agreement, the recipient will not suffer any liability to taxation, nor can the

payer obtain any significant relief. Thus in many situations payments must be financed in whole or in part out of taxed income. This obligation must be recognised when the order or agreement is being discussed and it may be considered advisable to transfer the ownership of income-producing assets, rather than enter into a commitment for the payment of maintenance. Where there are children of the marriage the possible obligation of a parent to make child maintenance payments to the Child Support Agency is a further factor requiring detailed review.

Payments made under 'old' orders or agreements may continue to obtain some relief, but this must be limited to the amount payable in 1988–89. It follows that where payments due under such an agreement or order are subsequently increased, the payer may fail to obtain any tax relief for the amount of the increase.

Although the transfer of assets between husband and wife 'living together' incurs no liability to capital gains tax, this exemption no longer applies once they are separated, or indeed divorced. Where the value of assets is substantial, a subsequent transfer often creates considerable liability to capital gains tax. It is essential that parties to a marriage breakdown take professional advice on their potential tax commitments at an early stage.

Interest

Unless payments of interest can be deducted in calculating business profits, or profits of a Schedule A business, stringent requirements must be satisfied before the outgoing will qualify for relief in calculating income chargeable to tax. No relief is available for interest payable on a bank overdraft, and whenever possible a more permanent form of borrowing should be used.

Interest on a loan applied to acquire an individual's only or main residence will usually qualify for relief, subject to a maximum ceiling of £30,000 and with relief limited to the reduced rate of 10 per cent for 1998–99. Some individuals may obtain a loan on the security of an existing dwelling but no relief can be obtained for the subsequent payment of interest, unless the loan is applied for a qualifying purpose. If the need to obtain additional finance can be anticipated, it may be advisable to await the need for funds to ensure that any borrowings are applied to a purpose which enables tax relief to be obtained.

The limited relief may continue for interest paid on loans applied before 6 April 1988 on the acquisition of a private residence for occupation by a separated spouse, divorced former spouse or a dependent relative. Relief may also be forthcoming where the loan was applied to improve the residence. However, if qualifying occupation is discontinued, or the old loan is replaced by a new loan, future relief for interest paid will be lost.

MIRAS

Income tax relief is obtained by deduction where MIRAS applies to interest payments. A number of conditions must be satisfactorily discharged before MIRAS can apply, and failure to observe those conditions may later have serious consequences. As a general rule, MIRAS is limited to interest paid on a loan applied to acquire a qualifying home. It cannot usually be obtained on property used for some other purpose or on property merely provided as security. Particular difficulties arise where two single individuals each have loans under MIRAS and subsequently marry. In the case of a husband and wife 'living together' there can be but one recognised 'only or main residence'. Relief is limited to interest paid on a loan applied to acquire that residence and cannot extend to a loan on some other property. Nor can the couple obtain relief for interest on aggregate loans in excess of £30,000.

It is of great importance that when completing the initial MIRAS documents, or where some future change in circumstances takes place, the lender is made fully aware of the position. Subsequent detection that MIRAS has been applied to a non-qualifying loan may not only lead to a demand for the recovery of excessive relief but can result in demands for interest and penalties also.

Children

Minor children are entitled to the basic personal allowance of £4,195 for 1998–99. Many children have little, if any, income, unless they leave school or undertake a part-time job. This means that the benefit of the personal allowance will be lost. To utilise that allowance, a grandparent, uncle or aunt would sometimes enter into a deed of covenant providing the child with income. Similar arrangements were used by parents having children over the age of 18 years and attending university or some other form of higher education establishment. On making payments under a deed of covenant the payer would usually deduct and retain income tax at the basic rate. The child could often obtain a repayment of the tax deducted from the Inland Revenue.

No payments made under such deeds will now be recognised for taxation purposes.

In substitution for payments under deed of covenant, grandparents may contemplate placing funds in a building society account, bank deposit account or other income-producing investment in the name of a child as this can provide income absorbed by the annual allowance. Parents may undertake similar arrangements for their minor children but where income exceeds £100 it may be treated as that of the parent for income tax purposes. It is as well to take professional advice before parents transfer assets to, or for the benefit of, their minor children.

Charitable covenants

No income tax relief is available to individuals making modest voluntary gifts to charity unless those payments are made under an approved payroll deduction scheme. However, regular donors should contemplate using deeds of covenant. Payments made under charitable covenants enable the payer to obtain tax relief at the highest rate of tax suffered, without any limitation on the amount paid for 1998–99.

Single donations of £250 or more under the Gift Aid scheme will provide relief on a basis similar to that for payments under deed of covenant. Those contemplating substantial donations of an irregular amount may prefer the flexibility of Gift Aid to a formal deed of covenant. Smaller donations may be made under the Millennium Gift Aid scheme where the objective is to support education and anti-poverty projects in poorer countries.

DIRECTORS AND EMPLOYEES

Living accommodation

An additional taxable benefit arises where a director or employee is provided with expensive living accommodation. This benefit applies if the cost of the accommodation, together with the cost of carrying out improvements, exceeds £75,000. Those occupying property acquired, perhaps many years earlier, at a cost falling below the £75,000 threshold should carefully consider the wisdom of moving to more expensive accommodation where the threshold is to be exceeded. The move may create a taxable benefit which would not otherwise arise.

Car benefits

Directors and higher-paid employees provided with motor cars for private motoring suffer tax on the car benefit. This benefit must usually be calculated by reference to the list price of a vehicle, perhaps increased by the list price of accessories. The basic benefit arising from the availability of vehicles less than four years old is 35 per cent of the list price, or aggregate of list prices where accessories are involved. This is reduced by one-third where there are 2,500 miles of business motoring in a year or reduced by two-thirds where business motoring exceeds 18,000 miles annually. Wherever possible attempts should be made to exceed these thresholds and reduce the amount of the taxable benefit.

Those making little use of a motor vehicle may wish to consider whether the arrangement should continue. It may be cost efficient for an individual to provide his or her own motor vehicle for business travel and to receive a 'tax-free' mileage allowance under the Fixed Profit Car Scheme, together with an increase in salary.

Particular consideration should be given to the proposed purchase by an employer of a 'classic' or 'veteran' motor car. Vehicles of this nature will usually be more than fifteen years of age and may well have a market value exceeding £15,000. It is the market value and not the original list price which governs the calculation of the taxable benefit for such vehicles. The magnitude of this benefit should always be considered before arranging for the purchase of an expensive or valuable motor car by an employer where that vehicle is to be used for private motoring.

Loss of office

The first £30,000 received as compensation for the loss of an office or employment is usually tax-free. Where dismissal or redundancy is likely and negotiations are taking place between the parties, there may be an advantage in accepting a tax-free lump sum, rather than an extended period of notice with taxable earnings.

A further alternative may involve a reduced lump sum and the provision of benefits, perhaps the use of a motor car, during future years.

BUSINESS CONSIDERATIONS

Accounting date

Many proprietors of businesses commenced before 6 April 1994 will have changed a perhaps long established annual accounting date in recognition of both the transitional approach to profit assessments for 1996–97 and the demands of the current year basis. Frequently the change will have been made to an accounting date falling on 31 March or perhaps 5 April. The main advantage of selecting these dates is the substantially reduced basis period which may arise on the future termination of a business.

Businesses commenced on and after 6 April 1994 are unaffected by the transitional arrangements as the current year basis will apply throughout. It will usually be found that the better approach to tax planning will be achieved by the careful selection of the basis period for the second year of assessment. Where the accounting date in the second year falls less than twelve months after the commencement of the business, the basis period for the second year will comprise the first twelve months. In those cases where the accounting date is more than twelve months after commencement it is the period of twelve months to the accounting date which establish the basis period. In the absence of any accounting date falling in the second year, the basis period will be the twelve months ending on 5 April. It is therefore the trend of profits which may indicate the ideal accounting date to select. Here also, the affect on future basis periods, particularly where a business comes to an end, must not be overlooked. Inevitably there will be commercial and other considerations which prompt a business proprietor to disregard the ideal tax planning date and to select an annual accounting date which reflects the needs of the business.

Discontinuing 'old' businesses

The taxable profits of 'old' businesses which commenced before 6 April 1994 and continue beyond 5 April 1997 will be determined by applying the transitional 'averaging' rules for 1996–97. The current year basis will then be used to determine profits chargeable for 1997–98 and future years, with the availability of transitional overlap relief. In two situations, however, special rules may be applied.

First, where such a business is discontinued on or before 5 April 1998 the Inland Revenue have the right to disregard both the current year basis and the transitional rules. Assessments for 1995–96, 1996–97 and 1997–98 may then be based on the former preceding year basis.

Secondly, where the business ceases during the twelve-month period ending on 5 April 1999 the Inland Revenue have the right to substitute the actual profits for the year ended 5 April 1997 when arriving at the assessment for 1996–97. This will displace the application of transitional rules.

The possibility of additional tax becoming payable where a business which was commenced before 6 April 1994 is discontinued during the two-year period ending on 5 April 1999, should never be overlooked.

Transfer of business

Individuals carrying on business on their own account, or as members of a partnership, may contemplate the transfer of that business to a newly incorporated company. A transfer of this nature will be treated as the discontinuance of the old business and require the application of special rules for determining liability to income tax in the closing years. Before deciding on the proposed date of transfer consideration must be given to the application of the current year basis of assessment. This basis may affect the most tax efficient date on which a business should be transferred as there may be either savings to be achieved or additional tax to be avoided.

Capital allowances

Annual writing down allowances are available for the cost of acquiring many assets used for business purposes. It is sometimes considered that by advancing the date of payment allowances may fall into an earlier basis period or company accounting period. This possibility must be approached with considerable caution. For example, in the case of plant and machinery not only must expenditure be incurred but an asset must usually 'belong to' the person incurring that expenditure before an allowance will become available. An invoice or other document backdated before the time on which ownership changes hands will not be sufficient.

National insurance contributions

Class 1 national insurance contributions are based on the level of 'earnings' paid to an employed individual. Primary contributions suffered by an employee are subject to a threshold. Once this threshold has been reached, contributions are not payable on the excess. No similar threshold applies to secondary contributions payable by the employer who must satisfy contributions on all earnings of higher paid employees. Some employers may consider whether employees should be offered 'perks' or 'benefits', rather than an increase in salary. Certain advantages of this nature, whilst creating taxable benefits in the hands of employees, are disregarded when determining the level of earnings on which contributions must be paid, although recent changes have substantially reduced this advantage. The availability of a car for private motoring and the provision of fuel for a similar purpose will involve the employer, but not the employee, in a further liability to discharge contributions.

In the case of closely controlled family companies advantages may arise from the payment of dividends, or possibly rent for the use of assets, rather than remuneration. Before any steps of this nature are taken detailed consideration must be given to the possible effect on other forms of taxation. In particular it will not be overlooked that with the forthcoming reduction in the rate of tax credits to one-ninth of a dividend and the repeal of liability to advance corporation tax many of the previous advantages from paying dividends have been eroded.

INVESTMENT OPPORTUNITIES

Life assurance
No tax relief is available for premiums paid on new life assurance policies made after 13 March 1984. However, relief continues for qualifying policies made on or before this date, unless the terms of the policy are altered. Relief reduces the cost of premiums by 12.5 per cent and this should be recognised before contemplating the surrender of older policies, or taking any steps which may terminate future relief.

Pensions for the employed
Employees who are members of a company, or other, occupational pension scheme obtain relief for contributions paid to secure benefits. The maximum relief is broadly limited to contributions not exceeding 15 per cent of earnings. Few schemes require contributions approaching this level but the employee may utilise the shortfall by paying additional voluntary contributions. The aggregate contributions paid must not result in the 15 per cent limit being exceeded, but subject to this the additional contributions may be paid to trustees administering the employer's scheme or to a 'free-standing' approved financial institution. These contributions produce relief at the employee's highest rate of income tax. For example, an individual paying additional voluntary contributions of £1,000 and suffering tax at the higher rate of 40 per cent for 1998–99 will reduce his or her tax bill by £400, so that the true net outlay is only £600. Membership of an employer's pension scheme is not compulsory but before ceasing to participate in such a scheme employees should carefully review the available alternatives. It may be found that these alternatives do not justify removal from the employer's scheme.

Pensions for the self-employed and others
Self-employed individuals and employees not covered by a pension scheme may contribute up to 17.5 per cent, or perhaps more for those aged over 35, of their earnings to a personal pension scheme. Premiums paid may be set against taxable income. Where insufficient premiums have been paid in any year the balance of unused relief may be carried forward for a maximum six-year period. Any unused relief remaining at the end of this six-year period is lost. Those able to contribute should consider the advisability of paying maximum contributions, particularly where they are approaching retirement age. Although the purpose of paying contributions is to provide a pension or annuity in retirement, it is possible to obtain a tax-free lump sum, with reduced periodic payments in the future.

Similar comments apply where contributions are paid to a retirement annuity scheme set up before 1 July 1988.

Claims can be made to treat personal pension contributions or retirement annuity contributions paid in one year of assessment as paid in an earlier year. Subject to the satisfaction of normal requirements, this will usually result in a repayment of income tax. However, it should not be overlooked that with the introduction of self-assessment, contributions which are related back in this manner often create a disadvantage. Whilst tax relief is calculated by reference to liabilities in the earlier year, the amount of those liabilities is not reduced. It follows that where income tax must be discharged by instalments, based on liabilities for the previous year, those liabilities will not now be regarded as reduced by pension contributions related back. This does suggest that where it is possible to discharge contributions without the need to relate back, this approach ought to be followed. Clearly, there will be many situations where it cannot, due to the absence of reliable information as 5 April approaches.

Enterprise investment schemes
Tax relief can be obtained for the cost of subscribing for shares in a qualifying company where the enterprise investment scheme requirements are satisfied. Maximum relief is available on share subscriptions up to £150,000 for 1998–99, although relief is limited to the lower rate of 20 per cent only. If any part of the £150,000 relief available remains unused, it may be possible to utilise all or part of the balance by making investments in the first six months of 1999–2000 which are related back to the previous year. Subject to this, any unused relief cannot be carried forward and will be lost.

Venture capital trusts

A subscription for shares in a venture capital trust will enable tax relief to be obtained at the rate of 20 per cent. This relief is limited to subscriptions not exceeding in aggregate £100,000 in 1998–99. Like subscriptions under the enterprise investment scheme, this effectively reduces the subscription cost by one-fifth. In addition, distributions from holdings in venture capital trusts incur no liability to income tax.

Enterprise zones

Capital allowances up to a maximum of 100 per cent are available for the cost of constructing buildings, including commercial buildings, in an enterprise zone. It is possible for these allowances to be set against income generally but the year in which relief is to be obtained should be carefully selected.

Personal equity plans

No new PEP holdings can be obtained after 5 April 1999. However, existing holdings may be retained and will continue to secure exemption from both income tax and capital gains tax. Holders requiring to secure benefits from this type of investment should endeavour to acquire the maximum PEP investment in 1998–99 and retain the aggregate investment for a future period of time.

Tax Exempt Special Savings Accounts

5 April 1999 is also the deadline for opening a TESSA. It will not be possible to open a new account after that date. Subject to this, existing TESSAs may be retained throughout the normal five-year period, with deposits not exceeding normal annual limits. Depositors with TESSAs may well conclude that the exemption conferred on interest arising is a valuable advantage and will be keen to retain their deposits until maturity on the fifth anniversary.

Individual Savings Accounts

The introduction of Individual Savings Accounts on 6 April 1999 will offer an opportunity to both receive tax-free income and avoid liability to capital gains tax. The terms and conditions, together with charges made by account managers, will reflect matters to be carefully analysed before ISAs become available.

Investment generally

A modest tax efficient investment is the purchase of National Savings certificates, as interest arising to the eventual date of realisation is not liable to income tax. An identical yield will be received by those who suffer tax at the higher rate and those who are not chargeable. This may prove a particular attraction for higher rate taxpayers as the tax free annual compound yield of 4.8 per cent which, for example, is available on the 46th issue held throughout the full five-year period, is equal to a gross yield of 8 per cent on which tax is suffered at 40 per cent.

Interest received from building societies, banks and some other financial institutions suffers income tax by deduction at the lower rate of 20 per cent for 1998–99. Investors not liable, or not fully liable, may obtain a repayment of any excessive tax deducted. Those of small means and not liable to tax may arrange for interest to be paid or credited gross. From 6 April 1998 interest on all government securities may be received gross without deduction of income tax. Holdings of this nature also avoid the need to claim any repayment of tax, although where the investor is liable any tax must be paid.

A note of caution

Newspaper advertisements sometimes list attractive opportunities for investment designed to secure tax advantages or to provide an excessive income yield. Before taking advantage of the opportunities offered, potential investors should fully understand the working of the scheme and establish that it is not vulnerable to attack by the Inland Revenue. If substantial sums are involved, it may be worthwhile taking independent professional advice.

CAPITAL GAINS TAX

Annual exemption

The first £6,800 of net gains, realised by an individual from the disposal of assets in the year ended 5 April 1999 are exempt from capital gains tax. If the exemption is not fully used the excess cannot be carried forward to the following year. Attempts should therefore be made to fully utilise the exemption, perhaps by bringing forward disposals to a date falling before 6 April 1999. In cases where the exemption limit has already been exceeded, disposals may possibly be deferred until the following year.

Losses

Where gains exceed the annual exemption of £6,800, it may be advisable to consider whether the excess gains can be reduced by creating losses. In some cases this may be achieved by bringing forward a disposal date which would otherwise fall after 5

April, or perhaps by arranging 'bed and breakfast' transactions whereby shares are sold to produce a loss and subsequently reacquired. However, when contemplating such a transaction it will not be overlooked that a period of at least 31 days must elapse before the reacquisition can take place. Should shares be reacquired within a shorter period, the anticipated advantage will not arise.

Government securities
No capital gains tax will be payable by individuals on the disposal of Government securities and many securities (but not shares) issued by listed and unlisted companies. Those retaining substantial holdings of securities should not overlook the accrued income scheme for calculating liability to income tax.

Deferment of tax
Liability to capital gains tax for disposals taking place in the year ended 5 April 1999 requires satisfaction on 31 January 2000. In some cases where the exemption of £6,800 has been used, it may be thought advisable to defer the contemplated disposal of assets until a date falling after 5 April 1999. This will delay payment of tax until 31 January 2001.

Tapering relief
The introduction of tapering relief to replace the indexation allowance for disposals made after 5 April 1998 may well have a considerable bearing on future investment decisions. For non-business assets this relief has little effect on that part of the gain chargeable to capital gains tax until the asset has been retained for four or five years. Increased relief is available where gains arise on the disposal of business assets but in many situations this may well be influenced by possible claims for business roll-over relief. Apart from a 'bonus' of one year for assets acquired before 17 March 1998, tapering relief is measured by the number of complete years of ownership falling after 5 April 1998. Where one of those years is approaching in the future it may be possible to obtain a modest advantage by postponing the disposal for a few days or weeks.

Retirement relief
Maximum rates of retirement relief will be available where the disposal or other event occurs before 6 April 1999. The relief is then rapidly phased out over the four following years. Where a selection of dates is possible, individuals qualifying for retirement relief should carefully consider the ideal time of proposed disposals.

Roll-over and deferral relief
There are several different forms of roll-over and deferral relief which can be applied to avoid or defer immediate liability to capital gains tax by acquiring shares. Of particular interest to some investors will be subscriptions in enterprise investment scheme shares or subscriptions in venture capital trust. The amount subscribed may be used to defer the payment of capital gains tax on the disposal of other assets.

Many individuals have taken advantage of reinvestment relief whereby gains arising on the disposal of assets may be rolled over and subtracted from the cost of acquiring shares in a qualifying trading company. The attraction of reinvestment relief is no longer available for shares acquired after 5 April 1998 and those requiring to defer tax on gains must examine deferral relief.

When contemplating the availability of relief on the acquisition of shares, potential investors should not only recognise the risks involved but, where they do proceed, ensure that the share transaction will secure the required advantages.

Rate of tax
The rate of capital gains tax due on chargeable gains will reflect an individual's marginal rate of income tax. Where income is expected to fluctuate considerably as between one year and another, this could become a factor governing the tax year in which a planned disposal should be made.

INHERITANCE TAX

Annual exemption
Few lifetime gifts and dispositions now incur liability to inheritance tax. However, where a lifetime transaction within the limited range producing liability is contemplated, the annual exemption of £3,000 should not be overlooked. This applies to gifts made in a year ending on 5 April, and if the exemption is not fully utilised in a particular year the excess can be carried forward and absorbed in the following year only. An aggregate exemption of £6,000 may therefore be obtained for the year to 5 April 1999 if no part of the exemption has been used in the previous year. Failure to absorb the amount brought forward in the second year will result in the exemption being lost. Wherever possible the available exemption should be used.

Gifts with reservation

The making of a lifetime gift which reserves some benefit to the donor may create liability to inheritance tax on death, unless the reservation ceased to apply more than seven years before the time of death. Gifts made subject to reservation which do not fall within a limited list of exceptions are to be firmly avoided.

Potentially exempt transfers

Many lifetime gifts made by an individual to a second individual or to a limited range of trustees comprise potentially exempt transfers. No liability to inheritance tax will arise should the donor survive the seven-year inter vivos period. There is an obvious attraction of making such gifts at the earliest possible date.

Gifts within seven years before death

Should the donor die within seven years of making a gift, liability to inheritance tax may arise on the value of the gift. Although this is mainly designed to frustrate 'deathbed gifts', it will apply equally to all gifts within the seven-year period. The subsequent date of a donor's death cannot usually be anticipated with any measure of accuracy, except in the case of terminal illness, and an unexpected death within the seven-year period may create substantial liability to inheritance tax. In some situations it may be thought advisable to secure funds for the possible satisfaction of tax payable on gifts by means of a term assurance policy.

Reliefs

Certain reliefs, notably business asset relief and agricultural property relief, will only be available if assets have been owned throughout a required period of time ending on the date of a lifetime disposition or death. The need to establish a qualifying period should be recognised before transferring assets, particularly between members of a family, where ownership must inevitably change. Other requirements must be satisfied between the date of a gift comprising a potentially exempt transfer and the time of death if reliefs are to be preserved.

The need to satisfy these requirements is of particular importance where relief is available at the rate of 100 per cent for many business assets, unlisted shares in trading companies and a range of agricultural property.

Other considerations

Savings in inheritance tax and other tax considerations must never reflect the sole reason for making gifts. Once the ownership of assets has been transferred those assets will cease to be available to the donor, if the transaction is to secure the required tax advantages. Those contemplating substantial gifts must recognise the depletion in their available funds and perhaps a reduction in future income which the transfer will create.

GENERAL MATTERS

Claims and elections

Many tax advantages are only available if a written claim or election is lodged with the Inland Revenue. There is a very long list of time limits governing different elections and claims and it is essential that these limits are fully observed. If they are not, unexpected tax liabilities may arise.

Numerous time limits previously expired on the last day of the tax year, namely 5 April. To accommodate self-assessment many dates have been changed to 31 January. Care must be taken to recognise the changes which have been made and the reduction of some claim periods by more than two months.

Disclosure of information

The law requires that taxpayers should disclose details of income, profits or gains to the Inland Revenue, although this is of limited significance to those whose only income is derived from an employment where the PAYE deduction scheme applies. Failure to disclose details of a part-time job, the existence of a business, or details of chargeable gains assessable to capital gains tax, may have serious consequences. Not only will tax become payable but the individual may incur additional liabilities to interest and penalties.

And finally...

The recent introduction of self-assessment is a matter which many taxpayers cannot afford to overlook. Those required to complete a self-assessment tax return form should carefully review the comments made in the chapter commencing on page 1 and the further chapter which begins on page 135. Others who do not receive a tax return but have income, profits or gains on which tax has not been paid must be prepared to advise the Inland Revenue at an early date. If they do not a liability to interest, penalties and surcharges may arise.

25

Action before
6 April 1999

AS THE END of the tax year approaches on 5 April 1999, taxpayers should consider whether any action is needed to reduce tax payable. Before this date is reached the Chancellor of the Exchequer is likely to deliver at least one Budget Statement disclosing details of any tax rate changes coming into operation on 6 April 1999. This will enable a comparison to be made with those matters in force for the year ending on the previous day. It should also identify those tax reliefs which are to be retained or perhaps withdrawn. In addition, the following matters may be significant, among many others:

☐ Claims for repayment of income tax must be made within a period of six years from the end of the year of assessment to which those claims relate. The time limit for submitting claims in respect of 1992–93 expires on 5 April 1999. (The 'old' six-year time limit continues to apply for claims relating to 1995–96 and earlier years.)

☐ Elections which may be of interest to a large number of taxpayers concern the married couple's allowance. A wife 'living with' her husband can elect to receive one-half of the basic allowance for 1999–2000 if action is taken not later than 5 April 1999. It is also possible for the entire basic allowance to accrue for the benefit of the wife only, if a suitable claim is submitted by the same date. New elections will not be necessary if an election has already been made, unless that election is to be varied. Those contemplating new elections will recognise that for 1999–2000 the married couple's allowance is likely to produce relief at the reduced rate of only 10 per cent. Whether this indicates that the allowance will shortly be withdrawn entirely remains to be seen.

☐ Few claims and elections now have time limits expiring on 5 April. For example, claims to relieve trading losses must usually be made not later than 31 January falling some 22 months after the end of the year of assessment concerned. An 'interest allocation election', which apportions interest paid between husband and wife, must be submitted not later than 31 January 2000 if it is to apply for 1997–98.

☐ Any additional voluntary pension contributions paid by an employed person must be satisfied by 5 April 1999 if they are to reduce the tax bill for 1998–99.

☐ Personal pension scheme contributions and retirement annuity premiums paid during the year ending on 5 April 1999 may be treated as satisfied in 1997–98, or perhaps earlier, if an election is made not later than 31 January 2000. The election may be particularly advantageous if the 17.5 per cent, or higher, maximum has not been fully used in the earlier year. Unused relief for previous years can be carried forward for a maximum of six years. This enables unused relief for 1991–92 to be used in the year ended on 5 April 1998 and that for 1992–93 to be utilised in the year ending on 5 April 1999. These are matters which an individual should carefully consider when paying premiums not later than 5 April 1999 which can, at his or her option, be allocated to the year ending on that date or to some previous year.

☐ There may be an advantage in entering into a deed of covenant in favour of a charity before 6 April 1999 to establish tax relief for a payment made under that deed in 1998–99. Those able to make donations under the Gift Aid scheme, or the special Millennium Gift Aid scheme, may consider action before 6 April 1999 if tax relief is to be obtained at the higher rate for 1998–99.

☐ No new TESSA arrangement can be entered into after 5 April 1999. Potential investors who do not maintain an existing TESSA should consider the advisability of taking action to obtain a tax efficient product.

☐ A maximum of £6,000 may be invested in a general PEP, or £3,000 in a single company PEP, during the year ending on 6 April 1999. Investors who have not taken advantage of these limits should consider their position as 5 April 1999 approaches as it will not be possible to undertake any further PEP investments subsequently.

☐ Investments up to a maximum of £150,000 can be made in an enterprise investment scheme during 1998–99 and obtain the relief at the rate of 20 per cent. A maximum of £100,000 and a similar rate of relief applies to investments in a venture capital trust. These are matters which should receive attention by potential investors who have not taken advantage of the investment possibilities as the end of 1998–99 looms.

☐ Employees earning £8,500 or more and directors provided with cars for private motoring should attempt to achieve 2,500 or 18,000 miles of business motoring before midnight on 5 April

1999 is reached. The mileage travelled will govern the amount of taxable benefit.

These individuals will be aware that the calculation of taxable benefits arising from the availability of motor cars is based on the list price of the vehicle and any accessories. The use of this basis should not be overlooked when replacing a car or adding expensive accessories to an existing vehicle. The application of this system could support a decision to change an existing model for the purpose of avoiding excessive liability to taxation.

☐ If the full exemption of £6,800 is to be used for capital gains tax purposes in 1998–99, it may be necessary to undertake the disposal of additional assets not later than 5 April 1999. Action may also be required to create losses which reduce that part of any gains which exceed the exemption limit. However, if 'bed and breakfast' devices are to be used to achieve this result a period in excess of 30 days must elapse before shares are reacquired.

☐ Those in business who are contemplating retirement should be aware that the rate of retirement relief to capital gains tax purposes will commence to be phased out after 5 April 1999.

☐ Any part of the annual inheritance tax exemption amounting to £3,000 and which has not been used in the year ending on 5 April 1998 will be lost unless it is utilised not later than 5 April 1999.

☐ There may be an advantage in making an unconditional gift of an asset between husband and wife, for the purpose of establishing the person on whom future income will be assessed for 1999–2000.

Note:

The above comments were based on the proposed tax law as it applied shortly after 5 April 1998. The possibility of significant changes being introduced subsequently and before 6 April 1999 should be recognised by readers when planning their tax affairs.

SOCIAL SECURITY BENEFITS

WHILST SOME social security benefits are taxable, many do not incur liability to income tax. The general rule is that benefits which replace lost earnings are subject to tax, whereas those intended to meet a specific need of the claimant are not. A list of the taxable and non-taxable benefits is shown below:

BENEFITS WHICH ARE TAXABLE

Incapacity benefit
Industrial death benefit pensions
Invalid care allowance
Jobseeker's allowance
Retirement pension
Statutory maternity pay
Statutory sick pay
Widowed mother's allowance
Widow's pension

BENEFITS WHICH ARE NOT TAXABLE

Attendance allowance
Child benefit
Child's special allowance
Disability living allowance
Disability working allowance
Earnings top-up grant
Family credit
Guardian's allowance
Housing benefit
Income support
Industrial disablement benefit
Jobfinders grant
Maternity allowance
One-parent benefit
Severe disablement allowance
Social fund payments
War widow's pension
Widow's payment
Work incentive grants

Notes:

1 Income support is taxable when paid to unemployed people who have to sign on, or to strikers or those directly interested in a trade dispute.

2 Child-dependent additions made to certain benefits are not taxable.

3 Although incapacity benefit is chargeable to income tax there are exceptions. No tax is due on that part of any increased incapacity benefit attributable to a child. Nor is tax due on that part of the benefit payable for the initial period of incapacity, namely the period for which incapacity benefit is payable otherwise than at the higher rate for the first 28 weeks. Those in receipt of invalidity benefit on 13 April 1995 did not pay tax subsequently while they remained incapable of work.

Tax on incapacity benefit is collected through the PAYE deduction scheme. This will be operated by the Benefits Agency unless the recipient is receiving income within some other PAYE scheme when tax will be collected by adjusting the code number.

4 Payments of short-term sick pay made by the recipient's employer are taxable through the PAYE deduction scheme. Statutory maternity pay is also discharged by employers, with PAYE being deducted where required.

5 A married woman's retirement pension paid on the basis of her husband's contributions is treated as income of the wife. Where the pension includes an adult dependency addition the entire pension will also be regarded as that of the recipient.

6 Jobseeker's allowance is taxable with tax being collected by the Benefits Agency who operate PAYE.

7 Grants paid under government pilot work incentive schemes are exempt from tax. These included jobfinders grant and earnings top-up grant introduced in 1996. The pilot schemes were replaced by a permanent jobwatch programme in 1997. Payments made under this programme, in addition to training vouchers, are exempt from income tax.

WORKING FAMILIES' TAX CREDIT

A new benefit system, the Working Families' Tax Credit (WFTC), is likely to replace family credit in October 1999. To qualify for the WFTC there must be a family with one or more children and at least one of the parents working 16 or more hours a week.

Where these requirements are satisfied the WFTC may contain the following elements, based on 1998–99 figures:

	Per week £
Basic tax credit per family	48.80
Tax credits for each child:	
0–11	14.85
11–16	20.45
16–18	25.40

Extra credit for working 30 hours or more per week 10.80

In addition, a child care tax credit worth up to 70 per cent of eligible child care costs may also be payable within the WFTC.

It is anticipated that where the net income of a family, calculated by excluding WFTC and also the child benefit, is less than £90 per week the full WFTC will be due. Once the threshold of £90 is exceeded WFTC will be reduced by 55p for each extra £1 of net income. The figure of net income is calculated after subtracting any national insurance contributions and income tax.

After a short introductory period WFTC will be paid together with wages by the employer. These payments are expected to commence in April 2000. Self-employed individuals will receive the WFTC direct from the Inland Revenue.

Payments of WFTC will usually be made to the wage earner. Where both parents are working it will remain for the couple to select the recipient.

It seems to be the intention that, like family credit, WFTC will not be chargeable to income tax.

RATES OF INCOME TAX AND ALLOWANCES FOR EARLIER YEARS

RATES OF INCOME tax and allowances for the past six years are shown below.

INCOME TAX

1992–93 Basic rate 25 per cent

Lower rate (*payable on first £2,000 of taxable income*)
20%
Higher rate (*payable on taxable income exceeding £23,700*)
40%

1995–96 Basic rate 25 per cent

Lower rate (*payable on first £3,200 of taxable income*)
20%
Higher rate (*payable on taxable income exceeding £24,300*)
40%

1993–94 Basic rate 25 per cent

Lower rate (*payable on first £2,500 of taxable income*)
20%
Higher rate (*payable on taxable income exceeding £23,700*)
40%

1996–97 Basic rate 24 per cent

Lower rate (*payable on first £3,900 of taxable income*)
20%
Higher rate (*payable on taxable income exceeding £25,500*)
40%

1994–95 Basic rate 25 per cent

Lower rate (*payable on first £3,000 of taxable income*)
20%
Higher rate (*payable on taxable income exceeding £23,700*)
40%

1997–98 Basic rate 23 per cent

Lower rate (*payable on first £4,100 of taxable income*)
20%
Higher rate (*payable on taxable income exceeding £26,100*)
40%

ALLOWANCES

	1992–93 £	1993–94 £	1994–95 £	1995–96 £	1996–97 £	1997–98 £
Additional personal allowance	1720	1720	1720	1720	1790	1830
Blind person's allowance	1080	1080	1200	1200	1250	1280
Married couples allowance						
age of elder spouse below 65	1720	1720	1720	1720	1790	1830
65 to 74	2465	2465	2665	2995	3115	3185
75 and over	2505	2505	2705	3035	3155	3225
Personal allowance						
Taxpayer's age below 65	3445	3445	3445	3525	3765	4045
65 to 74	4200	4200	4200	4630	4910	5220
75 and over	4370	4370	4370	4800	5090	5400
Widow's bereavement allowance	1720	1720	1720	1720	1790	1830

TAX DEDUCTION AND OTHER RATES – 1998–99

The complexity of United Kingdom taxation is demonstrated by the need to both recognise and use numerous different rates. In addition to the rates of income tax, capital gains tax and corporation tax, charged on profits, gains and income, the following tables summarise the main rates in operation for 1998–99.

DEDUCTION OF TAX

Where a person is required or entitled to deduct tax on making payments the following rates apply:

	Rate %
Interest:	
Paid by banks, building societies and other deposit-takers	20
On UK Government and other securities	20
On National Savings First Option Bonds	20
Distributions by authorised unit trusts	20
On cash deposits withdrawn from PEPs	20
Other annual interest payable under deduction	20
Annual payments and annuities:	
Deeds of covenant to charities	23
Distributions by unauthorised unit trusts	23
Income element of purchased life annuities	20
Other annuities where PAYE does not apply	23
Rents paid to non-resident landlords	23
Patent royalties	23
Payments to sub-contractors without certificates	23
Payments to foreign entertainers and sportsmen	23
Payments out of pension scheme AVC surpluses – by scheme administrators	33

Note. Interest on UK Government securities can be paid gross if required.

RELIEF AT SOURCE SCHEMES

Persons entitled to obtain relief at source on making payments should deduct tax at the following rates:

	Rate %
Interest payable under MIRAS – generally	10
Interest on loan used to buy a life annuity – under MIRAS	23
Vocational training payments	23
Life assurance premiums	12.5
Free-standing additional voluntary contributions	23
Contributions to approved personal pension schemes	23

DIVIDENDS AND OTHER DISTRIBUTIONS

Companies must account for advance corporation tax at the rate of one-quarter on dividends and other distributions.

The value of a tax credit attributable to such a dividend or distribution is also one-quarter. This represents 20 per cent of the aggregate dividend and tax credit.

DISCRETIONARY AND ACCUMULATION TRUSTS

Trustees administering discretionary and accumulation trusts incur liability to income tax at the rate of 34 per cent. If this income is distributed to beneficiaries it is treated as received net, also after deduction at the rate of 34 per cent.

INCOME TREATED AS PAID UNDER DEDUCTION OF TAX

The following income is deemed to have been received after deduction of tax although this tax is not recoverable:

	Rate %
Foreign income dividends	20
Stock dividends	20
Gains from certain events affecting life policies	23
Loans to company participators which are waived	20
Payments out of pension scheme AVC surpluses received by employees	23

It is important that these numerous different rates are carefully noted when dealing with the affairs of either payer or recipient.

RATES OF INHERITANCE TAX

Events after 17 March 1986
but before 17 March 1987

Portion of value	Rate per cent
£ £	
0– 71,000	Nil
71,001– 95,000	30
95,001–129,000	35
129,001–164,000	40
164,001–206,000	45
206,001–257,000	50
257,001–317,000	55
317,001 and above	60

Events after 16 March 1987
but before 15 March 1988

Portion of value	Rate per cent
£ £	
0– 90,000	Nil
90,001–140,000	30
140,001–220,000	40
220,001–330,000	50
330,001 and above	60

Events after 14 March 1988
but before 6 April 1989

Portion of value	Rate per cent
£ £	
0–110,000	Nil
110,001 and above	40

Events after 5 April 1989
but before 6 April 1990

Portion of value	Rate per cent
£ £	
0–118,000	Nil
118,001 and above	40

Events after 5 April 1990
but before 6 April 1991

Portion of value	Rate per cent
£ £	
0–128,000	Nil
128,001 and above	40

Events after 5 April 1991
but before 10 March 1992

Portion of value	Rate per cent
£ £	
0–140,000	Nil
140,001 and above	40

Events after 9 March 1992
but before 6 April 1995

Portion of value	Rate per cent
£ £	
0–150,000	Nil
150,001 and above	40

Events after 5 April 1995
but before 6 April 1996

Portion of value	Rate per cent
£ £	
0–154,000	Nil
154,001 and above	40

Events after 5 April 1996
but before 6 April 1997

Portion of value	Rate per cent
£ £	
0–200,000	Nil
200,001 and above	40

Events after 5 April 1997
but before 6 April 1998

Portion of value	Rate per cent
£ £	
0–215,000	Nil
215,001 and above	40

Events after 5 April 1998

Portion of value	Rate per cent
£ £	
0–223,000	Nil
223,001 and above	40

TAX PAYABLE ON SPECIMEN INCOMES[1] – 1998–99

	SINGLE PERSON OR MARRIED WOMAN[4]			MARRIED MAN[4]	
[5]On total income of	Persons under 65 years of age		Persons over the age of 65[2]	Persons under 65 years of age[2]	Persons over the age of 65[2]
	One person[2]	One parent family[3]			
£	£	£	£	£	£
4,500	61.00	—	—	—	—
5,000	161.00	—	—	—	—
5,500	261.00	—	18.00	—	—
6,000	361.00	76.00	118.00	76.00	—
6,500	461.00	176.00	218.00	176.00	—
7,000	561.00	276.00	318.00	276.00	—
7,500	661.00	376.00	418.00	376.00	—
8,000	761.00	476.00	518.00	476.00	22.25
9,000	976.15	691.15	718.00	691.15	222.25
10,000	1,206.15	921.15	926.70	921.15	430.95
12,000	1,666.15	1,381.15	1,386.70	1,381.15	890.95
14,000	2,126.15	1,841.15	1,846.70	1,841.15	1,350.95
16,000	2,586.15	2,301.15	2,306.70	2,301.15	1,810.95
18,000	3,046.15	2,761.15	2,973.70	2,761.15	2,477.95
20,000	3,506.15	3,221.15	3,506.15	3,221.15	3,113.15
25,000	4,656.15	4,371.15	4,656.15	4,371.15	4,371.15
30,000	5,806.15	5,521.15	5,806.15	5,521.15	5,521.15
35,000	7,586.00	7,301.00	7,586.00	7,301.00	7,301.00
40,000	9,586.00	9,301.00	9,586.00	9,301.00	9,301.00
45,000	11,586.00	11,301.00	11,586.00	11,301.00	11,301.00
50,000	13,586.00	13,301.00	13,586.00	13,301.00	13,301.00
75,000	23,586.00	23,301.00	23,586.00	23,301.00	23,301.00
100,000	33,586.00	33,301.00	33,586.00	33,301.00	33,301.00
150,000	53,586.00	53,301.00	53,586.00	53,301.00	53,301.00

NOTES
[1] Some reduction in the tax payable may arise if income includes income from savings which is not chargeable to tax at the basic rate.

[2] The tax shown is that due where there are no allowances other than the personal allowance and the married couple's allowance, as appropriate. Rather less tax will be payable by elderly persons aged 75 or over.

[3] A single person with a qualifying child receives both the personal allowance and an additional personal allowance of £1,900.

[4] The entire married couple's allowance has been allocated to the husband only.

[5] Total income is shown before subtracting any allowances.

READY RECKONER

Based on tax at 23 per cent

1p to 99p (to the nearest whole penny)

Amount	Tax	Amount	Tax	Amount	Tax
£	£	£	£	£	£
0.01	—	0.34	0.08	0.67	0.15
0.02	—	0.35	0.08	0.68	0.16
0.03	0.01	0.36	0.08	0.69	0.16
0.04	0.01	0.37	0.09	0.70	0.16
0.05	0.01	0.38	0.09	0.71	0.16
0.06	0.01	0.39	0.09	0.72	0.17
0.07	0.02	0.40	0.09	0.73	0.17
0.08	0.02	0.41	0.09	0.74	0.17
0.09	0.02	0.42	0.10	0.75	0.17
0.10	0.02	0.43	0.10	0.76	0.17
0.11	0.03	0.44	0.10	0.77	0.18
0.12	0.03	0.45	0.10	0.78	0.18
0.13	0.03	0.46	0.11	0.79	0.18
0.14	0.03	0.47	0.11	0.80	0.18
0.15	0.03	0.48	0.11	0.81	0.19
0.16	0.04	0.49	0.11	0.82	0.19
0.17	0.04	0.50	0.12	0.83	0.19
0.18	0.04	0.51	0.12	0.84	0.19
0.19	0.04	0.52	0.12	0.85	0.20
0.20	0.05	0.53	0.12	0.86	0.20
0.21	0.05	0.54	0.12	0.87	0.20
0.22	0.05	0.55	0.13	0.88	0.20
0.23	0.05	0.56	0.13	0.89	0.20
0.24	0.06	0.57	0.13	0.90	0.21
0.25	0.06	0.58	0.13	0.91	0.21
0.26	0.06	0.59	0.14	0.92	0.21
0.27	0.06	0.60	0.14	0.93	0.21
0.28	0.06	0.61	0.14	0.94	0.22
0.29	0.07	0.62	0.14	0.95	0.22
0.30	0.07	0.63	0.14	0.96	0.22
0.31	0.07	0.64	0.15	0.97	0.22
0.32	0.07	0.65	0.15	0.98	0.23
0.33	0.08	0.66	0.15	0.99	0.23

£1 to £22,000

Amount	Tax	Amount	Tax	Amount	Tax	Amount	Tax
£	£	£	£	£	£	£	£
1	0.23	46	10.58	91	20.93	136	31.28
2	0.46	47	10.81	92	21.16	137	31.51
3	0.69	48	11.04	93	21.39	138	31.74
4	0.92	49	11.27	94	21.62	139	31.97
5	1.15	50	11.50	95	21.85	140	32.20
6	1.38	51	11.73	96	22.08	141	32.43
7	1.61	52	11.96	97	22.31	142	32.66
8	1.84	53	12.19	98	22.54	143	32.89
9	2.07	54	12.42	99	22.77	144	33.12
10	2.30	55	12.65	100	23.00	145	33.35
11	2.53	56	12.88	101	23.23	146	33.58
12	2.76	57	13.11	102	23.46	147	33.81
13	2.99	58	13.34	103	23.69	148	34.04
14	3.22	59	13.57	104	23.92	149	34.27
15	3.45	60	13.80	105	24.15	150	34.50
16	3.68	61	14.03	106	24.38	200	46.00
17	3.91	62	14.26	107	24.61	250	57.50
18	4.14	63	14.49	108	24.84	300	69.00
19	4.37	64	14.72	109	25.07	350	80.50
20	4.60	65	14.95	110	25.30	400	92.00
21	4.83	66	15.18	111	25.53	450	103.50
22	5.06	67	15.41	112	25.76	500	115.00
23	5.29	68	15.64	113	25.99	550	126.50
24	5.52	69	15.87	114	26.22	600	138.00
25	5.75	70	16.10	115	26.45	650	149.50
26	5.98	71	16.33	116	26.68	700	161.00
27	6.21	72	16.56	117	26.91	750	172.50
28	6.44	73	16.79	118	27.14	800	184.00
29	6.67	74	17.02	119	27.37	850	195.50
30	6.90	75	17.25	120	27.60	900	207.00
31	7.13	76	17.48	121	27.83	950	218.50
32	7.36	77	17.71	122	28.06	1,000	230.00
33	7.59	78	17.94	123	28.29	1,500	345.00
34	7.82	79	18.17	124	28.52	2,000	460.00
35	8.05	80	18.40	125	28.75	2,500	575.00
36	8.28	81	18.63	126	28.98	3,000	690.00
37	8.51	82	18.86	127	29.21	3,500	805.00
38	8.74	83	19.09	128	29.44	4,000	920.00
39	8.97	84	19.32	129	29.67	4,500	1,035.00
40	9.20	85	19.55	130	29.90	5,000	1,150.00
41	9.43	86	19.78	131	30.13	7,500	1,725.00
42	9.66	87	20.01	132	30.36	10,000	2,300.00
43	9.89	88	20.24	133	30.59	15,000	3,450.00
44	10.12	89	20.47	134	30.82	20,000	4,600.00
45	10.35	90	20.70	135	31.05	22,000	5,060.00

READY RECKONER

Based on tax at 20 per cent

Amount	Tax	Amount	Tax	Amount	Tax	Amount	Tax
£	£	£	£	£	£	£	£
1	0.20	46	9.20	91	18.20	136	27.20
2	0.40	47	9.40	92	18.40	137	27.40
3	0.60	48	9.60	93	18.60	138	27.60
4	0.80	49	9.80	94	18.80	139	27.80
5	1.00	50	10.00	95	19.00	140	28.00
6	1.20	51	10.20	96	19.20	141	28.20
7	1.40	52	10.40	97	19.40	142	28.40
8	1.60	53	10.60	98	19.60	143	28.60
9	1.80	54	10.80	99	19.80	144	28.80
10	2.00	55	11.00	100	20.00	145	29.00
11	2.20	56	11.20	101	20.20	146	29.20
12	2.40	57	11.40	102	20.40	147	29.40
13	2.60	58	11.60	103	20.60	148	29.60
14	2.80	59	11.80	104	20.80	149	29.80
15	3.00	60	12.00	105	21.00	150	30.00
16	3.20	61	12.20	106	21.20	200	40.00
17	3.40	62	12.40	107	21.40	250	50.00
18	3.60	63	12.60	108	21.60	300	60.00
19	3.80	64	12.80	109	21.80	350	70.00
20	4.00	65	13.00	110	22.00	400	80.00
21	4.20	66	13.20	111	22.20	450	90.00
22	4.40	67	13.40	112	22.40	500	100.00
23	4.60	68	13.60	113	22.60	550	110.00
24	4.80	69	13.80	114	22.80	600	120.00
25	5.00	70	14.00	115	23.00	650	130.00
26	5.20	71	14.20	116	23.20	700	140.00
27	5.40	72	14.40	117	23.40	750	150.00
28	5.60	73	14.60	118	23.60	800	160.00
29	5.80	74	14.80	119	23.80	850	170.00
30	6.00	75	15.00	120	24.00	900	180.00
31	6.20	76	15.20	121	24.20	950	190.00
32	6.40	77	15.40	122	24.40	1,000	200.00
33	6.60	78	15.60	123	24.60	1,100	220.00
34	6.80	79	15.80	124	24.80	1,200	240.00
35	7.00	80	16.00	125	25.00	1,300	260.00
36	7.20	81	16.20	126	25.20	1,400	280.00
37	7.40	82	16.40	127	25.40	1,500	300.00
38	7.60	83	16.60	128	25.60	1,600	320.00
39	7.80	84	16.80	129	25.80	1,700	340.00
40	8.00	85	17.00	130	26.00	1,800	360.00
41	8.20	86	17.20	131	26.20	1,900	380.00
42	8.40	87	17.40	132	26.40	2,000	400.00
43	8.60	88	17.60	133	26.60	2,500	500.00
44	8.80	89	17.80	134	26.80	3,000	600.00
45	9.00	90	18.00	135	27.00	4,100	820.00

READY RECKONER

Based on tax at 40 per cent

Amount £	Tax £	Amount £	Tax £	Amount £	Tax £	Amount £	Tax £
1	0.40	46	18.40	91	36.40	136	54.40
2	0.80	47	18.80	92	36.80	137	54.80
3	1.20	48	19.20	93	37.20	138	55.20
4	1.60	49	19.60	94	37.60	139	55.60
5	2.00	50	20.00	95	38.00	140	56.00
6	2.40	51	20.40	96	38.40	141	56.40
7	2.80	52	20.80	97	38.80	142	56.80
8	3.20	53	21.20	98	39.20	143	57.20
9	3.60	54	21.60	99	39.60	144	57.60
10	4.00	55	22.00	100	40.00	145	58.00
11	4.40	56	22.40	101	40.40	146	58.40
12	4.80	57	22.80	102	40.80	147	58.80
13	5.20	58	23.20	103	41.20	148	59.20
14	5.60	59	23.60	104	41.60	149	59.60
15	6.00	60	24.00	105	42.00	150	60.00
16	6.40	61	24.40	106	42.40	200	80.00
17	6.80	62	24.80	107	42.80	250	100.00
18	7.20	63	25.20	108	43.20	300	120.00
19	7.60	64	25.60	109	43.60	350	140.00
20	8.00	65	26.00	110	44.00	400	160.00
21	8.40	66	26.40	111	44.40	450	180.00
22	8.80	67	26.80	112	44.80	500	200.00
23	9.20	68	27.20	113	45.20	550	220.00
24	9.60	69	27.60	114	45.60	600	240.00
25	10.00	70	28.00	115	46.00	650	260.00
26	10.40	71	28.40	116	46.40	700	280.00
27	10.80	72	28.80	117	46.80	750	300.00
28	11.20	73	29.20	118	47.20	800	320.00
29	11.60	74	29.60	119	47.60	850	340.00
30	12.00	75	30.00	120	48.00	900	360.00
31	12.40	76	30.40	121	48.40	950	380.00
32	12.80	77	30.80	122	48.80	1,000	400.00
33	13.20	78	31.20	123	49.20	1,500	600.00
34	13.60	79	31.60	124	49.60	2,000	800.00
35	14.00	80	32.00	125	50.00	2,500	1,000.00
36	14.40	81	32.40	126	50.40	3,000	1,200.00
37	14.80	82	32.80	127	50.80	3,500	1,400.00
38	15.20	83	33.20	128	51.20	4,000	1,600.00
39	15.60	84	33.60	129	51.60	4,500	1,800.00
40	16.00	85	34.00	130	52.00	5,000	2,000.00
41	16.40	86	34.40	131	52.40	7,500	3,000.00
42	16.80	87	34.80	132	52.80	10,000	4,000.00
43	17.20	88	35.20	133	53.20	25,000	10,000.00
44	17.60	89	35.60	134	53.60	50,000	20,000.00
45	18.00	90	36.00	135	54.00	100,000	40,000.00

GROSSING-UP TABLES

At 20 per cent

1p to 99p (to the nearest whole penny)

Net	Tax	Gross	Net	Tax	Gross	Net	Tax	Gross
£	£	£	£	£	£	£	£	£
0.01	—	0.01	0.34	0.09	0.43	0.67	0.17	0.84
0.02	0.01	0.03	0.35	0.09	0.44	0.68	0.17	0.85
0.03	0.01	0.04	0.36	0.09	0.45	0.69	0.17	0.86
0.04	0.01	0.05	0.37	0.09	0.46	0.70	0.18	0.88
0.05	0.01	0.06	0.38	0.10	0.48	0.71	0.18	0.89
0.06	0.02	0.08	0.39	0.10	0.49	0.72	0.18	0.90
0.07	0.02	0.09	0.40	0.10	0.50	0.73	0.18	0.91
0.08	0.02	0.10	0.41	0.10	0.51	0.74	0.19	0.93
0.09	0.02	0.11	0.42	0.11	0.53	0.75	0.19	0.94
0.10	0.03	0.13	0.43	0.11	0.54	0.76	0.19	0.95
0.11	0.03	0.14	0.44	0.11	0.55	0.77	0.19	0.96
0.12	0.03	0.15	0.45	0.11	0.56	0.78	0.20	0.98
0.13	0.03	0.16	0.46	0.12	0.58	0.79	0.20	0.99
0.14	0.04	0.18	0.47	0.12	0.59	0.80	0.20	1.00
0.15	0.04	0.19	0.48	0.12	0.60	0.81	0.20	1.01
0.16	0.04	0.20	0.49	0.12	0.61	0.82	0.21	1.03
0.17	0.04	0.21	0.50	0.13	0.63	0.83	0.21	1.04
0.18	0.05	0.23	0.51	0.13	0.64	0.84	0.21	1.05
0.19	0.05	0.24	0.52	0.13	0.65	0.85	0.21	1.06
0.20	0.05	0.25	0.53	0.13	0.66	0.86	0.22	1.08
0.21	0.05	0.26	0.54	0.14	0.68	0.87	0.22	1.09
0.22	0.06	0.28	0.55	0.14	0.69	0.88	0.22	1.10
0.23	0.06	0.29	0.56	0.14	0.70	0.89	0.22	1.11
0.24	0.06	0.30	0.57	0.14	0.71	0.90	0.23	1.13
0.25	0.06	0.31	0.58	0.15	0.73	0.91	0.23	1.14
0.26	0.07	0.33	0.59	0.15	0.74	0.92	0.23	1.15
0.27	0.07	0.34	0.60	0.15	0.75	0.93	0.23	1.16
0.28	0.07	0.35	0.61	0.15	0.76	0.94	0.24	1.18
0.29	0.07	0.36	0.62	0.16	0.78	0.95	0.24	1.19
0.30	0.08	0.38	0.63	0.16	0.79	0.96	0.24	1.20
0.31	0.08	0.39	0.64	0.16	0.80	0.97	0.24	1.21
0.32	0.08	0.40	0.65	0.16	0.81	0.98	0.25	1.23
0.33	0.08	0.41	0.66	0.17	0.83	0.99	0.25	1.24

Net column shows the actual amount of dividend or interest received.

Tax column shows the amount of the tax credit calculated at the rate of one quarter or income tax deducted at the rate of 20 per cent.

Gross column shows the total income for tax purposes.

£1 to £5,000

Net	Tax	Gross	Net	Tax	Gross	Net	Tax	Gross
£	£	£	£	£	£	£	£	£
1	0.25	1.25	34	8.50	42.50	130	32.50	162.50
2	0.50	2.50	35	8.75	43.75	140	35.00	175.00
3	0.75	3.75	36	9.00	45.00	150	37.50	187.50
4	1.00	5.00	37	9.25	46.25	160	40.00	200.00
5	1.25	6.25	38	9.50	47.50	170	42.50	212.50
6	1.50	7.50	39	9.75	48.75	180	45.00	225.00
7	1.75	8.75	40	10.00	50.00	190	47.50	237.50
8	2.00	10.00	41	10.25	51.25	200	50.00	250.00
9	2.25	11.25	42	10.50	52.50	210	52.50	262.50
10	2.50	12.50	43	10.75	53.75	220	55.00	275.00
11	2.75	13.75	44	11.00	55.00	230	57.50	287.50
12	3.00	15.00	45	11.25	56.25	240	60.00	300.00
13	3.25	16.25	46	11.50	57.50	250	62.50	312.50
14	3.50	17.50	47	11.75	58.75	260	65.00	325.00
15	3.75	18.75	48	12.00	60.00	270	67.50	337.50
16	4.00	20.00	49	12.25	61.25	280	70.00	350.00
17	4.25	21.25	50	12.50	62.50	290	72.50	362.50
18	4.50	22.50	51	12.75	63.75	300	75.00	375.00
19	4.75	23.75	52	13.00	65.00	350	87.50	437.50
20	5.00	25.00	53	13.25	66.25	400	100.00	500.00
21	5.25	26.25	54	13.50	67.50	450	112.50	562.50
22	5.50	27.50	55	13.75	68.75	500	125.00	625.00
23	5.75	28.75	60	15.00	75.00	550	137.50	687.50
24	6.00	30.00	65	16.25	81.25	600	150.00	750.00
25	6.25	31.25	70	17.50	87.50	650	162.50	812.50
26	6.50	32.50	75	18.75	93.75	700	175.00	875.00
27	6.75	33.75	80	20.00	100.00	750	187.50	937.50
28	7.00	35.00	85	21.25	106.25	800	200.00	1,000.00
29	7.25	36.25	90	22.50	112.50	850	212.50	1,062.50
30	7.50	37.50	95	23.75	118.75	900	225.00	1,125.00
31	7.75	38.75	100	25.00	125.00	950	237.50	1,187.50
32	8.00	40.00	110	27.50	137.50	1,000	250.00	1,250.00
33	8.25	41.25	120	30.00	150.00	5,000	1,250.00	6,250.00

Net column shows the actual amount of dividend or interest received.

Tax column shows the amount of the tax credit calculated at the rate of one quarter or income tax deducted at the rate of 20 per cent.

Gross column shows the total income for tax purposes.

Index